THE TARIFF CONTROVERSY IN THE UNITED STATES 1789-1833

WITH A SUMMARY OF THE PERIOD BEFORE THE ADOPTION OF THE CONSTITUTION

BY

ORRIN LESLIE ELLIOTT, P.H.D

Originally published in 1892 by Leland Stanford Junior University Monographs.
Copyright © 1892 by Leland Stanford Junior University Monographs.

This edition published by Bulkington Books.
This is a new edition of the 1892 text, with updated layout, format, and design, as
well as a new foreword, and annotations.
Copyright © 2025 by Bulkington Books.
ISBN: 978-1-966777-07-6

Bulkington Books
www.bulkingtonbooks.com
For typos, corrections, mistakes, or feedback contact
bulkington@bulkingtonbooks.com

Printed in the United States of America
First Printing of this Edition, 2025

BULKINGTON BOOKS

"Madman! Look through my eyes if thou hast none of thine own."

This Book Belongs to:

SA
PIEN
TIA

SCI
EN
TIA

IN
TELLEC
TVS

FOR
TITV
DO

CON
SILI
VM

PI
E
TAS

TIMOR
DÑI

THE TARIFF CONTROVERSY IN THE UNITED STATES 1789-1833

WITH A SUMMARY OF THE PERIOD BEFORE THE ADOPTION OF THE CONSTITUTION

By

ORRIN LESLIE ELLIOTT, P.H.D

THE TARIFF ISSUE AGAIN.

The House—How much longer can you hold on?
The Senate—Not long; let's adjourn.

From The Minneapolis Journal, April 13, 1906

TABLE OF CONTENTS

PUBLISHER'S NOTE

Blessed beloved bookreader, you have found this volume in your vision. We hope you read on, but let us offer a few humble words. Of making many books there is no end, and a long preface is a chasing after wind. We pray you give us a moment's indulgence.

Our mission is to build a bridge into the past, before film, television, copyright, and internet swallowed up the world. Before 'content' was culture. If the reader finds friends from before the echo chamber, they may find armor and sword against the dreadful noise machine.

We are convinced that many authors and many books are ready to rise like Lazarus and reenter the world to remind the readers that their life has purpose; that their time should be valued; and their history is an honorable home.

This book was chosen because it reveals a forgotten path, a bridge between the modern recovery movement, and the oldest American church tradition. It was written by a storied name, John Cotton Mather, and is an incredible tale of recovery and reformation. The original illustrations, though aged and stained, have been reproduced, because they are illuminating of the author's narrative.

We hope that if your first instinct is to scoff at such a narrative, that you read through and find light in the author's experience, strength and hope.

Your Most Humble and Obedient Servant (YMHOS),
Arthur Bulkington,
Melville Bay

PUBLISHER'S FOREWORD

We believe in monographs. Monographs are marvelous cre-
ations. They focus relentlessly on one thing. In so doing, they set
aside a great deal. They do this to pursue a topic to its depths. For
example, this book spends a lot of time on the period of the War
of 1812. It never once mentions the White House burning down
or the Battle of New Orleans. It stays on its topic, the Congressional maneuvering on war tariffs and peacetime adjustments.

The result is that in coming to understand one thing well, you
see further into all things. A monograph is like a corner piece of a
puzzle. It anchors the corner of one domain, and lets you go deeper into the subject. A monograph is one long unbroken shot of a
scene. No jump cuts, no editing, no reverse.

This is a monograph on tariffs in the early American Republic, from the founding to the Nullification Crisis in 1832. In this
single-minded pursuit of one topic, you acquire a narrow mastery.
This narrow mastery gives you insight and competence.

Most books nowadays are not monographs. They try and give
comprehensive surveys of a given thing, and touch all the key
points but shallowly. They try and imitate big box one stop shop-
ping, and offer you all the basics cheaply. But if you want professional tools, or you have special needs, or a finer taste, you need
to find a completely different establishment, you need to find a
professional who has mastered their craft.

We found this book to be a masterpiece of scholarship. And by this we don't mean the hundreds of footnotes. We mean the command of the material, and the way it weaves together a story greater than the sum of its parts. We admire this because it is dedication and craftsmanship. You do not find that in many books published today. The author mastered his subject and offers the Reader a few hard won pearls. That is after all why we read.

We return to our formula for what a foreword must do. We reiterate the three main points of a foreword, as we understand it.

1) We will tell you why we liked it, why it was worth our time to read, reformat, and republish.

2) We will suggest reasons why this book is relevant for our time.

3) We will suggest why it may be worth your precious reading time.

We will not lie. We are not economists or econometricians or accountants. We don't like numbers. We considered working on some other texts on this topic of tariff, but most of them are 500 page monstrosities with charts and graphs and numbers. This book is not that. It does not deal with the numbers. It deals with the legislation, the history, and the movement of forces. We liked it for that.

Another thing we liked about this book is how closely the author read the Founders. Nowadays we get, at best, a portrayal of the Founders that is all praise and no devotion. You are supposed to say nice things about the Founders and assume their goodness and wisdom, and move on to your aim. (Or, you are supposed to demonize them along the lines of the 1619 Project, write them off completely, and move on to your point.)

This author spent time reading the proceedings of Congress after Congress, and the complete works of most of the Founders we know, and some of the Founders we have never heard of, like Fisher Ames or Albert Gallatin or Richard Lee or General Dearborn. While we grant the Author was an exceptional scholar, we must admit that knowledge of the Founders has declined substantially. Their works remain unread, except for a handful of quotes you can quickly google, or a few lines that make it onto bumper stickers.

We liked being reminded of this fact. Because the Founders do have the answers to most of the questions our country faces. The first seven Presidents all favored tariffs. They saw no other solution in the face of a commercial manufacturing giant like Great Britain that continuously tried to overwhelm American markets with cheap goods. "I do not know that we can enter upon a war of imposts with Great Britain or any other foreign power" Washington wrote, fearing the economic shocks of a trade war.

Several of the Founders were idealistic free traders, especially Madison. They had read Adam Smith and David Ricardo and took their arguments seriously and believed in them sincerely. And yet, faced with events, they imposed protective tariffs because they understood that without reciprocity, American manufactures were at a disadvantage.

The Early Republic was remarkably weak. The Confederation was weak, and the states turned on each other. After they ratified the Constitution, they faced severe external threats from France, Spain, and Great Britain. Domestic rebellions, Indian wars, and division in Congress all threatened the Nation.

But they did not lie to themselves, and they knew they must remain united for the common good. They would not legislate nice theories that would not work in reality. They would meet the world as it is, and impose tariffs to protect the public from ruin.

Economics is where philosophy and idealism meets cynicism and selfishness. They put aside their naïve hopes and wishful thinking about the ideal state of affairs and played hardball to survive.

That is what came through to us as we read this text and worked on it. It was a pleasure to reacquaint ourselves with the Founders as they navigated a complicated issue.

One last thing we will note here. Because the author is so focused and thorough, the subtleties and varieties of the first presidential administrations acquire much richer variety and coloration. The Jefferson administration was committed to avoiding war with both France and Great Britain, and the author says that when he left office, there was a burst of youthful enthusiasm that overthrew the caution of the old: "*The paralysis which the Jefferson policy of peace at any price had laid upon the country was at last overcome, and under the leadership of younger men the country regained its moral tone. War was finally declared.*"

This notion that the Jefferson Administration had become sclerotic, old, averse to war, flies in the face of the popular conception of the founders, and reveals how dynamic, vitalistic, and ambitious the Republic was before the frontier closed.

Now, while we could in theory enjoy reading the Founders at our leisure, and musing over the intricacies of the period, we must move on to the second point of our foreword.

The relevance of this topic should be self evident, but we will answer the point more fully.

George Washington supported tariffs. John Adams supported tariffs. Thomas Jefferson supported tariffs. James Madison supported tariffs. James Monroe supported tariffs. John Quincy Adams supported tariffs. Andrew Jackson supported tariffs. They differed over specific rates on specific goods, but they were unanimous that tariffs were vital for the American Republic to survive, grow, and thrive. They threw away the old idea of Crown loyalists that America could be the provider of raw goods to the motherland, and receive furnished goods in return. They knew that political independence was only possible and sustainable with economic independence.

This was self-evident to all of them. But this is not self-evident to many of our leaders today. We leave it as an exercise to the Reader to conclude why that is the case.

Every argument for and against tariffs that you hear today you can find in this book. The Founders were sophisticated and fluent in economics, and they themselves could look to the preceding two centuries of British mercantilism for an idea of what creates economic success.

Free trade has never existed but for textbooks. Whether that's neoclassicals like Samuelson in our time, or Smith in the time of the Founders, it has never existed. Free trade without restriction or protection is consenting to be a colonial market, a captive economic dependency on a manufacturing nation that protects its interests. Free trade will never exist. From one of the footnotes: *Free trade is a pretty thing to talk about, but it cannot exist. What if England were to agree to receive American bread-stuffs? The taxes on lands could not be paid, nor the poor rates, nor the bellies priests be filled with the product of the labor of others" (30 Niles, 36 [1826]). And again (1831): "all the mighty capital of England—all her skill, industry, and scientific power, could not maintain an open trade with France for two years" (40 Niles, 289)*

Relative periods of open markets and low tariffs will exist from time to time, as they did in the period after the Second World War. These open markets are maintained and kept open for the benefit of one industrial hegemon. The British Empire of 1750 used the same playbook the American Empire of 1950 did.

One of the reasons we endeavored into bookmaking, and specifically the publication of old forgotten books, is because we believe that the long postwar era is coming to an end. The lessons and platitudes and truisms of that time period have lost their efficacy. What worked for Boomers will not work for Gen Z. To find what works in the future we must go deeper into the past, before World War Two and World War One. The copyright pocket universe of sequels and reboots and comic books, the social media echo chamber of slop and bait and one liners, these have no wisdom to give. Old books are the only way we can imagine a new world worth living in and passing on to our children and grandchildren.

An old book like this, on a narrow topic like tariffs, is of inestimable value in helping someone trapped in the postwar pocket universe to break out of amnesia and remember the wisdom of the Founders and the ancients, and reclaim their place in History.

For anyone who agrees with this thesis, this book is worth your time.

This book would also be worth the time of Readers who want to rediscover the founders. This book would also be worth the time of Beltway and Beltway adjacent types who want some breadcrumbs from the Founders to find some real reasons to enact the tariff agenda of the current administration. This book would be worth the time of people who want to help recapture what made America great, by recovering the old formula that demonstrably worked for most of the Republic's history. This book would be worth the time of Sensitive Young Men and E-girls who want to move past the shallow postwar myths and engage with real titans like Jefferson or Madison or Clay.

We believe that this conveys our point, and that we have justified our work on this book. As a housekeeping note, it has a dazzling array of footnotes, most of which are the work of the original author. We have only found fit to add a select few when certain topics needed a slice of context.

Your Most Humble and Obedient Servant (YMHOS),
Arthur Bulkington,
Melville Bay

CHAPTER I

THE COLONIAL PERIOD

The American colonies naturally inherited the political economy of Europe, and of one phase of it they were the unfortunate victims. The colonial system has supplied material for endless harangue and denunciation, and writers of a certain class have exhausted the vocabulary of invective in endeavoring to characterize the tyranny of the mother country toward her defenceless colonies. That England's policy was one of "deliberate and malignant selfishness," as even Lecky affirms,[1] may be granted, if the words be not understood too severely. Judged by modern standards it was so. The interests of the colonies were made strictly subordinate to those of the mother country, and her legislation bore with irritating severity upon the expanding industrial life of the New World. But it is not necessary to suppose a malignant intention on the part of English statesmen to oppress the colonies. In the political economy of the time, the prosperity of one nation seemed to demand the pulling down of others, and self-aggrandizement had almost universal sway, in home not less than in colonial administration. Yet the English government was as generous toward its colonial subjects as toward its home subjects, when such generosity did not run counter to generally accepted economic doctrines.[2] Indeed, in applying economic principles common to the age, England was far less oppressive than other powers; and the favor of princes—sometimes for selfish purposes, sometimes from indifference—left the colonies a comparatively free field for development. And in the general economic notions which underlay the policy of the mother country, the colonies in the main acquiesced.

The economic system which dominated England during the colonial period was the natural and perhaps necessary outgrowth of the time. Broadly speaking, it was an assertion, in legislation, of the new national life which marked the transition from mediaeval

---

1 2 Lecky's Hist. of 18th Century, 8, 11.
2 See Cunningham's Politics and Economics, 54, 66; also, Adam Smith's Wealth of Nations, Bk. 4, Ch. 7.

to modern times. Abnormal as it was, it realized, though crudely, what was most potent in the new industrial movement. Medievalism had not been favorable to trade or commerce. The church sternly repressed the desire for riches, and accounted worldly activity an evil. Necessary exchanges must conform strictly to the *justum pretium*,[3] or cost price, and commerce for gain was held to be wrong.[4] But the growth of an industrial and commercial spirit was encouraged in various ways. The Crusades, the revival of classical learning, especially the new discoveries and inventions, stirred the blood of all Europe; and gradually out of feudalism emerged a number of powerful states whose rivalries extended to commerce. In the pettiness of these rivalries, industry was saved from being plundered by the recognition of its immense importance in the new political struggles. To build up manufactures as the great resource of the state became the object of rulers, and a long series of restrictions, wise and foolish, was the fruit of their activity.

These new movements, the first fruits of national self-consciousness, came in time to be bulwarked and extended by certain economic doctrines known as the "mercantile system."[5] The application of this system, to the English colonies implied no feeling of unfriendliness toward them. The action was purely commercial, though at the same time determined by self-interest and with no

3 (Publisher footnote, henceforth P.N.): The just price, a Latin legal term later adapted by Aquinas, with an emphasis on fairness and avoidance of gouging. As opposed to the market price, whatever the market will pay for a good or service.
4 See Ashley's English Economic History, 126 *et seq.*
5 The economic errors of this system have been summarized as follows: It over-estimated the importance of gold and silver, often confounding them with wealth, and measuring the prosperity of a country by the excess of gold imported over that exported. It unduly exalted foreign over domestic trade, and manufactures over agriculture; this involved the balance-of-trade error, leading to what Hamilton styled "the vain project of selling everything and buying nothing." It placed too high an estimate on the value of a dense population as an element of national strength. It invoked too readily state aid for commercial purposes, filling the statute books with vexatious restrictions, and the borders of every little state with petty and hampering custom-houses. See Encyc. Brit. (ninth ed.), article Pol. Econ. (enlarged and reprinted as Ingram's History of Political Economy). The spirit of the mercantile system is admirably illustrated in 23 George II, Ch. 13, Laws of 1750, enforcing heavy penalties for enticing artificers out of Great Britain, or for exporting utensils of the woolen and silk manufactures. See especially the preamble. 20 Statues at Large, p. 14.

recognition of the colonies as independent factors, politically or industrially. Regulations affecting them were determined upon with regard to their effect upon the commerce and industries of the mother country. They were chiefly valued for the market they afforded for British manufactures, the carrying trade of which accrued to British seamen, and for what they could produce to supplement the agriculture of England, or as raw materials for her manufactures. This was considered the natural and proper function of colonies, and the general theory held that natural obstacles were sufficient to prevent the colonies from engaging in trades or manufactures prejudicial to the interests of the mother country.[6] Labor was dear and scarce, and machinery and skill almost entirely lacking. Fabrics could be obtained from England much cheaper than the colonies could make them, and there seemed little danger of collision. Yet British interests were not content with these general safeguards. In spite of the poverty of the colonies and their manifest dependence upon England, there was constant fear lest manufactures should somehow take root in them. Long before parliament was aroused to the political dangers lurking in colonial charters and customs, English merchants and manufacturers were alive to the possibilities of colonial competition. Everything except this they might forgive; but wherever an incipient manufacture showed itself, they were swift, through parliament, to strike at it with restrictive or prohibitive legislation. "The greatest and most general fear, and, indeed, what the colonies of late seem to threaten us with," wrote Cunningham, "is their going into manufactures, and thereby supplying themselves with what they now take from

6 The Navigation Act of 1660 begins: "For the increase of shipping and encouragement of the navigation of this nation, wherein under the good providence and protection of God, the wealth, safety, and strength of this kingdom is so much concerned." The preamble to the Wool Act of 1699 defines its purpose as follows: "Forasmuch as wooll and the woollen manufactures of cloth, serge, bayes, kerseys, and other stuffs made or mixed with wooll, are the greatest and most profitable commodities of this kingdom, on which the value of lands and the trade of the nations do chiefly depend; and whereas great quantities of the like manufactures have of late been made, and are daily increasing in the kingdom of Ireland, and in the English plantations in America, and are exported from thence to foreign markets heretofore supplied from England, which will inevitably sink the value of lands and tend to the ruin of the trade and the woollen manufactures of this realm; for the prevention thereof, and for the encouragement of the woollen manufactures within this kingdom, it be enacted," etc. 10 Statutes at Large, 249.

us. If this was likely to happen, the vigilance of our legislature would doubtless take measures to prevent it. ... Nothing, certainly, would create greater heart-burnings and discontent in Great Britain, than her colonies going into manufactures. On the other hand, nothing can be so agreeable, or so much for the interest of both, as the colonies turning their whole thoughts and powers to the cultivation of their lands."[7]

The beginning of commercial legislation which bore upon the colonies was the famous Navigation Act of 1651[8] This act, passed in no spirit of hostility to the colonies, was in pursuance of Cromwell's far-reaching policy to secure the commercial and maritime supremacy of England, and was aimed particularly at the Dutch, who were then monopolizing the carrying trade of the world.[9] The commerce of the colonies, until then too slight to attract much attention, was becoming important, and rapidly increasing. The Act provided that all commerce between England and the rest of the world should be conducted in English or colonial ships.[10] The Act of 1660 further provided that certain "enumerated article of colonial production should not be exported, even in English ships, to the general markets of the world, but only to England itself.[11]

---

7 Essay on Trade and Commerce, by J. Cunningham (?), pp. 194,197: London, 1770.

8 The Navigation Act is usually dated from 1660, for when the Commonwealth was overthrown the laws of Cromwell were declared invalid. The Navigation Act was re-enacted with the addition noted in the text.

9 The Navigation Act was not, of course, a new departure in English legislation, nor was it the first assertion of English control over colonial commerce. A statute of Richard IT, in 1381 (cited in Chalmers' Political Annals, p. 257), enacted "that to increase the navy of England, no goods or merchandise shall either be exported or imported, but only in ships belonging to the king's subjects." The patents granted by Henry VII to the Cabots provided that whatever commerce was the result of their discoveries must be brought to England. In his instructions to Berkeley in 1639, Charles I directed him "to oblige the masters of vessels, freighted with the productions of the colony, to give bond before their departure to bring the same into England; and to forbid all trade with foreign vessels, except upon necessity. (Chalmer's Political Annals, p. 120) Bancroft (vol. I, p. 146) gives the date as 1641.

10 "The Act was leveled against Dutch commerce, and was but a protection to British shipping; it contained no clause relating to a colonial monopoly, or specially injurious to an American colony. Of itself it inflected no wound on Virginia or New England." 1 Bancroft, 145.

11 The enumerated articles were of two kinds. 1. Those not produced in the moth-

The supplementary act of 1673 provided that articles of European growth or manufacture imported into the colonies should first pass through England, thus subjecting all colonial importations, not the product of England, to double charges in the interest of British merchants.

Still there was a loophole, and English merchants began to complain of the intercolonial trade, which had hitherto been permitted on the supposition that it would be confined to local demands. A profitable trade, however, had grown up between New England and the Southern colonies, and Eastern merchants, shipping to Boston tobacco and certain other colonial products in excess of local demand, sent the surplus to continental Europe without the payment of British or colonial duties, thus underselling the British trader who had paid heavy duties.[12]Accordingly, it was enacted, in 1672, that certain specified articles of intercolonial traffic should first go through England and be landed on English docks, or if trade were direct (and this was the practical clause of the act,) equivalent duties should be paid.[13]

Later acts were intended to supplement the general navigation acts, and especially to secure their more vigorous enforcement. But the measure which bore heaviest upon the northern colonies was the Molasses Act of 1733. A considerable trade grew up between these colonies and the French and Dutch West Indies, consisting of the exchange of lumber, fish, and horses for sugar, rum, and molasses. The British Islands protested and demanded the prohibition

---

er country at all. This was intended to enable English merchants to purchase cheaper in the colonies and sell with more profit at home, and also to make Britain the center of an important carrying trade. 2. Those produced in England, but not in sufficient quantities to supply the demand. These were to be so managed by proper duties as to be always dearer than the home product, thus preventing competition with home producers, but cheaper than the same articles imported from foreign countries. Other articles were not enumerated because they would interfere too much with home industries. See Adam Smith's Wealth of Nations, Bk IV, Ch. VII. The most important of the enumerated articles were sugar, tobacco, cotton, wool, indigo, ginger, fustic, and all other dyeing wood. This affected the West Indies and southern colonies more than New England, whose great staples, lumber, fish, oil, ashes, and furs, were free. See 6 Winsor, 7.

12 See 6 Winsor, 8.

13 Statutes at Large, 398.

of this trade between the colonies and foreign islands. The Molasses Act was nominally a compromise, but the duties levied on importations from the foreign islands amounted to prohibition.[14]

The Navigation Laws were passed in the interest of commerce, mainly through the influence of British shipowners and merchants. The manufacturing interest was not less prompt in appealing to the government, and with even greater success. On this point the nation was practically united, and from 1698 onwards stringent laws were passed designed to forestall any development of colonial manufacturing. In 1696 a Board of Commissioners for Trade and Plantations was created, with instructions to inquire into the means of making the colonies most useful and beneficial to England, and especially as to how they might be diverted from trades likely to prove prejudicial to England.[15]

Through inquiries of special agents and by letters, reports, and statistics from colonial governors, the board kept well informed in regard to colonial affairs and from time to time urged upon parliament legislation in the interest of home manufacturers. In 1699 measures were taken to crush out what seemed the beginning of woolen manufactures in some of the colonies. The household manufacture of coarse fabrics could not well be interfered with, but anything further was prohibited by declaring it unlawful to load wool upon any horse, cart, or other carriage.[16] In 1732 hats were added to the prescribed list, and hat makers were forbidden to have more than two apprentices each. An attempt to prohibit the manufacture of pig iron was temporarily defeated through the influence of the colonial agents; but the production became so important that, owing to the abundance and cheapness of fuel, the colonies were able to undersell their English competitors. The matter again coming up in parliament, the iron makers succeeded in placing heavy duties on American pig iron imported into England. But when the colonies thereupon turned their attention to the manufacture of steel and bar iron for their own use, they

---

14 9d. per gallon on rum and spirits and 6d. on molasses and syrup. 16 Statutes at Large, 374. See also 2 Bancroft, 242 *et seq.*

15 See 2 Bancroft, 73.

16 In part an extension to the colonies of the law of 1660 directed against Scotland and France (Charles II, Chap. 32, Laws of 1660.)

interfered with another and more powerful group of English manufacturers, who in turn appealed to the government. Parliament
then prohibited the manufacture of steel in the colonies, even for
their own consumption. All furnaces were ordered to be destroyed
as nuisances, but as some sort of compensation, the free admission
of pig and bar iron into England was provided for.[17] Presently the
colonies found that they could manufacture certain kinds of nails
cheaper than they could import them, and parliament again interposed with a prohibition of mills for the manufacture of spikes
and nails.

Yet although these restrictions bore with great verity upon the
colonies, there was for a long time no considerable protest against
the economic system which gave them force. Many causes conspired to this result. In the first place, under this system the trade
and manufactures of the mother country had so developed as to
make her the wealthiest and most powerful of European states.
The colonists were Englishmen with English feelings and prejudices. For British prosperity and British glory their hearts were

---

17 Pig iron could be imported free of duty into all parts of Great Britain; bar iron
only into the port of London, and it must not be taken more than ten miles from
London, nor re-exported.
The preamble reads: "Whereas the importation of bar iron from his Majesty's
colonies in America, into the port of London, and the importation of pig iron from
said colonies, into any port of Great Britain, and the manufacture of such bar and
pig iron in Great Britain, will be a great advantage, not only to the said colonies,
but also to this kingdom, by furnishing the manufacturers of iron with a supply of
that useful and necessary commodity, and by means thereof large sums of money, now annually paid for iron to foreigners, will be saved to this kingdom, and a
greater quantity of the woolen, and other manufactures of Great Britain, will be exported to America, in exchange for such iron so imported, be it therefore enacted,"
etc. The ninth and tenth sections of the Act read as followers: "And, that pig and
bar iron made in his Majesty's colonies in America may be further manufactured
in this kingdom; be it further enacted that from and after the twenty-fourth day of
June, 1750, no mill or other engine for slitting or rolling of iron, or any plateing
forge to work with a tilt hammer, or any furnace for making steel, shall be erected,
or after such erection, continued in any part of his Majesty's colonies in America ...
And it is hereby enacted ... that every such mill, engine, forge, or furnace so erected or continued contrary to the directions of this Act, shall be deemed a common
nuisance," and "within thirty days must be abated." 23 George II, Ch. 29 of the
Laws of 1750; 20 Statutes at Large, 97 *et seq.* See also 2 Bancroft, 356.

as warm as any Englishman's.[18] As Franklin put it, to be an "old England man" was of itself a character of some respect and gave a kind of rank among the colonies.[19] In all movements looking toward a better understanding between Great Britain and the colonies they insisted that the colonies need not cease being useful to the mother country. They were so many countries gained to Britain. Their interests were the same,[20] and for generations, and even centuries, the Americans would continue to buy what Britain wanted to sell, and sell what Britain wanted to buy.

Nor was the colonial system wholly one-sided. A large and profitable trade with the West Indies and with Asia and Africa was left untouched, and enjoyed the protection of the English naval power. Besides, there was a powerful appeal to British self-interest to encourage the colonies in those trades and industries which did not interfere with the home market. Governor Hunter of New York, in urging the Board of Trade, in 1715, to vigorously set on foot the production of naval stores, declared that there was no other way to prevent the poorer people from wearing homespun. 'Few that can afford it wear homespun,' said he, 'and a law to compel others would be equivalent to a law to compel them to go naked.'[21] The Lords Commissioners for Trades and Plantations, in 1721, concluded that it was necessity and not choice which sent the colonies to manufacturing, and if proper encouragement were given to naval stores and minerals, they could be diverted from thoughts of setting up any manufacturing of their own.[22]

---

18 1 Political Writings of John Dickinson, 119.

19 See 3 Franklin's Works, 416. Thomas Pownall said, in 1764 that "nothing could eradicate from the hearts of the Americans their natural, almost mechanical affection to Great Britain, which they conceive under no other sense, nor call by any other name than that of home." *The Administration of the Colonies*, by Thomas Pownall, p. 25: London, 1764.

20 "For one hundred years to this time there has not been an American to whom in the genuine feelings of his heart, the interest, welfare, and happiness of Great Britain was not as a dear as that of his own colony, having no other idea but that they were one and the same." Pownall's *Considerations on Taxing the Colonies* (1766), p. 2.

21 1 Doc. Hist. of New York, 713.

22 5 Doc's Relating to Colonial History of New York, 598, 604. The same recommendation was repeated in the Report of 1732; see 3 MacPherson's Annals of Commerce, 186 *et seq.*

In response to these and many similar appeals British legislation constantly favored colonial enterprise of the kind just mentioned. Discriminations in favor of colonial produce were made in English markets, and this was supplemented by bounties from the English government, and by premiums from private societies for the importation into England of silk, hemp and flax, indigo, naval stores, timber, and other articles. And in the case of tobacco, the growers were given the exclusive possession of the English market.[23]

But of far more moment was the practical nullity of the laws of trade. The English government at first attempted no vigorous enforcement, and the feeling regarding these regulations rendered evasions easy and widespread. Thus the Molasses Act of 1733, which was a nominal prohibition upon all lawful trade with the foreign West Indies, merely replaced this with a clandestine trade nearly as large. The Board of Trade was constantly reminded of this state of affairs, and concerted measures for securing the enforcement of the laws. But between the dissensions at home and the difficulties of dealing with colonial assemblies and charters, nothing effective was undertaken until after 1750. In a word, the colonies 'manufactured whatever they found to be for their advantage, and sent ships wherever they pleased, in spite of all navigation acts and laws of trade.'[24]

In their own internal affairs the colonies followed the example of England.[25] The royal veto generally prevented any legislation which would interfere with English interests, but within the narrower sphere mercantile principles had free play. Export bounties were granted, to encourage trade, manufactures, and agriculture, on linen and woolen cloths, silk, flax, pitch, hemp, yards, and other articles. Manufactures were promoted by bills of credit, exemptions from taxation, bounties, and premiums from private organizations.[26] Drawbacks were frequently given, though the opposition

23 7 Statutes at Large, 502, (Charles II, Chap. 34, Laws of 1660). See also George II, Chap. 20; 24 George II, Chap. 51; *et passim*.
24 See 6 Winsor, 9, 10.
25 See American Trade Regulations before 1789, printed in vol. iii of the publications of the American Historical Association.
26 In 1682 Virginia passed a law for the encouragement of domestic manufactures. In 1706 Maryland encouraged the manufacture of linen and even of woolen cloth, the assembly pleading in excuse of the weavers that they were driven to their task

of the South prevented their incorporation in the proposed tariffs under the Confederation. Bounties on imports were as freely resorted to. Virginia at times remitted the export duty on tobacco to encourage the importation of salt and negroes. Rhode Island, in 1777, granted a conditional bounty on the importation of salt. South Carolina, in 1716, granted a bounty of from £22 to £30 on imported servants. Maryland and Virginia allowed an abatement of from 10% to 25% on duties paid in imported gold or silver. Export duties were resorted to for revenue. In general they were low, but prohibitions both of importations and exportations were not unknown. Scarcity was sure to lead to such prohibitions, especially with regard to grain, flour, meats, salt, and military stores.

In import duties there was great diversity, but with a general tendency to higher rates. The early tariffs, in contrast to those of England, had a large free list, and even where the list was extended few articles were enumerated. In 1661 Virginia put a tariff on rum on the ground of its injurious effects. Massachusetts began by taxing beaver skins and wines. In 1703 South Carolina levied a general tariff of three percent on certain specified articles. In 1698 Maryland resorted to a tariff to secure funds for the erection of a capitol. During the disputes between Virginia and Maryland, hostile discriminations, embargoes, and three-fold duties were adopted to cut off inland trade to the northward.[27]

The Declaration of Independence threw off all restraint but the war itself was such a barrier to commerce that there was little incentive to tariff legislation. The Continental Congress had no power to regulate trade, and the cause of the colonies had, by this time, become, in some sense, a protest against the restrictive system of England. Before the final rupture various attempts were made by non-importation agreements and otherwise to break off trade with England and encourage home manufactures; such encouragement the war more effectually provided. On the return of peace the new

by absolute necessity. 2 Bancroft, 18, 22. In 1718 Massachusetts imposed a duty of one percent on English manufactures and gave a small discrimination in favor of its own shipbuilding. This was vetoed by the king. *Ib.* 239. The report of 1732 complained that Massachusetts had encouraged the manufacture of paper and other articles.

27 In 1676 New York was discriminating against Boston. See Randolph's report to the Council of Trade, 3 Doc's relating to Colonial Hist. of New York, 241.

republic sought reciprocity with all nations, and the failure to secure this, added to the commercial complications at home, brought the newly united states to the verge of dissolution.

The desperate financial straits of the Confederation, and the impossibility of raising money by requisitions on the states, first turned the attention of the country to the question of intrusting Congress with the power of regulating trade.[28] New Jersey, in 1778, soon after the Articles of Confederation were approved by Congress, laid before that body a proposition that, inasmuch as state control would lead to unavoidable confusion, Congress alone should have the power to regulate commerce and dispose of the resulting duties. In 1780 Hamilton, in a letter to James Duane, maintained that Congress should have the power of regulating trade, determining with what countries it should be carried on. The same idea found expression in the address of the Hartford Convention of 1780.[29] In December of that year Pennsylvania instructed its delegates in Congress that imposts on trade were absolutely necessary, and in order to prevent one state taking advantage of another, Congress should recommend to the several states a system of imposts.[30] In 1781 Congress itself asked for authority to levy an impost duty of five percent, the revenue to be applied only to war expenses, and to continue until the debts were paid. One by one the states replied until all had consented, with more or less reservations, except Georgia and Rhode Island. Congress again called upon these states to act. But Georgia made no response, and Rhode Island refused outright, alleging that such a duty would bear most heavily upon commercial states like herself, objecting to

---

28 Very slowly and reluctantly the prejudice against this step was overcome. The whole struggle of the century had been to secure the sole right of taxation to the local assemblies, and so little national feeling was there that the intrusting of any part of this power to Congress seemed like surrendering the chief result of the long struggle. The clause in Franklin's plan of 1754, giving the general Congress power to collect a revenue, insured its rejection by every colony. See letter of Governor Shirley to Secretary Robinson, Dec. 24, 1754, criticizing the Albany plan; 6 Doc's relating to Colonial History of New York, 930.

29 P.N. The Hartford Convention of 1780 was held to find ways to recruit troops and gather supplies for the Continental Congress and Army. Not to be confused with the later Hartford Convention of 1815, in which New England Federalists opposed the 1812 War.

30 6 Bancroft, 14.

collectors appointed by Congress, and insisting that it was far too much power to intrust to Congress.[31]

In 1783 Congress returned to the same plan, and a bill was drawn up calculated to meet the objections to the former measure. The concurrent right of taxation was still retained by the states, and the grant of power to Congress was limited to twenty-five years. Collectors of revenue were to be chosen by the states, and the grant was to take effect only when all the states had given their consent. This bill, approved by the almost unanimous vote of Congress, was sent out to the states accompanied by a solemn appeal, drawn from the desperate condition of the finances, written by Madison, and an elaborate answer to Rhode Island's former objections, written by Hamilton. After many delays and a second appeal from Congress, conditional acceptances were received from all the states except New York. In this refusal New York persisted, reiterating her position so late as February, 1787. In 1784 Congress called upon the states for a grant of power to regulate commerce for fifteen years, by prohibitions and discriminations against unfriendly powers. But the response to this request was even less favorable than to the other.[32]

Meanwhile the states, with different tariff and tonnage acts, began to make commercial war upon each other. When three New England states virtually closed their ports to British shipping, Connecticut threw hers wide open, and then laid duties upon imports from Massachusetts. Massachusetts retaliated by imposing heavier duties on imports from Connecticut than from Great Britain.[33] Pennsylvania discriminated against Delaware. New Jersey paid tribute to both her neighbors. New York exacted the same entrance fees and custom-house regulations from the sloops of Connecticut and New Jersey as from foreign vessels, and these states promptly retaliated. Articles which Connecticut and New Jersey excluded by heavy tonnage duties, entered New York virtually free. What Massachusetts encouraged, Virginia restricted. Virginia even proposed to impose enormous duties without regard

---

31 6 Bancroft, 33.

32 See John Fiske's Critical Period of American History, 144. For the animus of the opposition to these grants, see Van Buren's Political Parties in the United States.

33 See 1 Madison's Works, 216.

to the action of the other states.[34] New York was indifferent to the trade in indigo and pitch, South Carolina to that in furs. New England's revenues came from lumber, oil, and potash; Pennsylvania's from corn and grain; and neither was concerned as to the interests of the other.[35] Pending the action of the states on the five percent impost, Madison wrote: "In this suspense, the more suffering states are seeking relief from political efforts which are less likely to obtain it than to drive their trade into other channels and to kindle heart-burnings on all sides."[36] And six months later: "The states are every day giving proof that separate regulations are more likely to set them by the ears than to attain the common object."[37]

Inevitably the states drifted out towards anarchy and disunion, their credit daily sinking, and internal dissensions becoming more and more serious. The need of a stronger government and of a uniform revenue system came to be generally recognized, but the helplessness of the legislature prevented the adoption of any adequate measure. The Convention of 1787 gave the new government full powers in this respect, and prepared the way for a comprehensive tariff act.

Yet this movement toward restrictive legislation, necessary as it was, indicated a decided reaction from the position which had been reached; and to understand its significance it will be necessary to glance at the course of economic thought.

While colonial legislation reproduced much that was characteristic of the mercantile system, the logic of events had, in fact, emancipated American thought from the fetters of mercantilism much faster than either the colonies or England were aware. The voices of the new economic speculations were first heard in England, but the response was much readier in the colonies. Even while submitting to the part which mercantilism assigned them in building up the power of England, the colonies were not forced to believe that her infallibility extended to all details. They claimed all the rights of English subjects, resented the petty annoyances

34 See 1 Madison's Works, 271.
35 See John Fiske's Critical Period of American History, 144-147; and 1 McMaster, 206.
36 Madison to Jefferson, Aug. 20, 1785; 1 Madison's Works, 197.
37 Madison to Jefferson, March 18, 1786; 1 Madison's Works, 225.

with which the mother country sought to fetter their trade, and reached out after that larger liberty and more generous treatment which, they stoutly insisted, was not inconsistent with the prosperity of England. In all measures which they asked for they labored to make plain that they were not running counter to the interests of England. Yet they had other ideas of destiny than the narrow existence Great Britain proposed for them, and when British folly went so far as to force the fundamental issue of taxation without representation, the bond which connected them to the mother country was rudely snapped asunder.[38]

No one did more to establish the idea of a natural relation between the colonies and the mother country than Franklin.[39] In

---

38 The self-interest which impelled the colonies to revolt from the commercial fetters of England was powerfully reinforced by the writings of Petty, North, Locke, Dean Tucker, and Hume, in England, and of the economists in France, Quesnay, Turgot, and others,—the latter, especially, bulwarked in a social philosophy which took deep root in American soil. A hundred years before Adam Smith, Sir William Petty showed that value originates in labor, and pointed out some of the advantages of a division of labor. He anticipated Ricardo's iron law of wages, and strongly opposed governmental interference with industry. North maintained that as to trade the whole world were as one nation, and no trade was unprofitable to the public—if it were, it would be given up; and that no people could become rich by state regulations.

All this was mostly negative, but it set the current of economic thinking in a direction opposite to mercantilism. Then came the physiocrats with their positive ideas and system—the *jus naturae*—which called for the abolition of all prohibitions on exports and imports, in the interest of agriculture. Then followed Dean Tucker and Hume in England, and finally, in the same year that Independence was declared, appeared Adam Smith's *Wealth of Nations*.

39 The idea of the natural dependence of the colonies on the mother country was, of course, fundamental and at the basis, even, of the navigation acts and laws of trade. But the fear that their increasing numbers and wealth, joined to their great distance from Great Britain, would lead them to throw off their dependence, found constant expression. Some of the acts of the earlier assemblies were, indeed, tantamount to a renunciation of allegiance. But wiser men, while yielding none of the rights they believed themselves entitled to as British subjects, sought, with infinite tact and patience, to secure these liberties in the broad line of constitutional development. And preliminary to all it was necessary to show that the colonies had no inducements to set up for themselves. Jeremiah Dummer, in his defense of the colonial charters in 1721, declared that it was "not more absurd to place two of his Majesty's beef-eaters to watch an infant in the cradle that it don't rise to cut it's father's throat, than to guard those weak infant colonies to prevent their shaking

a pamphlet written in 1751, and reprinted in England, he point-ed out that notwithstanding the rapid increase of population in America, so vast was the territory that it would require many ages to settle it fully. Labor never would be cheap, where no man continued long a laborer for others, but got a plantation of his own. Labor, he declared, was no cheaper in Pennsylvania than it had been thirty years before, though many thousand laboring men had been imported. The danger, therefore, of the colonies interfering with the mother country in trades that depended on labor was too remote to require the attention of Great Britain. "But in proportion to the increase of the colonies, a vast demand is growing for British manufactures, a glorious market wholly in the power of Britain, in which foreigners cannot interfere, which will increase in a short time even beyond her power of supply-ing, though her whole trade should be to her colonies."[40] "They who understand the economy and principles of manufactures," he asserted in another pamphlet written in England, in 1760, "know that it is impossible to establish them in places not populous; and even in those that are populous, hardly possible to establish them to the prejudice of the places already in possession of them. ... A manufacturer is part of a great system of commerce which takes in conveniences of various kinds; methods of promoting materials of all sorts, machines for expediting and facilitating labor, all the channels of correspondence for vending the wares, the credit and confidence necessary to found and support this correspondence, the mutual aid of different artisans, and a thousand other particu-lars which time and long experience have gradually established."[41]

The occasion of the pamphlet just cited was the question before the British Cabinet as to whether Canada or Guadaloupe should be given back to the French. It was urged that Canada should be sacrificed, among other reasons, because its possession

off the British yoke." The most constant argument was the one drawn from the dearness and scarcity of labor. See, for instances, Doc. Hist. of New York, vol. I, pp. 714 et seq.; Doc's relating to Colonial Hist. of New York, vol. viii, p. 66, et passim.

40 Observations concerning the Increase of Mankind, etc.; 2 Franklin's Works, 223 et seq.

41 The Interest of Great Britain Considered, etc.; 3 Franklin's Works, 100. Cf. John Dickinson, infra, p. 40.

by the French would tend to keep the colonies in check. Franklin was alarmed at the idea of parting with Canada and strongly urged the commercial necessity of retaining it. Speaking now as an Englishman, he argued that the blood and treasure spent in American wars, was not spent in the cause of the colonies alone; nor did he omit to hold up the alternative of colonial manufactures. "A people spread through the whole tract of country on this side of the Mississippi, and secured by Canada in our hands, would probably for some centuries find employment in agriculture, and thereby free us at home effectually from our fears of American manufactures. Unprejudiced men well know that all the penal and prohibitory laws that were ever thought on will not be sufficient to prevent manufactures in a country whose inhabitants surpass the number that can subsist by the husbandry of it. That this will be the case in America soon, if our people remain confined within the mountains, and almost as soon should it be unsafe for them to live beyond, though the country be ceded to us, no man acquainted with political and commercial history can doubt. Manufactures are founded in poverty. It is the multitude of poor without law in a country and who must work for others at low wages or starve, that enables undertakers to carry on a manufacture and afford it cheap enough to prevent the importation of the same kind from abroad, and to bear the expense of exportation. But no man who can have a piece of land of his own sufficient by his labor to subsist his family in plenty, is poor enough to be a manufacturer and work for a master. Hence while there is land enough in America for our own people, there can never be manufactures to any amount or value."[42] It was not necessary, he insisted, that the American colonies should cease being useful to the mother country. It had been urged that finding no check from Canada, the Americans would extend themselves almost without bounds into the inland parts and increase infinitely from all causes. But that would take some centuries, and "in the meantime this nation must necessarily supply them with the manufactures they consume; because the new settlers will be employed in agriculture; and the new settlements will so continually draw off spare hands from the old that our present colonies will not find themselves in a condition to manufacture even for their own inhabitants. Thus our trade must,

42 3 Franklin's Works, 86. See also *ib. v*, 1 *et seq.*

till that country becomes as fully peopled as England (that is, for centuries to come) be continually increasing, and with it our naval power."[43] The exports to Pennsylvania, he said, had increased in twenty-eight years in the proportion of 17 to 1, while the population had increased only 4 to 1. "In fact, the occasion for English goods in North America, and the inclination to have and use them, is, and must be for ages to come, much greater than the ability of the people to pay for them."[44]

It must not be supposed, however, that Franklin adopted the English view with regard to colonial manufactures. He had a sincere preference for agricultural pursuits, and shared the common opinion that for a long time manufactures must be very slight. But the necessity for allaying the fears of English interests naturally led him to emphasize unduly the dependence of the colonies on the manufactures of England, as well as their supreme devotion to agriculture. The economic basis of England's policy he came more and more to question, and keeping well abreast of current criticism of mercantilism he lost no opportunity of cautiously enforcing a more generous policy.

As far back as 1729, in arguing for paper money, Franklin appealed to those who wished to see manufactures encouraged.[45]

---

43 3 Franklin's Works, 93. Cf. Views of Jefferson, Ellsworth, Adams, Washington, and Hamilton—*infra*, pp. 38 *et seq.*
In his examination before the House of Commons in 1766, he explained how the balance of trade was adjusted. Pennsylvania, he said, imported from England £500,000 a year, and exported to England £40,000. The balance was paid by produce carried to the West Indies and sold to the English, French, Spaniards, Danes, and Dutch; by the same produce carried to other colonies in North America, as to New England, Nova Scotia, Newfoundland, Carolina, and Georgia; by the same carried to different parts of Europe, as Spain, Portugal, and Italy. In all these places they received either money, bills of exchange, or commodities, suitable for remittance to Britain; which together with all the profits on the industry of merchants and mariners arising in those circuitious voyages, and the freights made their ships, centered finally in Britain to discharge the balance and pay for British manufactures continually used in the provinces or sold to foreigners by traders. (3 Franklin's Works, 417.) Franklin was here arguing that the Americans would be utterly unable to pay the Stamp duty, and it may be presumed that he made the case as strong as possible.
44 3 Franklin's Works, 109. See also *ib.* 417.
45 See 1 Franklin's Works, 359 *et seq.*

In 1747 Connecticut proposed a tariff of five percent on imports. In answer to an inquiry as to the advisability of this duty, Franklin said that undoubtedly, on the whole, the duty would be paid by the consumer; so that it would be another mode of taxing their own people, though perhaps meant to raise money on their neighbors. Yet if they could make some of the goods heretofore imported, the advanced price might encourage their own manufacture and in time make importations unnecessary, which would be an advantage. But he reminded them that their tariff might not only encourage smuggling, but also offend their neighbors, who by heavy counter duties might leave Connecticut's own exports a drug in the market.[46] Even when speaking most extravagantly of colonial dependence, he shrewdly inserted arguments tending to a less severe repression of colonial manufactures. In a pamphlet already cited, after referring to the vast and growing demand for British manufactures in the colonies—"a glorious market wholly in the power of Britain"—he added: "therefore, Britain should not too much restrain manufactures in the colonies. To distress is to weaken, and weakening the children weakens the whole family." Again, in the Canada-Guadaloupe pamphlet, after insisting that for ages to come the colonies would want more English manufactures than they could pay for, he continued: "And thus, if at any time they should manufacture some coarse article, which on account of its bulk or other circumstance cannot so well be brought to them from Britain, it only enables them the better to pay for finer goods that otherwise they could not indulge themselves in."[47]

Regarding the proposed representation of the colonies in the British parliament, he declared that such a course would be very acceptable to the colonies, provided they had a reasonable number of representatives allowed them; and that all the old acts of parliament restraining the trade or cramping the manufactures of the colonies be at the same time repealed, and the British subjects on this side of the water put, in those respects, on the same footing with those in Great Britain, till the new parliament representing the whole, shall think it for the interest of the whole to re-enact some or all of them. ... "I should hope, too, that by such a union

---

46 Franklin to Jared Eliot, July 16, 1747; 2 Franklin's Works, 78, 79.
47 3 Franklin's Works, 110.

the people of Great Britain and the people of the colonies would learn to consider themselves as not belonging to different interests, but to one community, with one interest; which, I imagine, would contribute to strengthen the whole and greatly lessen the danger of future separation. ... I look on the colonies as so many countries gained to Great Britain and more advantageous to it than if they had been gained out of the seas around the coasts and joined to its lands; for being in different climates, they afford greater variety of produce and materials for more manufactures, and being separated by the ocean they increase much more its shipping and seamen... And if through increase of people two smiths are wanted for one employed before, why may not the new smith be allowed to live and thrive in the *new* country."[48] Six years later he wrote to Hume: "I have lately read with great pleasure, as I do everything of yours, the excellent essay on the *Jealousy of Commerce*.... But I hope particularly from that essay an abatement of the jealousy that reigns here [i.e. in England] of the commerce of the colonies."[49]

But what Franklin regarded as the normal course of development for the colonies, he by no means believed to be the only course open to them; and in his examination before the House of Commons in 1766, pending the repeal of the Stamp Act, his attitude was one of defiance. He defined the difference between external and internal taxes by saying that an external tax was a duty levied on commodities imported and added to the cost; people could buy or not as they chose. But the Stamp Act proposed to force the people to pay whether they wished or not. When asked whether external taxes levied on necessaries of life would not be the same as an internal tax, he replied that he did not know a single article imported into the northern colonies, that they could not either do without or make themselves. Even English cloth was not absolutely necessary, for with industry and good management they might very well supply themselves with all they wanted. He was asked if it would not take a long time to establish the woolen manufacture, the Americans meanwhile suffering greatly. He thought not. They had made surprising progress already, and he was of the opinion

48 Franklin to Governor Shirley, Dec. 22,1754; 2 Franklin's Works, 384 *et seq.* Franklin's more mature ideas on the proper relations of trade are given in a letter to Pownall in 1768; see infra, p. 33.
49 Franklin to Hume, Sept. 27, 1760 ; 3 Franklin's Works, 127.

that before their old clothes were worn out they would have new ones of their own making. "Can they possibly find wool enough in North America?" "They have taken steps to increase wool," he replied. "They entered into general combinations not to eat any more lamb; and very few lambs were killed last year. This will soon make a prodigious difference; and the establishment of great manufactories like those in England are not necessary because the people will all spin and work for themselves." "But is it their interest to make cloth at home?" "They may at present get it cheaper from the British," was the reply, "but when one considers other circumstances, the restraints on their trade and the difficulty of making remittances, it is their interest to make everything." "Supposing the Stamp Act continued and enforced, do you imagine that ill-humor will induce the Americans to give as much for worse manufactures of their own, and use them, preferable to better of ours?" "Yes, I think so," Franklin answered. "People will pay as freely to gratify one passion as another, their resentment as their pride."[50]

In this examination Franklin asserted that the respect for parliament was greatly lessened among the colonies, but if the Stamp Act were repealed he thought their attempts to force manufactures would be given up. In 1767, after the repeal, the people of Boston, still smarting under the injustice of England's policy, passed resolutions recommending that all prudent and legal measures be taken to encourage the produce and manufactures of the province, to lessen the use of superfluities, and to refrain from purchasing a great number of imported articles.[51] These resolutions created no little commotion in England. The newspapers were in full cry against America, Franklin wrote. "Colonel Onslow told me in court last Sunday," he continued, "I could not conceive how much the friends of America were run upon and hurt by them, and how much the Grenvillians[52] triumphed. I have just written a paper for Tuesday's *Chronicle* to extenuate matters a little.... If our people [i.e. Pennsylvania] should follow the Boston example of entering

---

50 3 Franklin's Works 422 *et seq.*
51 See 4 Franklin's Works 59 *et seq.*
52 P.N.: George Grenville (1712-1770) was the Prime Minister of Great Britain from 1763-1765. This was during the Seven Years War. To help finance the costs of this war, he passed the Stamp Act and Quartering Act, which imposed heavily on the American colonists.

into resolutions for frugality and industry, full as necessary for us as for them, I hope they will, among other things, give this reason, that it is to enable them the more speedily and effectually to discharge their debts to Great Britain. This will soften a little, and at the same time appear honorable and like ourselves."[53]

This was very adroitly turning the edge of the weapon, but Franklin soon found an even better means of mollifying the outraged Englishman. Happening to hear Grenville complain in the House of Commons, that some of the colonial governors had not reported, as they had been directed, regarding the manufactures of their respective colonies, it occurred to him to look at those which had been sent in. They were all to one effect—that there were no manufactures of any consequence in the colonies,—and Franklin lost no time in making the public acquainted with their contents. "These accounts are very satisfactory here," he wrote, "and induce parliament to despise and take no notice of the Boston resolutions."[54]

In these representations Franklin reflected fairly enough the temper of the coolest headed Americans, a temper, indeed, which

53 4 Franklin's Works, 59-61.
54 4 Franklin's Works, 132, 133. In his *Chronicle* letter, Franklin insisted that the Americans complained justly of the action of the nailmakers and hatters of England in getting a prohibition of slitting mills and hat manufacture in the colonies. But a remonstrance against the English trade regulations, which he quoted from an American newspaper, he apologized for as "the wild ravings of the at present half-distracted Americans." The clipping, which at that time seemed to Franklin worthy of such epithets, is in part as follows:
"Our people have been foolishly fond of their [English] modes and manufactures to the impoverishing of our own country, carrying off all our cash, and loading us with debt; they will not suffer to restrain the luxury of our inhabitants, as they do that of their own, by laws; they can make laws to discourage or prohibit the importation of French superfluities; but though those of England are as ruinous to us as the French ones to them, if we make a law of that kind, they immediately repeal it. Thus they get all our money from us by trade; and every profit we can anywhere make by our fisheries, our produce, or our commerce, centers finally with them; but this does not signify. It is time, then, to take care of ourselves in the best means in our power. Let us unite in solemn resolution and engagements with and to each other, that we will give these new officers as little trouble as possible, by not consuming the British manufactures on which they are to levy duties. Let us agree to consume no more of their expensive gewgaws. Let us live frugally, and let us industriously manufacture what we can for ourselves." *Ib.,* 109.

he was doing much to form and direct. Loyalty to England—to larger England,—but resentment of injustice; submission to the general colonial policy as loyal subjects of the realm; a willing preference for agriculture, but the insistence, on certain necessary exceptions to the general rule; an opposition to oppression, firm and uncompromising where colonial action was possible, but wary and cautious in all conflicts with the British ministry—such was, in general, at the time, the dominant feeling of the colonies. All this involved little economic thinking, though it did imply a practical denial of some of the cherished principles of mercantilism. But the more eager minds in America, and Franklin's among the first, were coming in contact with ideas which were wholly revolutionizing their theories of trade and commerce, and undermining their abstract justification of the policy which all Europe was pursuing. Almost insensibly, but firmly, the new ground was taken until as the struggle went on in the conflict of arms the smaller question seemed swallowed up in the larger one of the vindication of the principles of free commerce.

We have already noted the cordiality with which Franklin greeted Hume's essay on *Commerce*, in which it was maintained that the prosperity of one nation, instead of being a hindrance, was a help to that of its neighbors, and which condemned the "numberless bars, obstructions, and imposts which all nations of Europe, and none more than England have put upon trade." "If the colonies are fitter for a particular trade than Britain," Franklin wrote Pownall, "they should have it, and Britain apply to what it is more fit for. The whole empire is a gainer. And if Britain is not so fit or so well situated for a particular advantage, other countries will get it, if the colonies do not. Thus Ireland was forbid the woolen manufacture and remains poor; but this has given to the French the trade and wealth Ireland might have gained for the British Empire. ... Advantageous situations and circumstances will always secure and fix manufactures."[55]

Franklin's contact with the physiocrats colored his economic thinking to the end of his life.[56] Their exaltation of agriculture

---

55 4 Franklin's Works, 64.
56 From London he wrote to Dupont de Nemours, July 1768, acknowledging the receipt "of your *Physiocratie*, which I have read with great pleasure. ... Am

accorded with his own tastes, and confirmed him in his distrust of manufactures, except in a narrow and very subordinate way.[57] To Joshua Babcock he wrote, in 1772, of a tour he had made through Ireland and Scotland, and of the sad contrast between the few noblemen living in the highest affluence and the bulk of the people living in the most sordid wretchedness. "I thought often of the happiness of New England," he continued, "where every man is a freeholder, has a vote in public affairs, lives in a tidy, warm house, has plenty of good food and fuel, with whole clothes from head to foot, the manufacture perhaps of his own family." Comparing this condition with that of England, Ireland, and Scotland, he declared that if any should envy the trade of these countries, they could have a share of it if they would go barefoot and shirtless, be content to wear rags, and live the year round on potatoes and buttermilk.[58]

In 1776, before departing for France as one of the special commissioners from Congress, Franklin sketched an outline of the terms upon which he supposed a peace might be made with Great Britain, in case opportunity for negotiation should be offered. Free trade was to be the basis of all commercial arrangements. Peace, he maintained, was as necessary to England as to the states, and although England would no longer have a monopoly her share of the growing trade would soon be greater than the whole had

perfectly charmed with the principles of your new philosophy, and wish I could have stayed in France for some time to have studied in your school that I might by conversing with its founders have made myself quite a master of that philosophy. ... I am sorry to find that wisdom which sees the welfare of the parts in the prosperity of the whole seems yet not to be known in this country. We are so far from conceiving that which is best for mankind, or even for Europe in general, may be best for us, that we are even studying to establish and extend a separate interest of Britain, to the prejudice of even Ireland and our own colonies. ... It is from your philosophy only that the maxims of a more contrary and more happy conduct are to be drawn, which I therefore sincerely wish may grow and increase till it becomes the governing philosophy of the human species." (4 Franklin's Works, 194.)

57 "After all," he wrote, echoing the physiocratic dogma, "this country [i.e. England] is fond of manufactures beyond their real value, for the true source of riches is husbandry. Agriculture is truly productive of new wealth; manufactures only change forms, and whatever value they give to the materials they work upon, they in the meantime consume an equal value in provisions, etc." (Franklin's Works, 120.)

58 4 Franklin's Works, 440.

been before.[59] When peace was made it seemed that the opportunity had come to begin a new and better system. "Restraints on the freedom of commerce and intercourse between us," Franklin wrote Hartley, "can afford no advantage equivalent to the mischief they will do by keeping up ill-humor and promoting a total alienation."[60] The failure to secure reciprocity he attributed to the want of united action on the part of the states,[61] and consoled himself with the thought that the United States could do as well without a commercial treaty as England.[62]

Franklin favored the five percent impost, and acquiesced in the probable existence of tariffs under the constitution. But his tone was one of apology, and he had no notion that the new republic would re-enact the foolish policy of England. To Mr. Small he wrote, in 1787: "I have not lost any of the principles of public economy you once knew me possessed of, but to get the bad customs of a country changed and new ones, though better, introduced, it is necessary first to remove the prejudices of the people, enlighten their ignorance, and to convince them that their interest will be promoted by the proposed changes, and this is not the work of a day. Our legislators are all landowners, and they are not yet persuaded that all taxes are finally paid by the land. Besides, our country is so sparsely settled, the habitations, particularly in the back countries, being perhaps five or six miles distant from each other, that the time and labor of the collector in going from house to house, and being obliged to call often before he can recover the tax, amounts to more than the tax is worth, and therefore we have been forced into the mode of indirect taxes —that is, duties on importation of goods, and excises."[63] "We shall, as you suppose," he wrote M. Le Veillard, " have imposts on trade and custom-houses, not because other nations have them, but because we cannot at present do without them. We want to discharge our public debt occasioned by the late war. ... When we are out of debt we may leave our trade free, for our ordinary charges of gov-

---

59 See 6 Franklin's Works, 18.
60 8 Franklin's Works, 337.
61 8 Franklin's Works, 349.
62 9 Franklin's Works, 279.
63 9 Franklin's Works, 414.

ernment will not be great."[64]

In this response to the new and stirring thought of the age, Franklin by no means stood alone. Many years the senior of most of the Revolutionary statesmen,[65] with large experience and renown, familiar with the thought and refinement of Europe, himself an important contributor to the scientific progress of his time, he first, perhaps, caught the new spirit, and in large measure, no doubt, imparted it to his countrymen. Yet the younger men were hardly less keen than the sage and philosopher. They too had something of a vision of "manifest destiny," and in their thought for the future of America they laid hold of those fresh ideas of human life and human society which characterized the philosophers of the eighteenth century, and became the severe though sober critics of the old economy and old civilization. The Adams's, Otis, Jefferson, Madison, Dickinson, Jay, Morris, Fisher Ames, and

---

64 In Franklin's Works, 460; see also *ib.* 471. In a pamphlet published in Europe, in 1782, for the information of those who thought of emigrating to America, Franklin pointed out that legislative aid to manufactures had been rare in America and of little success in establishing a manufacture which the country was not yet so ripe as to encourage private persons to set up; labor being generally too dear and hands difficult to be kept together. And when the governments had been solicited to support such schemes by encouragements in money, or by imposing duties on importation, it had been generally refused on the principle that if the country was ripe for manufacturing it would be carried on by private persons to advantage, and if not, it would be folly to think of forcing nature. (8 Franklin's Works, 179 *et seq.*) Franklin's "Wail of a Protected Manufacturer," written in 1789, may be quoted as his parting word on the protective system: "Messrs.—I am a manufacturer and was a petitioner for the act to encourage and protect the manufactures of this state. I was very happy when the act was obtained, and I immediately added to the price of my manufactures as much as it would bear so as to be a little cheaper than the same article imported and paying the duty. By this addition I hoped to grow richer. But as every other manufacturer whose wares are under the protection of this act has done the same, I begin to doubt whether, considering the whole year's expenses of my family, with all these separate additions I pay to other manufacturers, I am at all a gainer. And I confess I cannot but wish that, except the protective duty on my own manufacture, all duties of the kind were taken off and abolished. This, however, I must submit to the better judgment of our legislators. Yours, etc., Q." (10 Franklin's Works, 118.) See also 4 Franklin's Works, 21, in more serious vein, on how protective duties work.

65 Franklin was twenty-six years older than Washington, and fifty-one years older than Hamilton. He was seventy when the Declaration of Independence was adopted, and eighty-one when he sat in the Constitutional Convention of 1787.

others, were all, more or less, born into this newness of life, and all, with more or less agreement, felt the Revolution to be a protest against the Restrictive system of the Old World. All shared in the distrust of manufactures and labored and hoped for a commercial relation with Europe free from the barriers that had so long existed. Yet all were too patriotic to be willing to purchase commercial peace on the terms of a tame submission to British arrogance, and at last reached practically the same standpoint in the persuasion that their theories were, for the time at least, impossible of realization.

Madison, eminently a conservative, at twenty-three eagerly read Dean Tucker's tracts,[66] and a casual allusion to the *Wealth of Nations*, in 1785, shows him familiar with that great work. In a letter to Jefferson, in 1784, he argued for the free use of the Mississippi, holding that the settlement of the western country depended upon it, and that by the free expansion of the people the establishment of internal manufactures would not only be long delayed, but the consumption of foreign manufactures increased, creating in turn an increased demand for American products of the soil.[67] In acknowledging the receipt of a book on the commerce between France and the United States, Jefferson wrote, in 1786: "Were I to select any particular passages as giving me particular satisfaction, it would be those wherein you prove to the United States that they will be more virtuous, more free, and more happy, employed in agriculture than as carriers or manufacturers. It is a truth, and a precious one for them, if they could be persuaded of it."[68] Two years later he wrote: "In general it is impossible that manufactures should succeed in America, from the high price of labor. This is occasioned by the great demand of labor for agriculture."[69] In his "Notes on Virginia," published in 1781, Jefferson stated his position more strongly. The political economists of Europe, he said, had established it as a principle that every state should endeavor to manufacture for itself; and this principle like many others was transferred to America without calculating the difference of

66 See letter from Madison to Wm. Bradford, July 1, 1774; 1 Madison's Works, 17.
67 1 Madison's Works, 96.
68 Jefferson to M. De Warville, Aug. 15,1786; 2 Jefferson's Works, 11.
69 Jefferson to Thomas Digges, June 19, 1788; 2 Jefferson's Works, 412.

circumstances which should often produce difference of results. In Europe the lands were either cultivated or locked up against the cultivator. Manufacture must therefore be resorted to of necessity, not of choice, to support the surplus of their peoples. But in America there was an abundance of land courting the industry of the husbandman. "Those who labor in the earth are the chosen people of God, if ever he had a chosen people. ... While we have land to labor, then, let us never wish to see our citizens occupied at a work-bench, or twirling a distaff. Carpenters, masons, smiths, are wanting in husbandry; but for the general operations of manufacture, let our workshops remain in Europe."[70]

Washington, whose partiality for American manufactures was always pronounced, hardly looked for more than the employment of women and children.[71] In regard to the prospect of a closer commercial union with France, he wrote Lafayette, in 1786: "There are many articles of manufacture which we stand absolutely in need of, and shall continue to have occasion for, so long as we remain an agricultural people, ... that is to say, for ages to come."[72] As population increases, imports will necessarily increase, argued Ellsworth of Connecticut, urging the advantage of an indirect revenue, in the debate on the adoption of the Constitution, " because our citizens will choose to be farmers, living independently on their freeholds, rather than to be manufacturers and work for a groat a day."[73] " The American continental colonies," wrote John Dickinson in 1765, in his arraignment of the Stamp Act, "are inhabited by persons of small fortunes who are so closely employed in subduing a wild country for their subsistence, and who would labor under such difficulties in contending with old and populous countries which must excel them in workmanship and cheapness, that they have not time nor any temptation to apply themselves to manufactures.[74] John Adams, minister to Holland in 1780, in

---

70 8 Jefferson's Works, 405.
71 "Though I would not force the introduction of manufactures by extravagant encouragements, and to the prejudice of agriculture, yet I conceive much might be done in the way by women, children, and others, without taking one really necessary hand from tilling the earth."
72 9 Washington's Works, 192.
73 2 Elliot's Debates, 192.
74 1 Political Writings of John Dickson, 48.

correcting certain misconceptions regarding America, declared that agriculture ever was, and ever would be, the dominant interest in America. Manufactures in general had never flourished in America. They employed only women and children who could not work in the field, and men at certain seasons when they could not be employed in agriculture. Labor upon land was more profitable than in manufactures, which they could import and purchase with the produce of the soil, cheaper than they could make them. "Since the war, however, freight and insurance have been so high that manufactures have been more attended to. ... But these, for the reason before given, will last no longer than the war or than the hazard of their trade. America is the country of raw materials, and of commerce enough to carry them to a good market; but Europe is the country for manufactures and commerce. Thus Europe and America will be blessings to each other, if some malevolent policy does not frustrate the purposes of nature."[75]

But as time went on and the 'purposes of nature' were frustrated by the 'malevolent policy' of both France and England, as Britain resumed complete and insolent control of commerce, and embarrassments multiplied at home, the American temper underwent a great change. Much of the faith in the beneficent workings of free commerce vanished. To some, at times, it seemed Better to cut off all intercourse with the rest of the world. In this mood Jefferson wrote: "Were I to indulge my own theory, I should wish [the states] to practice neither commerce nor navigation, but to stand, with respect to Europe, precisely on the footing of China."[76] In the same strain Adams expressed himself to Jay: "If all intercourse between Europe and America could be cut off forever, if

---

75 7 John Adam's Works, 309 *et seq.* Jefferson wrote his "Notes on Virginia" (1780): "Our external trade has suffered very much from the beginning of the present contest. During this time we have manufactured within our families the most necessary articles of clothing. Those of cotton will bear some comparison with the same kinds of manufacture in Europe; but those of wool, flax, and hemp are very coarse, unsightly, and unpleasant; and such is our attachment to agriculture, and such our preference for foreign manufactures, that, be it wise or unwise, our people will certainly return as soon as they can, to the raising of raw materials and exchanging them for finer manufactures than they are able to execute themselves. (8 Jefferson's Works, 404.)

76 Jefferson to Hogendorf, Oct. 13, 1785; 1 Jefferson's Works, 465. Cf. Jefferson's credo in 1799; 4 Jefferson's Works, 268.

every ship we have were burnt, and the keel of another never to be laid, we might still be the happiest people upon earth, and in fifty years the most powerful."[77] Neither, however, meant to be taken seriously. This is theory only, Jefferson said. Our people have a decided taste for navigation, and would like to throw open all doors of commerce, but cannot unless others will do it for us; therefore it is necessary to shackle them as they shackle us. 'Our people' confessed Adams, 'are as aquatic as the tortoises and sea-fowl, and the love of commerce, with its conveniences and pleasures, is a habit in them as unalterable as their natures. It is in vain, then, to amuse ourselves with the thought of annihilating commerce, unless as philosophical speculations. We are to consider men and things as practical statesmen, and to consider what our constituents are, and what they expect of us. We shall find that we must have connections with Europe, Asia, and Africa; and therefore, the sooner we form those connections into a judicious system the better for us and our children.'

The retaliation here suggested soon became dominant in the policy of American statesmen." The effort to plant commerce on new and higher grounds, the belief that in commerce old things ought to pass away and a new era come in, was sincere, and the disappointment at the failure to secure reciprocity was keen. Adams, Franklin, and Jay pressed the matter diplomatically, and in the belief that they were acting for the advantage of England as well. Shelburne, one of the earliest disciples of Adam Smith, and a firm friend of America, was inclined to meet them half way. But upon the overthrow of the Shelburne ministry and the advent of the younger Pitt, a different tone was adopted.[78] Nor was England's coolness toward reciprocity without reason. The fear of losing the American trade at first inclined the commercial interest to liberal treaty relations. But as time went on the English merchants gradually resumed their old trade, and with it came back the old supremacy. Exaggerated reports of the disorders and weakness of the Confederation found willing acceptance in England until it

---

77 Adams to Jay, Dec. 6, 1785; 8 John Adams' Works, 357.

78 P.N. William Petty, 2nd Earl of Shelburne, was Prime Minister of Great Britain for less than a year, from 1782-1783. He had originally opposed the war, and during his tenure worked on negotiations. He was succeeded by the Duke of Portland for a short interim, until William Pitt the Younger became Prime Minister.

seemed hardly worth while to respect very rigidly the provisions
of the treaty of peace, much less to go to the trouble of negotiat-
ing new treaties with a government so imbecile and doomed to
speedy dissolution. The belief that the states must inevitably split
apart and most likely, be glad to get back under the protection of
England, was almost universal. At any rate, a trial had been made,
and English merchants had easily carried off the American trade.
The Americans were not slow to perceive this change of front, and
to understand that commercially the war had availed them nothing. Their offer of reciprocity was not only scornfully rejected, but
the West India trade which they had formerly enjoyed was now
snatched from them. There seemed nothing to do but to meet
restriction with restriction, and an eager inquiry arose as to what
could be done to secure decent recognition. The proposal to give
Congress power to lay a five percent impost and to regulate trade,
as well as the more complete grant of authority in the Constitution, received its backing largely from this cause.

"Will it not be good policy," Madison ventured to inquire, in
1784, "to suspend further treaties of commerce till measures shall
have taken place in America which may correct the idea in Europe
of impotency in the federal government in matters of commerce?"[79]

"Much indeed it is to be wished, as I conceive," he wrote a year
later, announcing a position which to the end of his life he scarcely
varied from even in phraseology, "that no regulations of trade, that
is to say, no restrictions on imposts whatever, were necessary. A
perfect system is the system which would be my choice. But before
such a system will be eligible, perhaps, for the United States, they
must be out of debt; before it will be attainable, all other nations
must concur in it. Whilst any one of these imposes on our vessels,
seamen, etc., in their ports, clogs from which they exempt their
own, we must either retort the distinction or renounce, not merely
a just profit, but our only defence against the danger which may
most easily beset us. Are we not at this moment under this very
alternative? The policy of Great Britain (to say nothing of other nations) has shut against us the channels without which our
trade with her must be a losing one; and she has consequently

79 Madison to Jefferson, April 25, 1784; 1 Madison's Works, 79.

the triumph, as we have the chagrin, of seeing accomplished her prophetic threats, that our independence should forfeit commercial advantages for which it would not recompense us with new channels of trade."The only means of redress, he held, were retaliating regulations of trade, adopted by Congress.[80] The same month he wrote again: "The machinations of Great Britain with regard to commerce have produced much distress and noise in Northern states. ... The sufferers are everywhere calling for such augmentation of the power of Congress as may effect relief. ... If anything should reconcile Virginia to the idea of giving Congress a power over her trade, it will be that this power is likely to annoy Great Britain, against whom the animosities of our citizens are still strong."[81] Of the proposed Annapolis Convention he wrote Jefferson: "If it should come to nothing, it will, I fear, confirm Great Britain and all the world in the belief that we are not to be respected nor apprehended as a nation in matters of commerce."[82]

Jefferson, then in France, noted the new tendency and its wholesome effect. "I am well informed," he wrote Madison, "that the late proceedings in America have produced a wonderful sensation in England in our favor. I mean the disposition which seems to be becoming general, to invest Congress with the regulation of our commerce, and, in the meantime, the measures taken to defeat the avidity of the British government grasping at our carrying business. I can add with truth, that it was not till these symptoms appeared in America that I have been able to discover the smallest token of respect towards the United States in any part of Europe."[83] "I do not know," wrote Washington at almost the same time, "that we can enter upon a war of imposts with Great Britain or any other foreign power; but we are certain that this war has been waged against us by the former; professedly upon a belief that we never could unite in opposition to it; and I believe there is no way of putting an end to it, or at least, of stopping the increase of it, but to convince them of the contrary. Our trade, in all points of view, is as essential to Great Britain as hers is to us; and she will

---

80 Madison to Monroe, Aug. 7 1785; 1 Madison's Works, 170 *et seq.*
81 Madison to Jefferson, Aug. 20, 1785; 1 Madison's Works, 173.
82 Madison to Jefferson, March 18, 1786; 1 Madison's Works, 226.
83 Jefferson to Madison, Sept. 1 1785; 1 Jefferson's Works, 413. Cf. 4 Jefferson's Works, 106.

exchange it upon reciprocal and liberal terms, if better cannot be had."[84]

In no one of the statesmen of the Revolution was this change of temper more marked than in John Adams. He went abroad as one of the commissioners to negotiate the treaty of peace, and became the first American minister to England. Like Franklin and Jay, he felt himself thoroughly cut loose from the mercantile system, and confident that the new order of things was inevitable, went jauntily forward prepared to accept provisionally almost anything in regard to trade. "I said to my brothers," he wrote in his diary, April 28, 1783, "I shall be very ductile about commerce. I would agree at once to mutual naturalization, or to the article, as first agreed on, by Dr. Franklin and Mr. Jay, with Mr. Oswald; or I would agree to Mr. Hartley's propositions, to let the trade go on as before the war, or as with Nova Scotia; I could agree to any of these things, because that time and the natural course of things will produce a good treaty of commerce. Great Britain will soon see and feel the necessity of alluring American commerce to her ports by facilities and encouragements of every kind."[85]

But this state of feeling did not last. Reciprocity not secured at first became less and less probable as England began to experience a decided reaction toward the treaty itself. Adams was received at court, but treated coldly or with studied neglect, and England sent no minister in return. The feeling against America was still very bitter, and now much heightened by the appearance of loyalist refugees who gained the ear of the government. Of the proclamation of July 2, 1783, cutting off at one stroke the whole American trade with the West Indies, except in British vessels, Adams wrote from Paris; "A jealousy of American ships, seamen, carrying trade, and naval power, appears every day more and more conspicuous. … This proclamation is issued in full confidence that the United States have no confidence in one another; that they cannot agree to act in a body as one nation; that they cannot agree upon any navigation act which may be common to the thirteen states. Our proper remedy would be to confine our exports to American

---

84 Washington to James McHenry, Aug. 22, 1785; 9 Washington's Works, 123.
85 3 John Adams' Works, 363. See also his Diary, May 21 and 22, 1783; 3 John Adam's Works, 371 *et seq.*

ships."[86] "The British proclamation of July 2," he declared, "is the result of refugee politics; it is intended to encourage Canada and Nova Scotia and their fisheries, to support still the ruins of their navigation act, and to take from us the carriage even of our own productions. A system which has in it so little respect for us, and is so obviously calculated to give a blow to our nurseries of ships and seamen, could never have been adopted but from the opinion that we had no common legislation for the government of commerce. ... I hope the thirteen states will unite in some measures to counteract this policy of Britain, so evidently selfish, unsocial, and I had almost said, hostile."[87]

Two years later, after his experience in London, he could write still more strongly: "The popular pulse seems to beat high against America. ...Their attachment to their navigation act, as well as that of all other parties here, is grown so strong, and their determination to consider us as foreigners, and to undermine our navigation, and to draw away our seamen, is so fixed ... that I despair of any equal treaty. ... It cannot therefore be too earnestly recommended to all the states to concur with the state of New York, in giving to Congress full power to make treaties of commerce, and, in short, to govern all our external commerce, for, I really believe, it must come to that. Whether prohibitions or high duties will be most politic is a great question."[88] A little earlier he had written Jay concerning the outlook: " The Britons boast that all the prophecies of the loss of the American trade from the independence of the United States have proved false; that the experiment has been tried and the contest decided; that there was at the peace a competition of the commercial nations of Europe for the prize; that the superior abilities of the British manufacturers, and the greater capital of their merchants, have enabled them to give our traders better bargains and longer credit than any others in Europe; that,

---

86 8 John Adams' Works , 97. Adams immediately had a conversation with Vergennes, the French minister, and learning that in the French West Indies the United States had two free ports, he wrote to Livingston: " Upon the whole, I was much pleased with this conversation and conclude from it that we shall do very well in the French West India Islands; perhaps the better in them, the worse we are treated by the English ;" *Ib.*, 100.

87 8 John Adams' Works, 101; see also letter to Livingston, *ib.* 105.

88 Adams to Jay, July 19, 1785; 8 John Adams' Works, 282.

as we love our interests and have small fortunes, we must come to
them who can furnish us with goods of the best qualities at the
cheapest rates, and allow us the longest time to pay... You will negotiate for reciprocity in commerce to very little purpose, while the
British ministers and merchants are certain that they shall enjoy all
the profits of our commerce, under their own partial regulations."[89]
Three months later he wrote again: "I find the spirit of the times
very different from that which you and I saw when we were here
together, in the months of November and December, 1783... Now
the boast is, that our commerce has returned to its old channels,
and that it can follow in no other; now the utmost contempt of
our commerce is freely expressed in pamphlets, gazettes, cof-
fee-houses, and in common street talk. I wish I could not add to
this the discourses of cabinet counsellors and ministers of state,
as well as members of both houses of Parliament. The national
judgment and popular voice is so decided in favor of the navigation acts, that neither administration nor opposition dare avow a
thought of relaxing them further than has already been done. This
decided cast has been given to public opinion and the national
councils by two facts, or rather presumptions. The first is, that in all
events this country is sure of the American commerce; the second
is, that the American states are not and cannot be united."[90]

As to ways and means Adams turned more and more to
retaliation as the only effective remedy. Among indirect methods
he suggested measures for encouraging the growth in the United
States of West India articles, the encouragement of manufactures,
especially of wool and iron, export and import duties on British
ships, and the immediate sending of ships to China. The states,
he told Jay, might lay such discouragements on British ships and
manufactures, as would not only benefit themselves but show England her own weakness. Heavy duties might be laid on luxuries
from Great Britain which would discourage the extravagant use
of them in America, place other nations upon as good or a better
footing than the English, "and raise a revenue for the public out of
that enthusiasm for England which has been, and is still, so unwise

---

89 Adams to Jay, May 5, 1785; 8 John Adams' Works, 240 *et seq.* Cf. letter of June
26, *ib.* 274.
90 Adams to Jay, Aug. 6, 1785; 8 John Adams' Works, 289.

in itself, and so hurtful to our country."[91] The refusal of the states to grant Congress power to levy a five percent duty and to regulate commerce was rather bewildering to Adams, who was persuaded, however, that the objections could be only technical. He could not conceive that there could be opposition to the policy itself, and felt sure the states individually would readily comply with a recommendation of Congress wholly to prohibit British vessels and merchandise. "If Congress should enter in earnest into this commercial war," he declared, "it must necessarily be a long one." But he would not stop at half measures. They must take higher ground than the British. They must take measures by which the increase of shipping would be not only encouraged but rendered inevitable. They must adopt in all the states the regulations that were once made in England. He should be sorry to adopt a monopoly; but driven by necessity, he would not do things by halves.[92]

August 10, 1785, Adams wrote to Jay, referring to the recent arrest of Louis XVI advocating liberality in trade: "As the French court has condescended to adopt our principle in theory, I am very much afraid we shall be obliged to imitate their wisdom in practice, and exclude from the United States, or suffer to be imported by our nation only, and in their own ships, those foreign goods which would be hurtful to the United States and their manufactories, make the balance of trade to be against them, or annihilate or diminish their shipping or mariners. We have hitherto been the bubbles of our own philosophical and equitable liberality; and, instead of meeting correspondent sentiments, both France and England have shown a constant disposition to take a selfish and partial advantage of us because of them, to turn them to the diminution or destruction of our own means of trade and strength. I hope we shall be the dupes no longer than we must. I would venture upon monopolies and exclusions, if they were found to be the only arms of defence against monopolies and exclusions, without fear of offending Dean Tucker or the ghost of Doctor Quesnay."[93] Adams told Pitt that the most judicious men in America had been long balancing in their minds the advantages and disadvantages of a commerce perfectly free on one side, and of a navigation act on

91 8 John Adams' Works 242.
92 8 John Adams' Works, 241, 274, 291, 292.
93 8 John Adams' Works, 299.

the other, that the present time was a critical one, and that the balance was inclining toward a navigation act. "But," he wrote Jay, "I do not expect any answer at all before next spring, nor then unless intelligence should arrive of all the states adopting the navigation act, or authorizing Congress to do it; and even in that case, I am inclined to think they will try the experiment and let our navigation acts operate, to satisfy themselves which people will first roar out with pain."[94] "Patience under all the unequal burdens they impose upon our commerce," he wrote a few days later, "will do us no good; it will contribute in no degree to preserve the peace with this country. On the contrary, nothing but retaliation, reciprocal prohibitions and imposts, and putting ourselves in a posture of defence, will have any effect. ... Confining exports to our own ships, and laying on heavy duties upon all foreign luxuries, and encouraging our own manufactures, appear to me to be our only resource."[95]

Adams' attitude toward the doctrines of free commerce, which he had once so thoroughly embraced, took on something of bitterness as America's condition became more and more alarming. "If the United States would adopt the principle of the French economists," he wrote Jay, "and allow the ships and merchants of all nations equal privileges with their own citizens, they need not give themselves any further trouble about treaties or ambassadors. The consequence, nevertheless, would be the sudden annihilation of all their manufactures and navigation. We should have the most luxurious set of farmers that ever existed, and should not be able to defend our sea-coasts against the insults of a pirate."[96]

The general trend of all these utterances is sufficiently evident. They were the expressions of men who, among other fruits of independence, counted the abolition of shackles upon trade as one of the most important. In their own achievement of independence and in the philosophy which environed it, they thought they saw the beginning of the new heavens and new earth in social and political relations. They put their hand to the work in full readiness to accept the most altruistic conception of human society. But their social philosophy was more securely grounded than their

94 Adams to Jay, Aug. 25, 1785; 8 John Adams' Works, 302-310.
95 Adams to Jay, Aug. 30 1785; 8 John Adams' Works, 313.
96 Adams to Jay, Feb. 20, 1786; 8 John Adams' Works, 381.

economic. Abstract *laissez-faire* as law in political economy they hardly got a glimpse of, or perceived the full bearing of its criticism upon mercantilism. And they were pre-eminently Americans and of heroic mould. When they found that commercial shackles were not to be struck off at their bidding, the effect varied with their several temperaments and the abandon with which they had given themselves to the new gospel. Conservatives like Madison retained their ideal unchanged, but resolutely separated it from the practical problem in hand. Timid republicans like Jefferson involuntarily shrank back from any foreign intercourse whatever. Sturdy, impetuous patriots like Adams never recovered from the shock to their vanity in the discovery that their youthful theories would not work, and in the reaction a feeling of resentment led them to go even beyond Europe in their advocacy of restrictions.[97] All this is easily understood, and, under the circumstances, perfectly natural. However, it was not a very scientific or logical position, and in itself was a rather inadequate support for the policy of a nation. While many of the old errors might creep back and become intrenched again, the mercantile system as a whole was too strongly discredited to be ever again accepted as the basis of a great public policy. For the present, indeed, the problem was comparatively simple, and never was a measure more completely sanctioned by common consent than the first tariff under the Constitution. What was needed was the placing of the inevitable policy on broader and stronger grounds,—a need which in due time was to be supplied by Hamilton.

Hamilton's position agreed in the main with that outlined by Madison and Adams, though it was not reached from the same starting-point. Of the notion of giving Congress power to regulate commerce he was one of the earliest and most persistent advocates, but he was not driven to this by the failure of other ideals of commercial policy. Unlike Madison and Adams he wasted no regrets for what was at best a policy impossible of realization. Unlike them he was feeling his way toward a system based not on the injustice of other nations, but springing from national needs and conditions. Already he was working over in his mind an American

---

97 Of course, the larger and more important result—free trade and commerce among the states—was secured.

policy, and in his attitude toward the new powers of Congress in
the proposed Constitution, he stood at the farthest remove from
the apologetic tone of Franklin. He failed to escape from some
of the errors of mercantilism, but his essential position was not
founded in them. He borrowed from Hume and Adam Smith
and physiocrats alike, but criticised all in the free and easy, though
sympathetic, fashion of a man who did his own thinking, and by
none was led away from practical problems from the American
standpoint. He recognized, as all did, the supremacy of agriculture,
but he had no predilection for workshops, in Europe. More than
this, and what made him essentially the leader in the new economic policy of America, he believed in the inherent usefulness, for the
time at least, of restrictive legislation.

"The vesting Congress with the power of regulating trade,"
wrote Hamilton, in 1782, "ought to have been a principal object of
the Confederation. ... It is as necessary for the purposes of commerce as of revenue. There are some who maintain that trade will
regulate itself, and is not to be benefited by the encouragements or
restraints of government. ... [This is] contradicted by the numerous institutions and laws that exist everywhere for the benefit of
trade, by the pains taken to cultivate particular branches and to
discourage others, by the known advantages derived from those
measures, and by the palpable evils that would attend their discon-
tinuance. ... To preserve the balance of trade in favor of a nation
ought to be a leading aim of its policy. The avarice of individuals
may frequently find its account in pursuing channels of traffic
prejudicial to that balance, to which the government may be able
to oppose effectual impediments. There may, on the other hand,
be a possibility of opening new sources, which though accompanied with great difficulties in the commencement, would in the
event amply reward the trouble and expense of bringing them to
perfection. The undertaking may often exceed the influence and
capitals of individuals. ... The contrary opinion, which has grown
into a degree of vogue among us, has originated in the injudicious
attempts made at different times to effect a regulation of prices. It
became a cant phrase among the opposers of these attempts, that
trade must regulate itself; by which at first was only meant that
it had its fundamental laws, agreeable to which its general opera-

tions must be directed, and that any violent attempt in oppositions to these would commonly miscarry. In this sense the maxim was reasonable, but it has since been extended to militate against all interference by the sovereign." The rapid progress of trade in England, he declared, was due, in great measure, to the fostering care of the government, and Dutch prosperity was due to the strictness of their commercial regulations. Owing to a different spirit in the government, France was much later in commercial improvements; "nor would her trade have been at this time in so prosperous a condition, had it not been for the abilities and indefatigable endeavors of the great Colbert. ... The establishment of the woolen manufacture in a kingdom where nature seemed to have denied the means, is one, among many proofs, how much may be effected in favor of commerce by the attention and patronage of a wise administration."[98]

One of the objects Hamilton kept in the foreground was the raising of a revenue, and for this he insisted that no mode could be so convenient as an impost. There would be no temptation to abuse this power, he argued, because experience showed that moderate duties were more productive than high ones. In his resolutions in Congress, June, 1783, for a general convention, he named, among other defects in the Confederation, that of not vesting in Congress a general superintendence of trade, "equally necessary in the view of revenue and regulation ... of regulation, because by general prohibitions of particular articles, by a judicious

---

[98] The Continentalist, No. 5, April 18,1782; 1 Hamilton's Works, 254263. Hamilton was only twenty-five, and in his maturity would hardly have subscribed to so much mercantilism. Still he was essentially a special pleader even when he argued most nobly and with most signal ability. In this same number of the Continentalist he asserted that the maxim that the consumer pays the duty had been admitted in theory with too little reserve, and was frequently contradicted in practice. True, he said, the merchant would be unwilling to let the duty be deducted from his profits, if the market permitted; but this often was not practicable, for price was determined by demand and supply. But in the report drawn up by Hamilton, Madison, and Fitzsimons, in 1782, in answer to Rhode Island's objections to the proposed impost, it was stated that the "concurrent opinions of the ablest commercial and political observers, have established beyond controversy, this general principle that every duty on imposts is incorporated with the price of the commodity and ultimately paid by the consumer, with a profit on the duty itself as a compensation to the merchant for the advance of his money." (2 Hamilton's Works, 2.)

arrangement of duties, sometimes by bounties on the manufacture
or exportation of certain commodities, injurious branches of commerce might be discouraged, favorable branches encouraged, useful
products and manufactures promoted."[99]

In No. 11 of the Federalist, he declared that Europe was
uneasy about the adventurous spirit which seemed to distinguish
the commercial character of the United States, and therefore
would naturally attempt to foster divisions among them, in order
to deprive them, as far as possible, of an active commerce in their
own ships. "By prohibitory regulations extending, at the same
time, throughout the states, we may oblige foreign countries to bid
against each other, for the privileges of our markets. This assertion
will not appear chimerical to those who are able to appreciate the
importance [to any manufacturing nation] of the markets of three
millions of people ... for the most part exclusively addicted to agriculture, and likely from local circumstances to remain so."[100]

All this was doubtless vague enough and loosely argued. But it
illustrates the general bend of Hamilton's mind toward a practical
solution of the question. "General principles in subjects of this
nature," he had said in a pamphlet already quoted, "ought always
to be advanced with caution; in an experimental analysis there are
found such a number of exceptions as tend to render them very
doubtful; and in questions which affect the existence and collective
happiness of these states, all nice and abstract distinctions should
give way to plainer interests and to more obvious and simple rules
of conduct."[101]

The picture commonly given of the period from 1783 to 1789
between the close of the war and the adoption of the Constitution,
is one of demoralization and almost total collapse. The effective
background which such a representation gives to a glowing canvas

---

99 1 Hamilton's Works, 292. Hamilton saw the obstacles which the dearness of
labor put in the way of manufactures, and in No. 6 of the Continentalist he frankly
declared that it ought to be a capital object of their policy to reduce the price of
labor. (1 Hamilton's Works, 264-273.) He was too tactful, however, to continue the
line of argument, and in his Report on Manufactures he endeavored to show that
the dearness of labor was not an obstacle to manufacturing.
100 9 Hamilton's Works, 60, 61.
101 The Continentalist, No. 5, April 18, 1782; 1 Hamilton's Works, 262.

of the United States under the Constitution, affords a temptation that few historical artists can resist. The times were bad enough and critical enough, it is true. They were certainly more critical than some of the statesmen of that time realized. Jefferson could see in Shay's rebellion[102] nothing but a sign of healthful vitality, and Patrick Henry, and George Clinton, and Benjamin Harrison found a constitution which gave Congress power to legislate for all the states far more unbearable than the disorders of the Confederation. Yet those who saw most clearly the gravity of the crisis saw also the inherent soundness of the body politic and the strong recuperative forces which would be at work could its organs once be gotten into healthy action. Washington, Madison, Jefferson, and even Franklin at times despaired and could see only gloom in the future. But the stronger possibilities of success nerved them for action, and kept firm, for the most part, their faith in the destiny of the Republic.

Want of unity and the weakness of the government had lost the states their great opportunity of pressing reciprocity to a successful issue. The advantage of capital and credit firmly reestablished English commercial supremacy, and now the West Indian trade was snatched from them. At home matters were in some respects worse. The states launched into reckless experiments with paper money, adopted hostile regulations against one another, and discontent not infrequently broke out into internal discords. Not a single state complied with the requisitions of Congress, not enough money could be coaxed out of the states to meet ordinary expenses, and the best men resigned and went home to their own legislatures. "No morn ever dawned more favorably than ours did," wrote Washington, "and no day was ever more clouded than the present."[103]

Yet all this expressed at most a vivid prophecy of what might happen if things did not begin to mend. But things were not past mending, and this the best men strongly felt. The harvests were

---

102 P.N. Shay's Rebellion was a tax protest in Massachusetts. Devalued paper currency was not accepted for tax payments. Crowds shut down courts and attempted to march on the Federal Armory. Distinct from the Whiskey Rebellion, which took place in Pennsylvania during George Washington's Presidency in the early 1790s.
103 Washington to Madison, Nov. 5, 1786; 9 Washington's Works, 206.

generally good, prices satisfactory, labor employed, and the country rapidly growing. In these circumstances it needed only a cure for political ills to start the states on that career of prosperity which Franklin and Washington and their compeers so strongly believed to be in store for them.

Even Madison did not fail to note that they were at times tasting some pleasant industrial fruits of independence, in better prices and more favorable trade.[104] Adams, in his optimistic letters from Holland, written in 1780, declared that as to poverty there was hardly a beggar in the country. The greatest source of grief and affliction was in the fluctuations of the paper money; but this, he said, although it occasioned unhappiness, had no violent or fatal effects.[105] In 1785, while noting the discouragement to shipping, seamen, and the carrying trade, he cited the high prices of American produce and the low prices of foreign merchandise, as proof of the prosperity of the preceding year.[106] He told Lord Carmarthen that the people were nineteen-twentieths of them farmers; that these had sold their produce dearer, and purchased the manufactures of Europe cheaper, since the peace, than ever; but that the situation of the merchants both in America and in England, had been, and continued to be, very distressing."[107]

For the Chevalier de la Luzerne, Washington drew, in 1786, a hopeful picture. After referring to the proposed grant to Congress of the power to regulate trade, he wrote: "In other respects our internal governments are daily acquiring strength. The laws have their fullest energy, justice is well administered; robbery, violence, or murder is not heard of from New Hampshire to Georgia. The people at large, as far as I can learn, are more industrious than they were before the war. Economy begins to prevail, partly from necessity and partly from choice and habit. The seeds of prosperity are scattered over an immense tract of western country. In the old states, which were the theatres of hostility, it is wonderful to see how soon the ravages of war are repaired. Houses are rebuilt, fields enclosed, stocks of cattle, which were destroyed, are replaced, and

---

104 See letter to Jefferson, Aug. 20, 1784; 1 Madison's Works 92.
105 See 7 John Adams' Works, 305.
106 8 John Adams' Works, 245.
107 John Adams' Works, 270.

many a desolated territory assumes again the cheerful appearance of cultivation. In many places the vestiges of conflagration and ruin are hardly to be traced. The arts of peace, such as clearing rivers, building bridges, and establishing conveniences for traveling, are assiduously promoted. ... I am sensible that the picture of our situation which has been exhibited in Europe since the peace, has been of a very different complexion; but it must be remembered that all the unfavorable features have been much heightened by the medium of the English newspapers."[108]

To Lafayette he wrote, with prophetic instinct, after the ratification of the Constitution had become a certainty: "And then, I expect that many blessings will be attributed to our new government, which are now taking their rise from that industry and frugality into the practice of which the people have been forced from necessity. I really believe that there never was so much labor and economy to be found in the country as at the present moment. If they persist in the habits they are acquiring the good effects will soon be distinguishable. When the people shall find themselves secure under an energetic government, when foreign nations shall be disposed to give us equal advantages in commerce from dread of retaliation, when the burdens of war shall be in a manner done away by the sale of western lands, when the seeds of happiness which are sown here shall begin to expand themselves, and when every one, under his own vine and fig tree, shall begin to taste the fruits of freedom, then all these blessings (for all these blessings will come) will be referred to the fostering influence of the new government. Whereas many causes will have conspired to produce them."[109] To Jefferson he wrote: "We may perhaps rejoice that the people have been ripened by misfortune for the reception of a good government. They are emerging from the gulf of dissipation and debt into which they had precipitated themselves at the close of the war. Economy and industry are evidently gaining ground. Not only agriculture, but even manufactures, are much more attended to than formerly. Notwithstanding the shackles under which our trade in general labors, commerce to the East Indies is prosecuted with considerable success. ... This year the exports

---

108 Washington to Luzerne, Aug. 1. 1786; 9 Washington's Works, 184.
109 Washington to Lafayette, June 18, 1788; 9 Washington's Works 382.

from Massachusetts have amounted to a great deal more than their imports. I wish this was the case everywhere."[110] "What has been considered at the moment as a disadvantage," he wrote Samuel Hanson, "will probably turn out for our good. While our commerce has been considerably curtailed, for want of that extensive credit formerly given in Europe, and for default of remittances, the useful arts have been almost perceptibly pushed to a considerable degree of perfection. ... No diminution in agriculture has taken place at the time when greater and more substantial improvements in manufactures were making than were ever before known in America. ... I hope it will not be a great while before it will be unfashionable for a gentleman to appear in any other dress [than home-spun]. Indeed, we have already been too long subject to British prejudices. I use no porter or cheese in my family, but such as is made in America."[111]

Jefferson's opinions were not less pronounced, though they perhaps exhibited faith rather than knowledge. To Baron Geismar he wrote, Sept. 6, 1785: "From the London Gazettes, and the papers copying them, you are led to suppose that all there [i.e. in the United States] is anarchy, discontent, and civil war. Nothing, however, is less true. There are not on the face of the earth, more tranquil governments than ours, nor a happier and more contented people. Their commerce has not as yet found the channels which their new relations with the world will offer to best advantage, and the old ones remain as yet unopened by new conventions. This occasions a stagnation in the sale of their produce, the only truth among all the circumstances published about them."[112] "With all the defects of our Constitution, whether general or particular," he affirmed two years later, "the comparison of our governments with those of Europe, is like a comparison of heaven and hell."[113]

Franklin, like Jefferson, was in France the greater part of this period, and therefore may not have been so keenly alive to the distresses among the states as those at home. But he had a juster appreciation of their resources and of the nature of their troubles.

---

110 Washington to Jefferson, Aug. 31, 1788; 9 Washington's Works, 427.
111 Washington to Samuel Hanson, Jan. 18, 1789; 9 Washington's Works, 464.
112 1 Jefferson's Works, 427.
113 2 Jefferson's Works, 249.

In a pamphlet, issued in 1784, on "The Internal State of America"
he examined the complaints of American newspapers regarding
hard times, deadness of trade, scarcity of money, and the like.
Admitting these, he could not believe the prospect was so gloomy
as had been imagined. The great business of the country, he said,
was agriculture. For one artisan or merchant there were at least
one hundred farmers, most of whom were cultivators of their own
fertile lands, from which they obtained not only food but materials
of their clothing, so that they needed very few foreign supplies. Although the crops of the year before had been generally good, never
was the farmer better paid for his surplus. His land was continually
rising in value with increase of population, and he was enabled to
give such good wages to those who worked for him that in no part
of the old world were the laboring poor so well fed, well clothed,
well lodged, and well paid, as in the United States. In cities since
the Revolution houses and lots had vastly increased in value. Rents
had risen to an astonishing height, which encouraged building,
thus giving employment to abundance of workmen. These workmen demanded and obtained better wages than any other part
of the world afforded them, and were paid in ready money. As to
the fisheries, they were not worse paid than before the Revolution. Merchants might calculate amiss and import too much, but
they would learn by experience. If artificers and farmers would
turn shopkeepers with the idea of leading easier lives, the business
might very well be too small for so many, and they might complain
that trade was dead. As to the growth of luxury which alarmed
so many, if the importation of foreign luxuries could ruin a people the states would have been ruined long ago; for the British
nation had claimed a right and practiced it, of importing among
them, not only the superfluities of their own products, but those of
every nation under heaven. The states bought and consumed them
and yet flourished and grew rich. At present these independent
governments might do what they could not then—discourage by
heavy duties or prevent by heavy prohibitions such importations
and thereby grow richer. Let the states attend to agriculture and
the fisheries, and the power of rivals with all their restraining and
prohibiting acts could not much hurt them.[114]

---

114 9 Franklin's Works, 35 *et seq.* See also 10 Franklin's Works, 69.

To Hartley he wrote: "All the stories in your papers relating to their divisions are fictions, as well as those of the people being discontented with Congressional government. Mr. Jay writes to me that they were at no time more happy or more satisfied. ... In truth, the freedom of their exports to all nations has brought in a vast plenty of foreign goods, and occasioned a demand for their produce, the consequence of which is the double advantage of buying what they consume cheap and selling what they can spare dear."[115] To the Amsterdam banker, Mr. Grand, he wrote after his return to Philadelphia: "By their accounts [i.e. in English papers] you would think we were in the utmost distress, in want of everything, all in confusion, no government, and wishing again for that of England. Be assured, my friend, that these are all fictions, mere English wishes, not American realities. ... I never saw greater and more indubitable marks of public prosperity in any country. The produce of our agriculture bears a good price, and is all paid for in ready hard money, all the laboring people have high wages, everybody is well clothed and well lodged, the poor provided for or assisted, and all estates in town or country much increased in value."[116]

---

115 Franklin to David Hartley, Jan 3, 1785; 9 Franklin's Works, 74. See also letter of Feb. 24, 1786, *ib*. 294.

116 Franklin to Mr. Grand, March 5, 1786; 9 Franklin's Works, 299. See also *ib*. 300, 348; vol. x, 63-70, *et passim*.

"In the Hist. Mag. March, 1871, there is a letter by H.B. Dawson to J.L. Motley, in response to some statements of that historian in the London *Times* in 1861, in which most of the symptoms of content during the Confederation days, which could be gleaned, are grouped together to point an argument." 7 Winsor, 221, note.

CHAPTER II

THE TARIFF OF 1789, AND HAMILTON'S REPORT ON MANUFACTURES

The first Congress of the United States under the Constitution met in New York City, March 4, 1789. A quorum of the House did not appear, however, until April 1, and of the Senate not until April 6. April 8, three weeks before Washington was inaugurated, the House took up, as the first business of the new government, the subject of an impost. The matter was brought forward by Madison, who introduced the measure of 1783 in blank, with the suggestion of an additional clause for discriminating tonnage duties, and recommended a general adherence to that plan. After a debate lasting five weeks, a bill was passed, May 16, retaining the five percent *ad valorem* rate of 1783 for the great majority of articles, but considerably enlarging the enumerated list. The specific duties were materially reduced in the Senate, and after numerous conferences, the House for the most part yielded. The bill received the President's signature July 4, 1789.

The bill on its final passage in the House, seems to have been agreed to without a division, though after a sharp struggle over many of the items. The Senate debates have not been preserved,[117] but the duties proposed by the House were modified on the general principle of securing as much revenue as possible, and on the ground that too high duties would encourage smuggling. In the House the debates ranged over the whole ground of tariffs and

---

117 But see "Sketches of Debate in the First Senate of the United States," by William Maclay; edited by George W. Harris. (Enlarged edition published by Appleton in 1890 under title of "Journal of William Maclay.") Maclay was the short-term senator from Pennsylvania, and his journal, covering a period of two years, contains the only connected account of the Senate discussions that has come down to us. He reports no speeches, but gives a strong picture of the tone and general drift of discussion. Maclay was a rather extreme republican, with little faith in the new Constitution, who abhorred Adams and Hamilton, disparaged Washington, distrusted Madison, and apparently saw no signs of leadership in Jefferson.

protective duties, and almost every question that has since come up in tariff discussion was touched upon. There was little of the intensity which marked later tariff struggles, and the rates which were fought over were small as compared with more modern tariffs. The responsibility of launching the new government, in the face of confident predictions of failure, and the pressing need of a revenue, moderated to an unusual degree the zeal of opposing interests. The differences between sections of the Union did not prove so great or so formidable as had been anticipated. This first Congress, which it was freely predicted would strangle the new government, really breathed into it the breath of life,[118] and the tariff of 1789, which foreshadowed the policy of a hundred years to come, was launched with astonishingly little friction. The sentiment for free trade, and the desirability of planting the nation on the principles of greater freedom from commercial restrictions, was voiced by Madison, who took his argument, as Fisher Ames said, direct from Adam Smith.[119] Yet these views, cautiously as they were expressed, had little effect other than to give their author a reputation for bookishness and want of practical sagacity.[120]

But even Madison had little conception of *laissez-faire* as a principle of economic life, and in its application he stopped far short of the conclusions of the school of Ricardo and Mill.[121] Reciprocity he earnestly advocated, but he did not conceive that one nation, particularly the United States, could adopt free trade independently of other nations. Indeed, it remained for him to give the only broad argument for protection heard during the debate. Madison was eminently a conservative. He spoke with power, vigor, and directness, but rarely with enthusiasm or abandon. His theories never led him far away from practical considerations, and he stood ready to have his position modified by new facts and phases; and for this he was termed vacillating by those who understood him least. He expressed himself strongly at times against what he considered a speculative rage for manufactures, and in favor of a

118 See Annals of Congress, vol. i, page 309.
119 1 Life of Fisher Ames, 49.
120 1 Life of Fisher Ames, 35.
121 P.N. David Ricardo (1772-1823) was an MP and classical economist who supported free trade and central banking. James Mill (1773-1836) was another free trade classical economist and father of John Stuart Mill.

larger commercial freedom. But he never ventured to base the offer of free trade upon other terms than reciprocity. While somewhat jealous of manufactures, he freely conceded their necessity to a certain extent, and stoutly maintained the propriety and duty of Congressional assistance and direction. Under changed conditions he would have been the sturdiest opponent of a protective tariff, but the logic of events made him more and more a defender and advocate, though he never ceased to retain his theoretical feeling for free trade.[122]

The argument for protection was blunt and practical. Manufactures already established should not be allowed to go down; especially in those states where legislative aid had been granted. These states, argued Madison, had surrendered this power to the general government in the confident expectation that the protecting arm would not be withdrawn. The country ought to be independent of foreign countries for supplies, and this could be accomplished by extending the aid of the government to certain industries for which the country was well adapted. The general answer was equally blunt and innocent of abstract reasoning. Certain sections of the country, particularly the south, were not interested in manufactures and were interested in foreign markets for their produce; protective duties would bear heavily and unequally against them. Madison's maxims regarding an ideal commercial relation probably found little response; no more did the opponents of the tariff grant that in the end all parts of the country shared equally in the benefits of protective duties. Tucker and Smith of South Carolina, and Bland, Parker, and the Lees of Virginia,[123] who mainly represented the Southern hostility to imports for other than revenue purposes, contented themselves with pointing out the depression of agriculture in their respective states, and the burdens which protective tariffs would impose upon them. However, they expressed themselves as willing to stand their share of loss, and to grant some encouragement to the manufacturing interests, though protesting that it was a clear concession on their part, and that the burdens would be unequally distributed.[124] They were by no

122 See his annual message, 1815; also 3 Works, 158-161, *et passim.*
123 Senator Richard Henry Lee and Representative Richard Bland Lee.
124 See remarks of Tucker, Annals of Congress, vol i., p. 308. Not all were so moderate. Thus in the Senate, Grayson of Virginia declared against all impost as the

means consistent free-traders, as the term would have been understood later, and were quite willing that their own local productions should share in the protection accorded to the industries of the North. There was as yet no organized movement on either side and no powerful interest, save that of commerce, needing to be conciliated. There was no union of protected interests whereby all should stand or fall together, and in the discussion over details, local interests had a pretty free expression. Fitzsimons of Pennsylvania did, indeed, urge Tucker of South Carolina to get rid of local considerations, declaring that unless such considerations were dropped every State would feel itself oppressed by the duty on particular articles, whereas when the whole system was perfected the burden would be equal on all.[125] Yet Fitzsimons, who especially wanted candles protected, was quite indifferent in regard to nails, a distinctively Eastern manufacture, and positively opposed to any tax on hemp, though the only one which seemed directly to favor the South. Ames of Massachusetts, who expressed himself as uniformly desirous of encouraging manufactures, persistently fought the tax on molasses, and, in general, the New England members united to oppose duties bearing against their section. Bland and Parker of Virginia were quite willing to have a duty on coal, because Virginia had mines that might be worked to advantage, and they asked for three cents per bushel. Hartley of Pennsylvania, one of the leading advocates of protection, grudgingly conceded one cent per bushel, but for hemp he would have a bounty rather than a tariff.

After all, the debate followed other lines than those of protection and free trade.[126] Various sections were alive to the interests

---

most unjust and oppressive mode of taxation; and Pierce Butler of South Carolina, who did not take his seat until June, signalized his appearance by arraigning the whole impost law and charging Congress with a design of oppressing South Carolina. In the debate on drawbacks, "Butler flamed away," says Maclay, "and threatened a dissolution of the Union, with regard to his state, *as sure as God was in the firmament*. He scattered his remarks over the whole impost bill, calling it partial, oppressive, etc., and solely calculated to oppress South Carolina … His State would live free, or die glorious, etc., etc." See Sketches of Debate in the First Senate, pp. 64, 75, 77.

125 H.R., April, 15, 1789; Annals of 1st Congress, vol. I, p. 155.

126 "If the duties shall be raised too high, the error will proceed as much from the popular ardor to throw the burden of revenue on trade as from the premature poli-

of various manufactures, but these interests were neither large nor powerful. Agriculture was tacitly assumed to be the great and controlling occupation of the people, and perhaps no one looked to see any very extensive manufacturing in the country. Fisher Ames' picture of the children making nails around the household forges on long winter evenings, perhaps suggests correctly enough the prevailing conception of the kind of manufacturing activity protection would foster.[127] Manufactures were treated with respect and consideration, and the constitutional question seems not even to have been suggested.[128] Manufacturing interests were allowed to monopolize a good part of the debate, but it was not supposed that they were speedily to become very large, or seriously to interfere with importations from abroad. Revenue was the principal consideration; and the powerful commercial interest, while not unfriendly to manufactures, instinctively and successfully opposed any tendency toward rates which would seem to threaten a diminution of foreign trade.[129]

In opening the tariff discussion, Madison reminded the House that the subject was one of the greatest magnitude, and required their first and united exertions. Every one knew the impotency of the last Congress. The Union, by establishing a more effective government, and having recovered from its former imbecility,

cy of stimulating manufactures." Madison to Edmund Pendleton, April 19, 1789; 1 Madison's Works, 465.

127 See *infra*, p. 84

128 The constitutional question, however, appeared in another form. Some of the members, notably the senators from Virginia, had been elected by the anti-federal party and rather in the spirit of continuing the opposition. These, hardly as yet accepting the new government as a finality, denounced the Constitution itself rather than its interpretation. Thus in the later debates on the assumption of the state debts, Maclay reports Bland of Virginia as supporting assumption with the avowed design, as he said, of showing to the world, that the present constitution aimed directly at consolidation, and the sooner everybody knew it the better. See Sketches of Debate in the First Senate, p. 179.

129 "The senators from Jersey, Pennsylvania, Delaware, and Maryland, in every act, seemed desirous of making the impost productive, bot has to revenue, and effective for the encouragement of manufactures; and seemed to consider the whole of the imposts (salt except) much too low. Articles of luxury, many of them would have raised one half. But the members both from the North and, still more particularly, from the South, were ever in a flame when any articles were brought forward that were in any considerable use among them." Sketches of Debate, 77.

ought, in its first act, to revive those principles of honor and honesty that had too long lain dormant. The deficiency in the treasury was too notorious to need mention. Let Congress content itself with remedying the evil. To do this a national revenue must be obtained, and by a system which, while securing revenue, should not be oppressive. Two points concerned them: First, the general regulation of commerce, which, in Madison's opinion, ought to be as free as the policy of nations would admit; and secondly, revenue. Since they were without the necessary data on which to base a permanent system, and as the situation would admit of no delay, he would propose such articles only as would occasion the least difficulty. The proposed measure of 1783 had received the assent of all the states in some form, and should be taken as a basis for a new tariff.[130]

It is barely possible that, had the government been fully organized, the tariff of 1783 would have been immediately enacted as a temporary measure, though no doubt against the protest of those states which were then collecting considerably higher rates,[131] the failure of the Confederation to secure the adoption of its proposed tariff in any acceptable form had discouraged further efforts to raise a revenue. After putting the machinery in motion for action upon the proposed Constitution the old Congress practically ceased to exist, though its sittings were continued even after the new Congress had met. The interval was one of great trial and uncertainty. When the ratification of the Constitution by the requisite number of states was known, the necessary steps were taken as promptly as circumstances would permit, and the first meeting of Congress appointed at this unfavorable season of the year in order, as Madison explained, to take advantage of the spring importations.[132] But as the time dragged wearily by, first without a quorum in either House, then waiting for the inauguration of Washington, the prospect of getting any revenue from the spring

---

130 Annals of 1st Congress, 107.

131 That Congress would lay an impost was well understood. The North Carolina Convention, in adjourning without action on the Constitution, in August, 1788, declared that as the new Congress would probably lay an impost, they recommended North Carolina to lay a similar impost and to appropriate the proceeds to the use of Congress. (7 Winsor, 251.)

132 1 Madison's Works, 459; see also *ib.* 453.

trade vanished,[133] and the debate once launched was soon under such headway that it could not be readily stopped.[134]

When Madison concluded his opening speech by proposing the measure of 1783, Boudinot of New Jersey promptly moved that the blanks be filled up with the rates of 1783. Objection followed from various quarters. Lawrence of New York objected to any specific duties at that time because they had not materials for even the basis of a system. Fitzsimons would go further than a temporary system, and adopt one adequate to the situation regarding agriculture, manufactures, and commerce. White of Virginia feared such a course would consume too much time and lose a greater sum than the additional impost would yield. Tucker of South Carolina thought a permanent system would be most likely to be satisfactory to their constituents, but a temporary system might be expedient and he would have no objection to an *ad valorem* rate as proposed in 1783. As to tonnage, he asked for delay until other representatives from the South should arrive.

At this point Hartley of Pennsylvania made the first appeal in behalf of manufactures. He objected to entering into the subject in a limited and partial manner, but would do it on as broad a bottom as practicable. Tucker's point regarding tonnage might have some weight, but no argument of that sort should discourage the House from taking such measures as would tend to protect and promote domestic manufactures. "I think it both politic and just that the fostering hand of the general government should extend to all those manufactures which will tend to national utility. I am therefore sorry that gentlemen seem to fix their mind to so early a period as 1783; for we very well know our circumstances are

---

133 The impatient Fisher Ames wrote to Minot, March 25, 1789; "We lose £1000 a day revenue. We lose credit, spirit, everything. The public will forget the government before it is born. The resurrection of the infant will come before its birth. Happily, however, the federal interest is strong in Congress. The old Congress still continues to meet and it seems to be doubtful whether the old government is dead, or the new one alive." 1 Life of Fisher Ames, 32.

134 "The plan of a hasty and temporary impost loses ground daily from the apparent impracticability of reaping the spring harvest from importations." Madison to Randolph, April 12, 1789 (1 Madison's Works, 463). Even Madison was obliged to admit that the plan of 1783 was inadmissible without alteration on some points; *ib. 467.*

much changed since that time. We had then but few manufactures among us, and the vast quantities of goods that flowed in upon us from Europe, at the conclusion of the war, rendered these few almost useless; since then we have been forced by necessity and various other causes, to increase our domestic manufactures to such a degree as to be able to furnish some in sufficient quantity to answer the consumption of the whole Union, while others are daily growing into importance. Our stock of materials is, in many instances, equal to the greatest demand, and our artisans sufficient to work them up even for exportation. In these cases I take it to be the policy of every enlightened nation to give their manufactures that degree of encouragement necessary to perfect them, without oppressing the other parts of the community."[135]

Madison again urged immediate action from considerations of revenue. The general interest, he declared, must be considered, and any system must be founded on the principles of mutual concession. Those states most advanced in population and ripe for manufactures, ought to have their interests attended to in some degree. By adopting the Constitution they had thrown the power of regulating trade out of their hands, and doubtless with the expectation that these interests would not be neglected by the national government. "I own myself," he said, "the friend to a very free system of commerce, and hold it as a truth, that commercial shackles are generally unjust, oppressive, and impolitic. It is also a truth that if industry and labor are left to take their own course, they will generally be directed to those objects which are the most productive, and this in a more certain and direct manner than the wisdom of the most enlightened legislature could point out. Nor do I think that the national interest is more promoted by such restrictions than that the interests of individuals would be promoted by legislative interference directing the particular application of its industry. ... For example, it would be of no advantage to the shoemaker to make his own clothes to save the expense of the tailor's bill, nor to the tailor to make his own shoes to save the expense of procuring them from the shoemaker. It would be better policy to suffer each of them to employ his talents in his own way. The case

---

135 1 Annals of 1st Congress, 114, 115 (April 9). For confirmation of statement as to progress of manufactures, see remarks of Madison, ib., 248.

is the same between the exercise of the arts and agriculture, between the city and the country, and between the city and the town; each capable of making particular articles in abundance to supply the other; thus all are benefited by exchange, and the less this exchange is cramped by government, the greater are the proportions of benefit to each. The same argument holds good between nation and nation, and between parts of the same nation."

To this unequivocal enunciation of the conclusions of the *Wealth of Nations*, Madison hastened to add that there were exceptions, important in themselves, and which claimed the particular attention of Congress. "If my general principle is a good one, that commerce ought to be free, and labor and industry left at large to find its proper object, the only thing which remains will be to discover the exceptions. ... Although the freedom of commerce would be advantageous to the world, yet in some particulars one nation might suffer to benefit others, and this ought to be for the general good of society. If America were to leave her ports perfectly free and make no discrimination between vessels owned by her citizens and those owned by foreigners, while other nations make this discrimination, it is obvious that such a policy would go to exclude American shipping altogether from foreign ports. ... By encouraging the means of transporting our products, we encourage the raising of them. ... Duties on imports may have an effect which comes within the idea of national prudence. It may happen that materials for manufacture may grow up without encouragement for this purpose; it has been the case in some of the states, but in others, regulations have been provided and have succeeded in producing some establishments which ought not to be allowed to perish. ... It would be cruel to neglect them and divert their industry to other channels; for it is not possible for the hand of man to shift from one employment to another without being injured by the change." Another exception, Madison said, would be an embargo in time of war. Another which had been argued with great plausibility, namely, that each nation should have within itself the means of defence, independent of foreign supplies, he thought had been carried too far, although there might be some truth in it.[136]

Later in the debate, in reply to Lawrence of New York, who

136 1 Annals of 1st Congress, 115-118 (H.R. April 9, 1789).

insisted that the United States was not in a condition to engage in commercial war, and who wanted commerce let alone,[137] Madison committed himself more unreservedly to government interference with industry. 'I am a friend of free commerce,' he said, 'and at the same time a friend to such regulations as are calculated to promote our own interest, and this on national principles. ... I wish we were under less necessity than I find we are, to shackle our commerce with duties, restrictions, and preferences; but there are cases in which it is impossible to avoid following the example of other nations in the great diversity of our trade. ... Although interest will, in general, operate effectually to produce political good, yet there are causes in which certain factitious circumstances may divert it from its natural channel, or throw or retain it in an unnatural one. Have we not been exercised on this topic for a long time past? Or why has it been necessary to give encouragement to particular species of industry, but to turn the stream in favor of an interest that would not otherwise succeed? But laying aside the illustration of these causes, so well known to all nations where cities, companies, or opulent individuals engross the business from others, by having had an uninterrupted possession of it, or by the extent of their capitals being able to destroy a competition, let us proceed to examine what ought to be our conduct on this principle, upon the present occasion. Suppose two commercial cities, one possessed of enormous capitals and long habits of business, whilst the other is possessed of superior natural advantages, but without that course of business and chain of connections which the other has; is it possible in the nature of things, that the latter city should carry on a successful competition with the former? Thus it is with nations; and when we consider the vast quantities of our produce sent to the different parts of Europe and the great exportations from the same places, that almost all of this great commerce is transacted through the medium of British ships and British merchants, I cannot help conceiving that from the force of habit and other conspiring causes, that nation is in possession of a much greater portion of our trade than she is naturally entitled to. Trade, then, being restrained to an artificial channel is not so advantageous to

---

137 See 1 Annals of 1st Congress, 211, 243. The question was to a discriminating tonnage duty. Madison had no fears, he said, as to the results of entering into a commercial war with Great Britain, *ib.* 248.

America as a direct intercourse would be; it becomes, therefore, the duty of those to whose care the public interest and welfare are committed, to turn the tide to a more favorable direction?"[138]

The debates as reported give little evidence of further abstract discussion of the general principles of protection and free trade. In the arrangement of details, however, great diversity of views was discovered, ranging from Fitzsimons' maxim that whatever operated to benefit one part of the Union would eventually benefit the whole, to Bland's assertion that in the then condition of manufacturing in America they would certainly be laying a tax upon the whole community in order to put money into the pockets of the few.

The items which occasioned most difficulty were molasses and rum, wines, salt, steel, nails, candles, hemp, and tonnage.

On molasses a tax of eight cents per gallon was proposed. Ames, who violently opposed this, explained that his constituents exchanged for molasses the fish which they could not dispose of anywhere else. It would be scarcely possible to maintain their fisheries if the market for summer fish were injured, and a tax of eight cents would carry devastation throughout all the New England States, and would ultimately affect all the Union. "Will gentlemen who declare themselves the friends of manufactures," he exclaimed, "support the opinion that a raw material ought to be saddled with an excessive duty, that the imposition should be at a higher rate than what is laid upon manufactured articles?" He would have a low duty on molasses and an excise on rum. He insisted that not much more than three-fourths as much rum was distilled in Massachusetts as formerly, that the nations which used to supply them with raw material were becoming their rivals, and that even the home market was not secured to them. He reiterated his belief that the proposed tax would ruin the rum manufacturing industry. Thatcher of Massachusetts declared that six cents on molasses would be as great a burden on Massachusetts as fifty dollars a slave would be in the South. Parker thought a higher tax on rum would be a good thing because it would discourage its use; Lawrence wanted a low duty because it was a necessity to the poor.

---

138 1 Annals of the 1st Congress, 192, 193 (H.R. April 21, 1789).

Fitzsimons brought forward his maxim that each particular duty must be regarded as a part of a system bearing equally upon all. He would support the molasses tax, but moved a corresponding drawback on all distilled rum exported. Madison opposed this as opening the door for frauds on the revenue; but Fitzsimons insisted that otherwise the manufacturer would be greatly injured. Bland predicted that if a duty of fifty cents were laid on Madeira wine not a gallon would be imported. Lawrence affirmed that it would encourage smuggling, but was Willing to allow twenty cents a gallon. Sinnickson of New Jersey wanted a prohibitive duty on beer because he thought the materials could be easily produced in the United States, and with such encouragement enough would be supplied, and this would tend to advance the agricultural interest.[139]

Fitzsimons moved a duty of two cents a pound on candles. Tucker objected that while some states made enough for their own consumption others were obliged to import, and the tax would burden particular states. Fitzsimons replied that the manufacture was an important one and far on the way toward perfection. In a few years they could supply the continent. Pennsylvania had a tax of two cents, and the manufacture had been greatly encouraged. Boudinot declared that if a small encouragement were held out by the government candles would soon be made cheaper than they could be imported. Lawrence thought that in any event they should be taxed for revenue.[140]

A duty of 66 Cents per 112 pounds was proposed on steel. Clymer of Pennsylvania admitted that the manufacture was in its infancy, but as the materials were produced in almost all the states, and the manufacture was already established with considerable

---

139 1 Annals of 1ˢᵗ Congress, 134, 139, 140, 143, 145, 180, 231. On molasses the amount finally fixed in the House was five cents. The Senate gradually reduced this to two and a half cents. Ames wrote to Minot, April 14: "Another molasses battle has been fought. Like modern victories it was incomplete, but we got off one cent;" (1 Life of Fisher Ames, 37). Jamaica spirits were finally rated by the Senate at ten cents per gallon; all others at eight. Madeira wine was reduced from thirty-three cents and one-third cents to eighteen cents; all other wines from twenty cents to ten.

140 1 Annals of 1st Congress, 151,152 (H. R. April 15,1789). Two cents was agreed to and remained the rate until doubled in the war of 1812.

success, he deemed it prudent to emancipate the country from the manacles of foreign manufactures. A single furnace in Philadelphia would, with a little encouragement, supply enough for the consumption of the Union. Lee objected to any duty, as the consumption of steel was large and essential to agricultural improvements. Tucker thought it impossible for some states to obtain steel except by importation, and that it was more deserving of a bounty than a tax. The smallest tax would be a burden on agriculture, and he was at a loss to imagine with what propriety gentlemen could propose a measure big with oppression and tending to burden particular states. The situation of South Carolina was melancholy. The state was deeply in debt, and produce was daily falling in price. However, he would be willing to grant a five percent *ad valorem*, tax. Madison agreed with Tucker, that as the object of the tax was solely the encouragement of manufactures and not revenue, it would be more proper to give a bounty on the manufacture. The duty would tend to depress many mechanic arts in the proportion that it protected this, and he thought it best to include it in the five percent list. Fitzsimons maintained that the evils of a small duty would soon be overbalanced by the establishment of such an important manufacture.[141]

Fisher Ames wanted nails protected. The manufacture, he said, had grown up with a little encouragement to an astonishing degree of perfection. It had become usual for the country people in Massachusetts to erect small forges in their chimney corners, and in winter and on evenings when little other work could be done, great quantities of nails were made even by children. Perhaps enough might be manufactured in this way to supply the continent. The business could be prosecuted in a similar manner in every state. Fitzsimons was not solicitous about a duty. The manufacturer would have little to fear, he thought, if the legislature should decide against him. The fact was, nails were at that moment made cheaper and, in the judgment of some, better than those coming from England. Before the Revolution the Americans were not permitted to have slitting mills. Now they had several and were independent of all the world for materials necessary for carrying on

141 1 Annals of 1st Congress, 154. In the bill as it finally passed unwrought steel was rated at 56 cents per 112 pounds, which as Hamilton pointed out the next year, was less than five percent *ad valorem* (2 Hamilton's Works, 110).

the business in the most extensive manner. Yet he was willing to allow a small duty because it conformed to the policy of the states which thought it proper thus to protect their manufactures. Madison feared the tax would increase the cost of shipbuilding. Bland deemed the tax unequal, burdening the South but not the North. Tucker observed that from what had been admitted regarding the little expense and great facility of manufacturing nails, it stood in no need of encouragement; at least, five percent *ad valorem*, would be sufficient. Ames warned the House against jumping to such a conclusion as Tucker's. The commerce of America, he said, particularly the southern parts, had by force of habit and English connections, been setting strong upon the British coasts; it required the aid of the general government to divert it to a more natural course. Laying a small duty on foreign manufactures might induce, from motives of interest as well as inclination, one citizen to barter with another what he had long been accustomed to take from strangers. In Europe the artisan was driven to labor for his bread; stern necessity, with her rod of iron, compelled his exertion. But in America invitation and encouragement were necessary; without them the infant manufacture would droop, and its patron seek with success a competency from the cheap and fertile soil.[142]

Madison doubted the propriety of taxing cordage,[143] because shipbuilding itself was a worthy object of legislative attention. If, however, it was necessary to lay a duty on cordage in order to make the United States independent of the world as to that article, it was also politic to endeavor to become alike independent of the raw material. A large portion of western land was peculiarly adapted to the growth of hemp, and Congress ought to pay as much respect to the encouragement and protection of husbandry as they did to manufactures. Boudinot said that hemp was a raw material necessary for an important manufacture and ought not to be subject to a heavy duty. If it were the product of the country in general a duty plight be proper, but he considered the soil of the country ill adapted to the cultivation of hemp. Partridge of Massachusetts thought a duty on hemp would tend to discourage American navigation, trade, and fisheries, without any good resulting to warrant

142 1 Annals of 1ˢᵗ Congress, 163, 164 (H.R. April 16, 1789). In the tariff act nails were rated at one cent per pound.

143 P.N. 'Cordage' refers to the ropes made for ship rigging on masts and sails.

such an injury. He was in favor of encouraging agriculture, but not at the expense of shipbuilding. Ames doubted the propriety of taxing either cordage or hemp because, while tending to encourage agriculture or manufacturing, it would discourage the maritime interest. Lawrence said, regarding the proposed duty on hemp, that the manufacture would be annihilated unless the duty on cordage was correspondingly raised. Hartley would give a small bounty to hemp growers, because the existence of the manufacture and of shipbuilding also was involved in the price of the raw material; he hoped America would soon become what nature desired her to be—a maritime nation. White of Virginia said that what might be good policy for Great Britain, a maritime nation, might be bad policy of the United States, an agricultural country. If the legislature took no notice the people would be led to believe that hemp was not an object worthy of encouragement, and the spirit of cultivation would be damped. Moore of Virginia declared that the southern states were well calculated for the cultivation of hemp, and well inclined thereto. Congress should pay as much attention to the encouragement and protection of husbandry as they did to manufactures. Burke liked the idea of encouraging hemp, as the present productions of South Carolina hardly paid, and the State was well adapted to raising hemp. Scott, who represented western Pennsylvania, granted that manufactures were useful establishments, but the circumstances of the United States did not admit of their becoming an extensive manufacturing country. They could not expect to export manufactures to foreign nations; they could not, on account of the demand for labor, vie with Europe. He was as well acquainted with the western country as any member of the House. The lands along the frontier were well calculated for the cultivation of hemp. If encouragement were given vast quantities would soon be brought at little expense to Philadelphia. Fitzsimons supposed there was a clear distinction between taxing manufactures and raw materials well known to every enlightened nation. He had no doubt that enough hemp could be raised, and was unable to see why enough was not raised. If eight dollars a hundred was not sufficient inducement to farmers, it was proof that they directed their labors to more profitable productions, and why should legislative authority be exercised to divide their attention? No duty which they could agree to lay could give encouragement to the cultivation of hemp, if the present price was insufficient.[144]

The duty on salt occasioned an animated discussion. Lawrence favored a tax because it was an article in such general use that it could be much depended on for revenue, but would grant a drawback on salted fish and provisions. Burke opposed any duty, because salt was a necessity of life, and a tax would be particularly odious to the inhabitants of South Carolina and Georgia, to whom the price was already oppressively great. Moore characterized the tax as both unpopular and unjust. Tucker declared that it would bear harder on the poor than on the rich. Every one should contribute to the support of the government in proportion to the value of his property; but the poor man consumed as much salt as the rich and more of salted provisions. The duty would enter into the price and the consumer would pay the retailer a profit on the tax. Scott was decidedly against the duty. The old argument in favor of manufactures did not apply, for no duty would be sufficient to establish it. If a high duty were laid on such an indispensable necessity of life, it would be bad policy and go nigh to shipwreck the government. He feared it would have a tendency to shake the foundations of their system, which he looked upon as the only anchor of their political salvation. Smith said it was understood that the inhabitants of the interior of South Carolina were opposed to the new government, and he warned the House that no stronger impulse for opposition could be given than this tax. Madison remarked that while it might be just to lay a considerable duty generally on imported articles, yet it would not be prudent or politic to do so then. In order to determine whether a tax on salt was just or unjust it must be considered as part of a system; so considered the equilibrium was restored. He would make the duty moderate. Huntingdon of Connecticut promised that when his constituents found that the tax was imposed from principles of justice and to promote the public good, they would pay without reluctance.[145]

---

144 1 Annals of 1st Congress, 156-161, 217, 219 (April 15, 16, and 27). In the tariff act cordage was rated at 75 cents and hemp at 60 cents per cwt. The following year cordage was raised to $1.00 and hemp reduced to 54 cents; but in 1792 hemp was placed at $1.00, which according to Gerry (*ib.* 217), would just neutralize the protection to cordage.

145 1 Annals of 1st Congress, 165 *et seq.* (April 16, 17). In the tariff act salt was rated at ten cents per bushel.

Two points were under consideration regarding a tonnage duty, first, as to the rate on foreign vessels, and secondly, as to whether there should be a discrimination against nations not in treaty relations, that is, against England as compared with France. Baldwin of Georgia said the expectation of the country was that there should be a discrimination. This sentiment was believed to be the cause of the Revolution. The selfish policy of Great Britain gave rise to an unavailing clamor and excited the feeble attempt of several state legislatures to counteract the detestable regulations of a commercial enemy. These ineffectual efforts led to the Annapolis Convention,[146] and then to the Constitution. Lawrence questioned the statement that public sentiment favored discrimination. No privileges worth mentioning were accorded the United States by France. He acknowledged the propriety of discriminating between their own citizens and foreigners, but saw no good reason for establishing a preference between foreign nations. Perhaps England might be disposed to adopt a similar discrimination and destroy what carrying trade still remained to the United States. On the whole he thought it good policy to let commerce take its own course. The United States were not in a condition to enter into a commercial war, and in the present condition of the country they ought not to express satisfaction or dissatisfaction with foreigners. Fitzsimons had no doubt that the nation should meet the commercial regulations of foreign powers with regulations of its own. The idea that the tax would fall upon the United States was founded in the presumption that foreigners could draw their supplies from other parts of the world. This was not true; they could not be obtained any where else than from America. But it would not be prudent to lay a duty so high as to deprive the United States of foreign shipping. Virginia had a duty of one dollar and found no difficulty in getting British ships to carry its produce. He did not think sixty cents much, if any, above the average laid by the state governments.[147] Madison said that, in the first place, public sentiment favored discrimination, and in the second place, while

146 P.N. The Annapolis Convention was held in 1786, with state delegates gathering to discuss trade policy. This was before the Constitution was adopted, when the central government had no power or authority to regulate trade.

147 In the larger part conflicts between Hamilton and Jefferson which soon followed, Fitzsimons retreated from this position and opposed discrimination between foreign nations. (See Annals of Congress, H.R. Jan 15, 1794.)

France had relaxed considerably her rigid policy, Great Britain had not. He instanced Vermont, Pennsylvania, and Maryland as examples of state that bad laid discriminating duties. He believed with Fitzsimons that foreigners must receive American tobacco, rice, etc., in American shipping if they could not get it in any other way. Tucker thought there ought to be some discrimination, but the proposed rate was too high. He would vote for thirty cents and twenty cents. Madison suggested a gradually increasing duty. Tucker did not want the burdened citizens of South Carolina to get the idea that their burdens were to be increased at a later time. He hoped gentlemen who wished for national encouragement to shipbuilding would be moderate, as they plainly saw that it must be at the expense of their neighbors. Madison admitted that laying fifty cents on foreign vessels, and but six cents on American, would put a considerable part of the difference into the pockets of American ship owners. This he considered a sacrifice of interest to policy; and were it not for the necessity of having some naval strength, he would advocate throwing wide open the doors of our commerce to all the world and making no kind of discrimination even in favor of American citizens.[148]

Although the bill as amended passed the House without opposition, there was much dissatisfaction with some of its provisions. Some were disappointed because the rates were not higher, but there was a more general fear lest the duties should prove so high as to defeat the objects of the bill and many were quite willing that the Senate should exercise a pruning hand. Ames, who rather voiced the commercial feeling of the East, wrote under date of May 27: "The Senate has begun to reduce the rate of duties. Rum is reduced one-third. Jamaica, ten cents, common, eight. Molasses from five to four. I feel as Enceladus would if Etna was removed. The Senate, God bless them, as if designated by Providence to keep rash and frolicsome brats out of the fire, have demolished the absurd, impolitic, mad discriminations of foreigners in alliance

---

148 1 Annals of 1st Congress, 189-246 (April 21-May 4). For a more elaborate speech of Madison in the same connection see 8upra, p. 79. The provisions regarding tonnage were incorporated in a separate bill which received the President's signature July 20, 1789. The Senate struck out the discrimination between foreign nations, the rates being 6 cents on American vessels, 80 cents on American built vessels owned wholly or in part by foreigners, and 60 cents on all others.

from other foreigners."[149] The House as a whole, however, was irritated at the manner in which its work had been overhauled, and was inclined to assert its right to dictate, as it constitutionally had to originate, revenue measures. Especially was this true as regarded the tonnage bill, into which political divisions of a far-reaching character had crept. But in the end moderation and good sense triumphed, and the House agreed to the best terms it could get.[150]

By the Constitution the power of originating financial legislation was lodged in the House of Representatives. But the starting of the new government was of such moment that upon the appointment of Hamilton to the newly created department of finance, the House was quite willing to turn over to him the work of initiation.[151] Resolutions were accordingly passed calling upon the Secretary for plans in various directions. The reports in answer to these resolutions were made the bases of bills, which were introduced into Congress. The great questions thus brought to the front were regarding the funding system, the assumption of the state debts, and the establishment of a national bank. On these party lines were drawn, and the issue sharply defined. The opposition, led by Madison and inspired by Jefferson, alarmed at the centralizing character of Hamilton's measures and suspecting his good faith toward republican principles, represented him as aiming to overthrow the constitution and establish a monarchy. Backed by state jealousies, they attacked his measures as dangerous and unconstitutional. The struggle became more and more acrimonious, and Washington who had reluctantly obeyed the call to the presidency in the first instance, and who confidently looked for release at the expiration of his term of office, was moved from his resolution by the solemn assurance of both Jefferson and Hamilton that his continuance in office was essential to the stability of the

149 1 Life of Fisher Ames, 45. For Senate amendments, see Senate Journal, vol. I, pp. 32-35.

150 See H.R. June 15, 1789; 1 Annals of 1st Congress, 427. For workings of the first tariff, see 2 Hamilton's Works, 110, 161.

151 Not without opposition however. Remonstrance was made at the outset against surrendering this power to the executive departments, and as party divisions developed the objection became more pronounced. The suggestion undoubtedly came from Hamilton. He considered that his office carried with it the prerogatives which belonged to an English minister of finance, and Hamilton was preeminently the party leader of the Federalists.

government. In these party struggles Hamilton won, and the great state papers in which he laid down the fundamental principles which should govern the financial administration of the country became the model and standard of all future finance ministers.

The tariff policy of the government stood in a somewhat different relation to the Treasury Department. The question most pressing when the government was established, and the one admitting of no delay, was that of revenue; and this, as we have seen, received the first attention of Congress. The Treasury Department was not established until September 2, 1789, and by this time the new tariff was in operation. The question, therefore, did not engage Hamilton's attention until his other measures were disposed of. The resolution of Congress under which the report on manufactures was prepared was adopted January 15, 1790; and when his hands were somewhat freed from other duties, Hamilton turned with deliberateness to the preparation of his reply, which was not transmitted to Congress until December 5, 1791.

At this time there was no pressing demand for action on the part of Congress. The tariff of 1789 was in operation, was yielding already more revenue than had been anticipated, and the limit of duties, even for protection, had, on most articles, Hamilton judged, been reached.[152] But although it launched no new policy, this third report of Hamilton was not less enthusiastically wrought out than the other two, and perhaps fell behind neither in the influence it was to exert upon the policy of the nation. Hamilton felt the ebb tide of that new economic thought which, starting from English and French criticisms of mercantilism, had reached its culmination in Adam Smith's great work on the *Wealth of Nations*, and whose reasoning had so strongly tinctured the thought of Franklin, Jefferson, Adams, Madison, Washington, and others of the first group of American statesmen. We have seen how eagerly the American diplomatists grasped after reciprocity, and how easily the freedom of commerce might have been secured, had not the selfishness of England interposed. But that time had gone by, and the current had set in the other direction. Already the tariff of 1789 had broken with *laissez-faire* and re-asserted mercantilism. Yet the sentiment for freedom of trade, the distrust of bungling

152 See his Report on Public Credit, Dec. 13, 1790; 2 Hamilton's Works, 161.

interference on the part of the government, the feeling that tariffs were partial and oppressive, was by no means silenced, and Hamilton felt the insufficiency of the old basis and the in part illogical character of the reasoning behind the first tariff legislation. Something more was needed to disarm the opposition of the South and to counteract the jealousy of the commercial interests, and he set about to make the encouragement of manufactures a part of his great national policy of strengthening the general government and binding together the interests of the various sections. In pursuance of this he accepted and enforced Adam Smith's refutation of the more obvious physiocratic and mercantile errors, but challenged his *laissez-faire* conclusions in the name of national defence and national welfare.

As to details, Hamilton had little to suggest in the way of addition to the tariff of 1789. In the main the rates were satisfactory both for revenue and protection. Experience had shown, he said, that some articles would bear a higher rate. Some objects demanded more protection, and new industries might soon invite the attention of Congress. And from revenue considerations alone the whole *ad valorem* list should be advanced a step. But in general things were working well, and his immediate recommendations were not specially significant.[153] What gave the report unity and significance was the broadly national ground on which the argument for protection was based, and the scope which was given to the powers of the government in its application.

Hamilton began by defining the scope of his inquiries as relating particularly to the means of promoting such manufactures as would tend to render the United States independent of foreign nations for military and other essential supplies. The opening sentence is significant: "The expediency of encouraging manufactures in the United States, which Was not long since deemed very questionable, appears at this time to be pretty generally admitted." The obstructions to commerce and the restrictions upon the foreign market for agricultural productions had turned attention, he said, to the desirability of encouraging domestic trade and markets. The complete success of some manufactures and the promising

---

153 The increase which he asked for was substantially granted, though sustained and opposed as a party measure.

beginning of others justified the hope that the obstacles were less formidable than had been thought, and that the further extension of manufactures would fully make up for any external disadvantages, and also add to the resources favorable to national independence and safety.

Yet there were those who still objected to the encouragement of manufactures, and their objections he first proceeded to answer.

The first objection, as Hamilton stated it, was the notion that agriculture was the most productive industry, especially true in the United States with its immense tracts of uncultivated lands; and that to endeavor to accelerate the growth of manufactures would be to endeavor to transfer the natural current of industry from a more to a less beneficial channel. Government, it was held, could not wisely undertake to give direction to the industry of its citizens. Private interest, if left to itself, would infallibly find its own way to the most profitable employment for itself. This principle again, had special force in the United States. The small population and large territory, the constant allurements from the settled to the unsettled parts of the country, the ease with which the artisan became a farmer—these, and similar causes, must occasion for a long time to come a scarcity of labor for manufacturing, and dearness of labor generally. Add to these the want of capital, and the prospect of successful competition with the manufactures of Europe became little less than desperate. And if, contrary to the natural course of things, an unreasonable and premature development of certain manufactures could be brought about by heavy duties, prohibitions, bounties, and the like, this would only be to sacrifice the interests of the community to those of particular classes. Monopolies would be created, and the enhancement of price, the inevitable consequence of every monopoly, would fall upon the other parts of society. It would be far preferable that those persons should be engaged in the cultivation of the earth, and that the country should procure, in exchange for its productions, the commodities which foreigners were able to supply in greater perfection and upon better terms.

In reply, Hamilton conceded the pre-eminence of agriculture, but maintained that its interests would be advanced rather than injured by the due encouragement of manufactures, and that the expediency of such encouragement was urged by the most cogent and persuasive motives of national policy. Of the general physiocratic doctrine that agriculture is the only productive industry, he entered into an elaborate refutation along the familiar line of reasoning of the *Wealth of Nations*.[154] He then proceeded to enforce the general argument for manufacturing as a wealth producing factor, summarizing its benefits under the following heads: the division of labor, the extension and use of machinery, the additional employment to persons not ordinarily engaged in business, the promotion of immigration from foreign countries, the greater scope for diversity of talents and dispositions, the more ample field for enterprise, the new and more certain and steady demand for the surplus produce of the soil.

As to the benefits of a division of labor, Hamilton merely repeated Adam Smith's analysis.[155] Regarding the additional employment which would be afforded, he had in mind, he said, the industrious farmers, their wives and daughters, and persons who would otherwise be idle and a burden on the community. Four-sevenths of all the persons employed in the cotton manufactories of England were women and children, mostly children of tender age. Again, manufactures would promote immigration. If they could be assured of encouragement and employment, foreign manufacturers would be tempted by the prospect of better price, cheaper provisions and raw materials, exemptions from taxes, burdens, and restraints endured in the old world, greater personal independence and consequence, more equal government, and religious liberty. Thus manufactures could be pursued without interfering with agriculture; and even if some hands were drawn from agriculture, their places would be supplied by others who had come over as manufacturers. If it were true, he said, as had often been remarked, that there was in the United States a peculiar aptitude for mechanical improvements, this was a forcible reason for encouraging manufactures. To cherish and stimulate the activity of the human mind by multiplying the objects of enterprise, was an

154 The only form, probably, in which the physiocratic objection met Hamilton was in a lingering hostility to manufactures as being of lower grade than tilling the soil. However, the question was quite aside from his main line of argument.
155 Cf. *Wealth of Nations*, Bk. 1, Ch. 1.

important means by which the wealth of the nation was promoted. Every new scene opened to the busy nature of man to rouse and exert itself, was the addition of a new energy to the general stock of effort.

It was by means of the home market, he declared, that the establishment of manufactures principally increased the produce and revenue of a country. It had an immediate and direct relation to agriculture, since the pursuit of farming was vigorous or feeble in proportion to the steadiness or fluctuation of the market for surplus produce. A domestic market was greatly preferable to a foreign one because in the nature of things it was more reliable. Every nation tried to supply itself with provisions from its own soil, and hence a foreign demand for agricultural products was casual and occasional; and as regarded the United States, even independently of artificial impediments, there were natural causes, such as the increase of agricultural products consequent upon the progress of new settlements, which rendered the foreign demand too uncertain for reliance. Such being the case the only way to secure a home market was to promote manufactures; for manufacturers were the principal consumers of the surplus productions of the soil.

These considerations, Hamilton observed, seemed sufficient to establish the general proposition that it was the interest of nations to diversify industry. But it might be further objected, that, while a state possessing large tracts of fertile lands and secluded from foreign commerce would find its interest to divert men from agriculture to manufactures, it did not follow that the same reasoning would hold where all that was needed could be procured on good terms from abroad. This latter condition would at least secure the great advantage of a division of labor, and leave the farmer free to pursue exclusively the culture of his land.

If the system of perfect liberty to industry and commerce were the prevailing system of nations, Hamilton replied, the arguments which dissuade a country like the United States from the zealous pursuit of manufactures would doubtless have great force. He would not affirm that they might not, with few exceptions, be permitted to serve as a rule of national conduct. Each country would then have the full benefit of its peculiar advantages to compensate for its deficiencies or disadvantages; and though nations merely agricultural would not enjoy the same degree of wealth in proportion to numbers, yet the progressive improvement of lands might in the end atone for this; and when considerations were pretty equally balanced, the option ought always to be in favor of leaving industry to its own direction. But the opposite was the general policy of nations ; consequently the United States were to a certain extent in the situation of a country excluded from foreign commerce. They could, indeed, obtain without difficulty the manufactures they wanted; but numerous and very injurious impediments interfered with the export of their own commodities. The United States could not exchange with Europe on equal terms; and the want of reciprocity would render them the victim of a system which should induce them to confine their views to agriculture and refrain from manufactures. The constant and increasing necessity on their part for the commodities of Europe, and the only partial and occasional demand for their own in return, could not but expose them to impoverishment. Americans did not complain of this state of affairs; nations must judge for themselves. It only remained for the United States to consider by what means they could render themselves least dependent on foreign policy. It was no small consolation that already measures which had embarrassed the trade of the country had accelerated internal improvements, and, upon the whole, bettered the condition of affairs. To diversify and extend these improvements was the surest and safest method of indemnifying the country for its inconveniences. If Europe would not take our agricultural products upon terms consistent with our interest the natural remedy was to contract as fast as possible our wants of Europe. Though the settlement of the country might be retarded by manufactures, this did not countervail the powerful inducements for encouragement. Besides, it was better that a smaller quantity of land should be well cultivated than that more should be poorly cultivated.[156]

156 Thus far Hamilton's argument, while both adroit and able, was but incidental, and added nothing to the modified mercantilism generally current. Had he stopped with this his report would have inspired no system and had no currency beyond the ordinary circulation of Congressional documents. It is interesting to note how much the modern tariff position is thrown back on this general preliminary argument, as the powerful reasons which Hamilton next proceeded to urge have one by

But it was said that industry if left to itself would naturally find its way to the most useful and profitable employment. Manufactures without the aid of government, would grow up as soon and as fast as the natural state of things and the interest of the community required. Hamilton enumerated as objections to this: The strong influence of habit, and the spirit of imitation; the fear of failure in untried enterprises; the intrinsic difficulties of first attempts in competition with business already perfected; and the bounties, premiums, and other artificial encouragements which foreign manufactures enjoyed. The simplest and most obvious improvements were adopted with hesitation, reluctance, and slow gradations. Spontaneous transition to new pursuits was even more difficult, and the apprehension of failure still more serious. To inspire confidence there must be prospect of countenance and support from the new government. The superiority of nations whose manufactures were already perfected, was still more formidable, the greatest obstacle being the bounties, premiums, and the like, enjoyed by foreign manufacturers, and the combinations to crush out new enterprises by temporary sacrifices. To enable new enterprises to contend with success against these disadvantages and to fortify them against the dread of such combinations, the assurance of interference and aid from the government was indispensable.

Manufacturing could not succeed in the United States, it was further claimed, because of the scarcity of hands, the dearness of labor, and the want of capital. The first two obstacles, Hamilton admitted, were to a certain extent real; but various considerations lessened their force. Certain parts of the country were pretty fully peopled, with flourishing and increasing towns, and these were fairly mature for manufacturing establishments. Furthermore, a much greater use could be made of women and children, and a vast extension had been given to the employment of machinery. Besides, artisans would transport themselves to the United States as soon as the serious prosecution of manufactures was encouraged. So far as dearness of labor might be a consequence of large profits, it was no obstacle to success; the undertaker could afford to pay the price. Undertakers could afford to pay higher wages than in Europe. The cost of materials on the whole favored the

_____

one ceased to exist.

United States; in the expense of buildings, tools, and the like, there was perhaps an equality; but commissions, transportation across the Atlantic, insurance, taxes, duties, and fees—amounting to from 15 percent to 30 percent—were all in favor of America, and this more than counterbalanced the difference in labor. As to the alleged want of capital in the country, aside from the fact that no one knew how much capital there was or how much was wanted, Hamilton looked to the introduction of banks, the aid of foreign capital, and the funded debt, to remove all disquietude in this regard.[157]

Finally this whole objection was disposed of by the flourishing manufactures already established. These Hamilton classified under seventeen heads, including leather, iron, ships, cabinet wares, flax and hemp, bricks, ardent spirits and malt liquors, paper, wool and fur hats, refined sugars, oils, soaps, candles, copper and brass wires, tin-ware, carriages, snuff, tobacco, starch, lampblack, gunpowder, and many others, besides great quantities of household manufactures.

As to the objection that the encouragement of manufactures would create a monopoly to particular classes at the expense of the rest of the community, Hamilton admitted that in some cases there was an enhancement of prices. But in several instances a reduction of price had immediately succeeded the establishment of a domestic manufacture; and even were it true that the immediate effect was an increase of price, the contrary was the ultimate effect with every successful manufacture. Free from the heavy charges which attended the importation of foreign commodities, it could be afforded cheaper, and internal competition soon did away with everything like monopoly. It was therefore the interest of the community to suffer an increased price with a view to eventual and permanent economy. This had a direct and very important tendency to benefit agriculture, enabling the farmer to procure with a smaller quantity of labor the produce of manufacturing.

Certain general considerations which Hamilton advanced as supporting his main argument were, the moral certainty that the trade of a country both manufacturing and agricultural would be

---

157 For a criticism of this last point, see Sumner's Hamilton, pp. 150, 174.

far more lucrative than that of a country merely agricultural, the greater attractions which a diversified market offered to foreign customers and the greater scope for mercantile enterprise, and the greater danger of stagnation in the trade of a nation which brought few articles to market. From these facts Hamilton drew two inferences: First, that there was always a higher probability of a favorable balance of trade in countries having a diversified industry; and secondly, that these countries were likely to possess more money than agricultural countries. Corroboration of this theory Hamilton affected to find in the fact "that the West India Islands, the soils of which are the most fertile, and the nation which, in the greatest degree, supplies the rest of the world with the precious metals, exchange to a loss with almost every other country," and in a comparison of the monetary condition of the colonies with that of the states in which since the Revolution manufactures had most flourished.[158]

As to the supposed conflict of interests between the North and the South, Hamilton reiterated the idea that the aggregate prosperity of manufactures and the aggregate prosperity of agriculture were intimately connected. Everything tending to establish substantial and permanent order in the affairs of a country, to increase the total mass of industry and wealth, was ultimately beneficial to all. Even if manufactures should be chiefly established in the northern and middle states, the South would be immediately benefited by the increased demand for its productions.

The present moment, then, Hamilton concluded, was a critical one for entering with zeal upon the encouragement of manufactures. Owing to the disturbed state of Europe her citizens were inclined to emigrate, and the money of foreigners was at the disposal of the United States. There was, too, a certain fermentation of mind, a certain activity of speculation and enterprise, which if properly directed, might be made subservient to useful purposes, but which, if left entirely to itself, might be attended with pernicious effects.

As to means, Hamilton named eleven ways which had been successfully employed in other countries: (1) protective duties,

---

158 See Sumner's Hamilton 180.

(2) prohibitions or prohibitive duties, (3) prohibition of the exportation of raw materials, (4) pecuniary bounties, (5) premiums, (6) exemption of raw materials from duty, (7) drawbacks on raw materials, (8) encouragements of new inventions and discoveries, (9) regulations for the inspection of manufactures, (10) the facilitating of pecuniary remittances from place to place, and (11) the facilitating of transportation; and indirectly, by avoiding certain kinds of taxation, such as poll and income taxes, which were apt to be oppressive and unfriendly to manufactures.

Protective duties were a virtual bounty on the domestic fabrics, since by enhancing the charges on foreign articles they enabled the home manufacturers to undersell all foreign competitors; in addition they were a source of revenue. Prohibitive duties were an efficacious means of encouraging manufactures, but in general were only fit to be employed when a manufacture had made such progress and was in so many hands, as to insure a due competition and an adequate supply on reasonable terms.[159] The prohibition of the exportation of raw materials was an encouragement to manufactures which, Hamilton thought, ought to be adopted with great circumspection and only in very plain cases. Yet although its immediate operation was to abridge the demand, and keep down the price of the produce of some other branch of industry—generally speaking, of agriculture—if it were really essential to the prosperity of any very important national manufacture, those injured in the first place might be eventually indemnified by the superior steadiness of an extensive domestic market. Still in a matter in which

---

159 *Laissez-faire* champions have been asking ever since, why in such cases, even on protectionist reasoning, a prohibitive or even protective duty would be necessary. The difficulty in answer is that the justification of protection under such circumstances seems to involve a practical denial of the 'young industries' argument, or at least of the statement that the ultimate effect of protection is a permanent reduction of prices. The best answer which the early controversy could give was perhaps that made by McLane in 1820, who having in mind the foolish prejudice for imported goods as well as the many advantages in taste, experience, and capital, of foreign manufacturers and merchants, declared that the 'American manufacturers did not ask to be allowed to sell at higher prices, but to sell at all.' Modern protectionism, with what President Andrews call its "theory of nutrient restriction," is, of course, not embarrassed by the question.

there was so much room for nice and difficult combinations prudence seemed to dictate that the expedient in question should be indulged with a sparing hand—a perfectly safe conclusion, since the Constitution specifically prohibited export duties!

Of all forms of encouragement Hamilton declared bounties to be one of the most efficacious and, in some views, the best. They acted more positively and directly than any other, and for that reason had a more immediate tendency to stimulate and uphold new enterprises.

They avoided the inconvenience of a temporary augmentation of price. Even if the fund for the bounty was derived from a protective duty, the increase of price was less, for one percent duty converted into a bounty was equal to a duty of two percent. If the bounty were drawn from another source it was calculated to reduce the price, because without laying any new charge on the foreign article it served to introduce a competition with it and to increase the total quantity of the article in the market. Again, bounties, unlike high protecting duties, had no tendency to produce scarcity. Bounties would settle the vexed question of raw materials. The true way to conciliate the interests of the farmer and the manufacturer was to lay a duty on foreign manufactures of the material, the growth of which was desired to be encouraged, and to apply the produce of that duty, by way of bounty, either upon the production of the material itself, or upon its manufacture at home, or upon both. The prejudice against bounties from the appearance of giving away public money without an immediate consideration, and from the supposition that they served to enrich particular classes at the expense of the community, would not bear serious examination. In no way could money be better employed than in gaining a new industry, and the further objection would bear equally against other modes of encouragement. As to the constitutional right of the government to grant bounties, Hamilton thought there could be no question. Congress had express authority "to lay and collect taxes, duties, imposts, and excises, to pay the debts, and provided for the common defence and general welfare." The latter term was as comprehensive as any that could have been used, because it was not fit that the constitutional authority of the Union to appropriate its revenues should have been restricted within narrower limits than the "general welfare," and because this necessarily embraced a vast variety of particulars, which were susceptible neither of specification nor of definition.

Premiums also were very economical means of exciting the enterprise of a community. Much had been done in this way in England, mostly by voluntary associations. From a similar establishment in the United States, supplied and supported by the government, vast benefits might reasonably be expected.[160] To the general rule that raw materials should not be taxed, Hamilton noted certain exceptions, as where a raw material was an object of such general consumption that it might properly be taxed for revenue, and where by encouragement the material could be produced in the country in sufficient abundance to furnish a cheap and plentiful supply to the manufacturers. As to the encouragement of inventions and discoveries, there might be some constitutional question. But it was customary for manufacturing nations to prohibit the exportation of implements and machines which they had either invented or improved, and already there were objects in the United States to which a similar regulation should be applied. This was not very much in accord with the spirit of the country, he admitted, but while other nations pursued their selfish and exclusive policy, the United States could do no better than to follow their example. Another thing much needed was the improvement of roads and canals, and it was much to be wished that there was no doubt of the constitutional power of the government to lend its direct aid on a comprehensive plan.

As articles proper for encouragement Hamilton named iron, copper, lead, coal, wood, skins, grain, flax and hemp, cotton, wool, silk, glass, gunpowder, paper, printed books, refined sugars and chocolate. Of these lead and sugar were already sufficiently protected. Iron should be protected because it was found in great abundance and the fuel used in its manufacture was cheap and plenty. Iron works had greatly increased, and the manufacture was

---

160 A species of protection of which lavish use has been made, though without the interference of the national government. Witness the bonding of towns for railroads, granting free right of way, exempting corporations from taxations, and other like favors. The River and Harbor bills and various educational and other grants of public money, may perhaps be regarded as national subsidies to the same purpose.

prosecuted with much more advantage than formerly. The duty on steel could be safely advanced from 75 cents to 100 cents per cwt., and a duty of two cents per pound should be put on nails to stop the importation, which had amounted to 1,800,000 pounds in 1790. The *ad valorem* duty on all manufactures of iron should be extended to 10 percent. Free pig and bar iron would certainly favor manufactures and probably not interfere with home production. As to copper, the material not being a product of the country, it ought to be put on the free list, while the duty of 5 percent on brass wares and 7 1/2 percent on tin, pewter, and copper ware might be raised to 10 percent. Coal being important for manufactures, bounties on home production and premiums on the opening of new mines were suggested. Wood used in shipbuilding and cabinet-making should be put on the free list. The abundance of timber afforded no objection to this, for the United States should commence and pursue systematic measures to preserve their forests. Tanneries were important, and an increase of duty on leather, together with a prohibition of the exports of bark, was suggested. Glue should be raised from 5 percent to 15 percent. Exclusive possession of the home market should be secured for spirits and malt liquors by an additional duty, and perhaps by an abatement on home-made spirits. Molasses had been rising in price for some years, and the duty of three cents might make it difficult for distillers to compete with the West Indies. A high duty on hemp would be objectionable as a tax on raw material, were there not great facilities for raising it in the United States. However, bounties and premiums were considered by many a more direct method of encouraging the growth of both flax and hemp. Sail-cloth should be raised to 10 percent, with a bounty of 2 cents per yard on the domestic manufacture to counteract the English export bounty. For the same reason the duty on certain linens should be raised to 7 1/2 percent, to counteract an average English export bounty of 12 1/2 percent.

As to cotton, the duty of three cents per pound was undoubtedly a very serious impediment to manufactures. Cotton had not the same pretensions to protection as hemp because not being a universal product of the country it afforded less assurance of adequate supply. Besides, foreign cotton was considered to be of

better quality, and it was certainly wise to let the infant manufacture have the full benefit of the best materials on the cheapest
terms. For the success of these manufactures the repeal of the duty
was indispensable, and a bounty of one cent per yard would be an
expense well justified by the magnitude of the object. As to wool,
household manufactures were carried on to an interesting extent.
The branch of hat-making had reached maturity, and nothing but
an adequate supply of materials was needed to render the manufacture commensurate with the demand. It was certainly most
desirable to encourage the raising and improving of sheep, but it
was yet a problem whether American wool was capable of being
made fit for the finer fabrics. Premiums would probably be found
the best means of promoting the domestic, and bounties, the foreign supply. The silk manufacture might well be encouraged by free
raw material and premiums on production. The materials for the
manufacture of glass were found everywhere. The existing duty of
12 1/2 percent was a considerable encouragement, and if anything
more were needed it should be supplied by a direct bounty on win-
dow glass and bottles. Sulphur should be included with saltpetre
in the free list, in the interest of the manufacture of gunpowder. As
to printed books, there was no need of being indebted to foreign
countries, and the duty should be raised from 5 percent to 10 percent, with free importation for seminaries and public libraries.

In conclusion, Hamilton recurred to the subject of bounties,
urging that in some cases at least they were indispensable. He
indicated ways in which they could be guarded from excess, and
assuming that a surplus could be counted on from the existing
revenue system, he advocated the setting aside of a fund for paying
bounties to be granted by Congress, and another fund to be under
the control of a board created for promoting the arts, agriculture,
manufactures, and commerce. This board should be composed of
not less than three commissioners, who should have power to apply the fund, to assist the immigration of artists and manufacturers
in particular branches of extraordinary importance; to promote
useful discoveries, inventions, and improvements, by rewards
judiciously held out and applied; to encourage special exertions
in promoting certain objects, by premiums; and to afford various
other aids. "It may confidently be affirmed," he said, "that there

is scarcely anything which has been devised, better calculated to excite a general spirit of improvement than the institutions of this nature. ... In countries where there is great private wealth, much may be effected by the voluntary contributions of patriotic individuals; but in a community situated like that of the United States the public purse must supply the deficiency of private resource. In what can it be so useful, as in promoting and improving the efforts of industry?"[161]

---

161 For full text of the Report, see 3 Hamilton's Works, 294-416.

CHAPTER III

COMMERCE VERSUS MANUFACTURES

Hamilton's Report on Manufactures could hardly have failed of having an immediate and important effect in strengthening and solidifying the protective system. Its strong Americanism and admirable temper must have insensibly but powerfully reinforced and directed the general sentiment in favor of legislative encouragement to industry. Not free from economic errors of a serious kind, these, even if perceived, would not have vitiated the appeal to national consciousness and national independence. Yet on its main lines the report provoked no discussion in Congress. With the tariff of 1789 in successful operation, Congress had come to a state of rest in the matter, and inertia was bard to overcome. Even Hamilton had little disposition to meddle with the schedule save for revenue purposes. He meant to lay down a policy far-reaching and adequate to the growth and needs of the country; but it was hardly for immediate action that he prepared. He Had already admitted that in the great majority of cases the rates were as high as the articles would bear, and a little later, in asking for additional rates (which he hoped would be temporary,) to defray the expenses of the Indian war, he declared that he did so with reluctance, for the reason already given, and because changes in the rates of duties by the uncertainty they caused in mercantile operations were injurious to commerce.[162] He did not fail, however, to note the beneficial effects which such increase might have on the "industry, wealth, strength, independence, and substantial prosperity of the country." He aimed to create a feeling toward manufactures so friendly that no needed encouragement would be withheld, but further action at the time was not essential to his general policy, and he was perfectly aware that his system must wait the slow ripening of events. The manufacturers were not wholly satisfied with the status quo, as was manifested by the frequent petitions which found their way

---

162 Report on Additional Supplies, H. R. March 17,1792; 2 Hamilton's Works, 223

into Congress; but to these there was no one to listen, for other and more exciting questions were absorbing public attention.

The great wheels of government had hardly got into motion when the storm of factional controversy burst forth. The background of the drama presently to be enacted was the old struggle between the friends and foes of the Constitution—between those, at the one extreme, with whom democracy was still synonymous with anarchy, and who saw success in the new government only as it should make itself felt as supreme and guiding instead of as an agent of discordant state governments; and those, at the other extreme, who looked with jealousy upon every exercise of power by the general government, and who, at first attacking the Constitution itself, presently rested their case on a strict construction of that instrument. Moderate men who approached neither extreme were finally drawn into taking sides as party divergence became more marked. The democratic element took alarm at the very organization of the government. John Adams began his official career as vice-president with a vainglorious display of pomp which disgusted and alarmed the Republicans. While waiting for the arrival of Washington the Senate toyed with the forms of monarchy in the etiquette it proposed to adopt in its relations with the Executive and the House. Even the dignity which Washington deemed essential to the executive office was offensive to the radical element in the country. Jefferson returned from France on the eve of her great democratic upheaval to find, "with wonder and mortification," the table conversations filled with sentiments in favor of royalty and kingly government.[163] Hamilton, in particular, was so unguarded in his approval of the English Constitution as to convince Jefferson that he was not loyal to the new Constitution and only waited an opportunity to overturn it.[164] "His system," Jefferson complained to Washington, " flowed from principles adverse to liberty, and was calculated to undermine and demolish the republic."[165] In Hamilton's financial policy Jefferson professed to see only two things—a puzzle to exclude popular understanding and inquiry, and a machine for the corruption of the legislature.[166]

163 See Jefferson's Anas; 9 Jefferson's Works, 91; also *ib*. vii, 367, 390.
164 See 3 Jefferson's Works, 450.
165 September 9, 1792; 3 Jefferson's Works, 461.
166 Jefferson's Anas; 9 Jefferson's Works, 91.

Matters were all going wrong, and all the evil machinations were traced to the sinister mind of Hamilton. He had deceived Washington and moulded him to his will, and by cabals with members of the legislature, and high-toned declamations, was forcing his system down the throats of the people. As Secretary of the Treasury he had assumed the aristocratic position of an English prime minister and usurped the functions of the House of Representatives. A morbid sensitiveness to the letter of the Constitution began to manifest itself. Already a sectional turn was given to the struggle. The South, it was said, had been chiefly opposed to the Constitution, and Congress had done nothing to allay its fears, but, on the contrary, whenever Northern and Southern prejudices had come into conflict, the latter had been sacrificed and the former soothed.[167] The national sentiment was still feeble, and it was not then to the interest of the Republicans to discourage this outburst of State jealousy. "We hear incessantly from the old foes of the Constitution," wrote Fisher Ames, "'this is unconstitutional, and that is'; and indeed, what is not? I scarce know a point which has not produced this cry, not excepting a motion for adjournment. ... The fishery bill was unconstitutional; it is unconstitutional to receive plans of finance from the Secretary; to give bounties; to make the militia worth having; order is unconstitutional; credit is tenfold worse."[168] Washington's proclamation of neutrality was bitterly denounced, not only for its hostility to France, but as violating the forms and spirit of the Constitution.[169]

Soothingly as Hamilton's Report on Manufactures fell upon the general discussion regarding protection, it was a firebrand in these wider political struggles. The tariff of 1789, passed before

167 See letter of Washington to Hamilton, July 29, 1792; 10 Washington's Works, 249 et seq.
168 Ames to Minot, March 8,1792; 1 Life of Fisher Ames, 114.
169 See 1 Madison's Works, 584. June 12,1789, Senator Maclay wrote in his journal: " My mind revolts in many instances against the Constitution of the United States. Indeed, I am afraid it will turn out the vilest of all traps that ever was set to ensnare the freedom of an unsuspecting people. . . . Mem. Get if I can the Federalist without buying it. It is not worth it. But being a lost book, Izard or some one else will give it to me. It certainly was instrumental in procuring the adoption of the Constitution. This is merely a point of curiosity and amusement, to see how wide of its explanations and conjectures the stream of business has taken its course" (Sketches of Debate in the First Senate, p. 79.)

party lines had been sharply drawn, had, seemingly at least, a distinctively non-partisan character. But some features of the first debate had revealed more than cursory differences and disclosed for a moment the party divisions and angry smuggles of the near future. Then came the plans of Hamilton, the resistless sweep of whose measures filled the Republicans with terror. His extension of the protective system, his proposal of bounties and premiums, his assumption that the general government had power to do whatever would promote the general welfare, seemed almost like treason. " [It] broaches a new constitutional doctrine of vast consequence" wrote Madison with more than usual feeling, " I consider it myself as subverting the fundamental and characteristic principles of the government; as contrary to the true and fair, as well as the received construction, and as bidding defiance to the sense in which the Constitution is known to have been proposed, advocated, and adopted."[170] Jefferson tried to put Washington on his guard against plans which would draw all the powers of government into the hands of the general legislature;[171] but what was more to the purpose, now thoroughly alarmed, with tireless energy he knit together the opposition into a compact body waging relentless war upon every detail of Hamilton's insidious policy. Had Hamilton's report preceded the adoption of a revenue system the question concerning the constitutionality of protective tariffs might have been tested a half century earlier than it really was. But there was a tacit agreement not to disturb the existing system; and such changes as Hamilton recommended, including his excise system, which Jefferson pronounced "an infernal tax," were adopted as strict party measures.

The disastrous ending of St. Clair's Indian campaign,[172] in November, 1791, made new demands upon the Treasury. Hamilton's proposals included a general advance of 2 1/2 percent *ad valorem* and some few changes in the enumerated list. In the debate that ensued the positions of 1789 were re-affirmed with somewhat more sharpness. The proposal to remove the duty from cotton was

---

170 Madison to Edmund Pendleton, Jan. 21, 1792; 1 Madison's Works, 546.
171 Jefferson to Washington, Sept. 9, 1792; 3 Jefferson's Works, 461, 463.
172 P.N. Major General Arthur St. Clair, with a force of about 1400 men, was ambushed by an Indian force led by Little Turtle, in November 1791. It was the most decisive defeat the Americans suffered from Native Americans.

opposed by the South, while the enhanced duty on hemp was as generally supported. Page of Virginia, while favoring the duty on cotton, denounced the bill as not really intended for the protection of the frontiers, but as a compromise for the assumption of the State debts and as an encouragement of the manufacturers and the fisheries. Encouraging manufactures he thought foreign to the business of Congress, and if not so, a mere taking from one hand, and giving to another.[173] Mercer of Maryland declared that a manufacture which would not after a sufficient stimulus support itself, ought not to be encouraged; and when it no longer needed aid the tax ought to be withdrawn. The bounties on certain articles were in fact paid from the staples of the Southern States by producing retaliating regulations in their only markets abroad.[174] But the stress of opposition did not fall upon the protective character of the bill Madison, arguing that the proposed bounty on fish was unconstitutional, took occasion to define again the limits of the federal power. This was not an indefinite government, he said, deriving its powers from the general terms prefixed to the specific powers, but a limited government tied down to the specified powers which explain and define the general terms. Were the power of Congress to be established in the latitude contended for it would subvert the very foundation, and transmute the very nature of the limited government established by the people of America.[175]

The Administration, Mercer declared, would not even permit Congress to defend the helpless women and children of the frontier from the brutal ferocity of a savage foe, but on condition that they surrender up forever the sacred trust of the Constitution and place in the power and under the control of the Executive and Senate a perpetual tax. The Treasury department, he complained bitterly, was the really efficient legislature of the country, so far as related to revenue, which was the vital principle of government.[176]

But aside from the general political struggles which forbade any further application of the protective system, there was a much stronger reason for not disturbing the existing arrangement. The

---

173 Quoted in Young's Custom-Tariff Legislation, pp. xxi, xxii.
174 H.R. January 27, 1793; 1 Annals of 2nd Congress, 352.
175 H.R. February 6, 1792; 1 Annals of 2nd Congress, 386, 389.
176 H.R. January 27, 1792; 1 Annals of 2nd Congress, 350, 351.

industry which thrust itself forward, and on which legislation so often turned during the years that followed, was not manufactures but commerce" Commerce was the controlling interest of the Northeast, audits international character gave it an exceptional importance. That the Constitution originated in a commercial necessity was a truism at the East, and the commercial and mercantile interests, rather than either agriculture or manufactures, had traced the limits of the tariff of 1789. Of all these industries commerce was destined to the most rapid growth; and the extraordinary condition of European affairs which was first to make the United States common carriers for all the world, and then to involve that whole commerce in ruin, prevented, while it prepared the way for, that peculiar national feeling out of which the American system was to emerge. Upon this mercantile and commercial interest Hamilton planted his whole policy. That the moneyed interest of the country should support the new government, he considered a prime necessity, and he strained every nerve to bind it to the new order of things. Though demanding a generous policy toward manufactures, not flinching when this seemed opposed to the selfish ends of commerce, he was careful to antagonize no real interest of the moneyed classes. When he called for additional duties, as in the bill for the protection of the frontiers, his opponents endeavored to make capital out of the apparent hostility to commerce;[177] but in all this an immense advantage lay with Hamilton whose advocacy of protection was frank, cordial, and unaffected. To Madison, indeed, belonged the chief credit for the tariff of 1789, but Madison could never separate his advocacy of protection from an avowal of preference for free trade, and besides he represented a constituency as indifferent to commerce as it was averse to further legislation in favor of manufactures.

However, a turn in foreign relations gave an opportunity to antagonize Hamilton's anglicism, which manifested itself in a steady promotion of trade with England. Hamilton had not objected to a discrimination in favor of American shipping as against all the world, but since nearly all their commerce was with the British

177 In the debate on the bill just referred to, Mercer called attention to the petitions from the great commercial capitals of America, which represented that the impositions on commerce were already oppressive and intolerable. H.R. January 27, 1792; 1 Annals of 2nd Congress, 351.

Empire, he regarded the attempt to discriminate between France and England in favor of the former as a piece of folly and commercially disastrous. Outside of the commercial centers, however, this rebuke to England chimed in with popular feeling. Madison had made it a special feature of the first tariff bill, and it had been adopted by the House with practical unanimity. Its rejection by the Senate, Madison charged, was due to the deep anglicism in which New York was steeped,[178] and their excuse that they wanted something more efficacious he regarded as the evasion it undoubtedly was.

Early in 1791, in a special message to Congress, Washington recounted the steps he had taken in endeavoring to come to an understanding with England on several points, particularly regarding reciprocity, and stated that as a result of informal conferences with British ministers he did not infer any disposition on their part to enter into such an arrangement.[179] The message was referred to a select committee, whose action in turn was referred to the Secretary of State with instructions to report to Congress the privileges and restrictions of commercial intercourse with foreign nations, with such measures as he deemed proper to be adopted. Jefferson noted, as he thought, an unfriendly design on Hamilton's part, and as he set about his report to Congress he tested Hamilton's views by mentioning that he should recommend a commercial retaliation against Great Britain. Hamilton strenuously objected, and this action Jefferson regarded as an invasion of his own prerogative as Secretary of State. "My system," he complained to Washington, "was to give some satisfactory distinctions to the French, of little cost to us, in return for the solid advantages yielded us by them; and to have met the English with some restrictions, which might induce them to abate their severities against our commerce. I have always supposed this coincided with your sentiments; yet the Secretary of the Treasury, by his cabals with members of the legislature and by high-toned declamations on other occasions, has forced down his own system, which was exactly the reverse."[180]

178 1 Madison's Works, 472, 467; see also Sketches of Debate in the First Senate, p. 94.
179 H.R February 14, 1791; 2 Annals of 1st Congress, 2015.
180 Jefferson to Washington, Sept. 9, 1792; 3 Jefferson's Works, 459 *et seq.*; also 10 Washington's Works, 517 *et seq.*

Jefferson felt this interference the more keenly because of his ardent sympathy with the French Revolution, then in its greatest promise. The beginning of that Revolution had stirred the blood of American patriots as it had not been stirred since their own great struggle. Not only was it a revolt against tyranny and oppression, but it held aloft the banner of liberty and equality. Besides, France had borne toward the struggling Republic the only sympathetic and generous countenance in all Europe, and had brought timely aid in its dire extremity. Every sentiment of self-respect as well as of gratitude seemed to demand that France in turn should be aided in every way consistent with national honor. A considerable portion of the country would have responded to a declaration of war against England, and the whole French party would barely have come short of such a proceeding. The coolness of the government under these circumstances, the determination to maintain strict neutrality and avoid all foreign complications, seemed to the Republicans the basest ingratitude. Washington's proclamation of neutrality was offensive because of its discourtesy and unfriendliness toward France rather than because of its alleged unconstitutionality. Jefferson had given a reluctant consent to its issuance, but he privately explained that its form and spirit had been totally changed.[181] For a time it seemed likely that the Federalists would be overthrown; but the reckless extravagance of the French faction and the insolence of Citizen Genet[182] soon turned the scale. This episode, however, while temporarily discrediting the French party, cleared the atmosphere of much foolish sentimentalizing and prepared the way for a more rational attempt to express sympathy with France.[183]

Meanwhile the situation was becoming complicated by the growing carelessness, not to say insolence, of Great Britain regarding American trade. Not only was there no indication of granting any commercial privileges with the West Indies, but in June, 1793, the British ministry issued orders for the seizure of

---

181 4 Jefferson's Works, 29.

182 P.N. Edmond-Charles Genêt (1763-1834) was French minister to the United States. He worked to recruit volunteers, raise funds, and outfit privateers to support the French revolutionary government. His actions violated American neutrality and put immense pressure on the fragile peace with Great Britain.

183 See 1 Schouler, 259, 260.

all vessels carrying provisions to France. In the irritation which this act produced came Jefferson's opportunity to strike, and Dec. 16,1793, just before retiring from the Cabinet, he submitted his Report on the condition of trade with foreign countries. The report consisted of an exhaustive examination of the restrictions upon American trade and a discussion at length of the principles upon which the United States should proceed. Jefferson found that American bread-stuffs were at most times under prohibitive duties in England, and considerably dutied on re-exportation from Spain to her colonies. Tobacco was heavily dutied in England, Sweden, and France, and prohibited in Spain and Portugal. Rice was heavily dutied in England and Sweden and prohibited in Portugal. Fish and salted provisions were prohibited in England and under prohibitive duties in France. Whale oils were prohibited in England and Portugal; and American vessels were denied naturalization in England and France. In the West Indies all intercourse was prohibited with the possessions of Spain and Portugal. Salted provisions and fish were prohibited by England, and salted pork and bread-stuffs, except maize, were received under temporary laws only in the dominions of France, salted fish even there paying a high duty. As to navigation, American carriage of their own tobacco was heavily dutied in Sweden and France, no article not of home production could be carried to the British ports in Europe, and not even American produce could be carried to the British West Indies in American ships.

Turning to remedies, Jefferson declared that of the two methods of dealing with such restrictions he would prefer that of a friendly arrangement. Instead of embarrassing commerce under piles of regulating duties and prohibitions, he would have it relieved from all its shackles in all parts of the world, with every country employed in producing that which nature had best fitted it to produce, and each free to exchange with others mutual surplusses for mutual wants. Would even a single nation begin with the United States this system of free commerce, it would be advisable to begin it with that nation. But free commerce and navigation were not to be given in exchange for restrictions and vexations; and should any nation continue its system of prohibitions, duties, and regulations, it behooved The United States to protect its citizens by counter-prohibitions, duties, and regulations. Following closely in Hamilton's footsteps, Jefferson saved himself from inconsistency by referring to the State governments those forms of encouragement to manufactures which, in his opinion, the general government had no power to offer. He would select such manufactures as were obtained from the offending nation in greatest quantities, and could be soonest developed within the United States or obtained from other foreign countries, and by gradually increasing duties, endeavor to draw the foreign manufacturer to America. He would have the State governments open their resources and extend them liberally to those manufactures for which their soil, climate, population, and other circumstances had matured them, especially fostering the precious efforts and progress of household manufactures.

So far Jefferson seemed but echoing Hamilton's own ideas of reciprocity; but the drift of his report was made sufficiently evident in the concluding statement that while France of her own accord had proposed negotiations for a new treaty of commerce, England had rejected all such proposals on the part of the United States. However, no positive deductions were drawn, and there was no deviation from the judicial tone which characterized the report. But this was only the first step, and in the House Madison promptly introduced a resolution proposing, among other things, to lay additional *ad valorem* duties on various manufactures of countries not in treaty, additional tonnage duties, to the same purpose, countervailing regulations and restrictions, and providing for the payment from such duties of losses sustained in consequence of the illegal regulations of other countries.[184]

The debate which followed is interesting as fore shadowing a struggle which was to bring the Union to the verge of dissolution, but more particularly as marking the limits of protective legislation and the strong forces which held the tariff to its original moorings. January 13, William Smith of South Carolina, in an elaborate speech prepared by Hamilton, combatted the conclusions of Jefferson's report, and opposed Madison's resolutions. Their ears were accustomed, he said, to a panegyric on the generous policy

184 For Jefferson's Report, see Annals of 3rd Congress (Appendix) pp. 1290 *et seq.*; also 7 Jefferson's Works, 637 *et seq.*

of France, and to as constant a philippic on the unfriendly, illiberal, and persecuting policy of Great Britain. The reverse was really the case, England granting far more substantial advantages than France. From Jefferson's report it appeared that three-fourths of the imports of the country came from Great Britain and her dominions. This was considered by some a grievance, but to an unbiased mind it demonstrated the great importance and utility of the trade with Britain. Nor could an alteration be made but by means violent and contrary to the interests of the country, except in one way, which was not the object of the report, namely, an efficacious system of encouragement to home manufactures. Imports from Great Britain were large because England was the first manufacturing country in the world and could supply them on the best terms, and because her merchants had large capitals and could give extensive credit. Manifestly it was the interest of the United States to be supplied with the manufactures it wanted, of the best quality and on the best terms, and to take them from that country which was most able to furnish them.

The Navigation Act was deemed by England the palladium of her riches, greatness, and security, and would not be surrendered without a struggle—a war of arms or of commercial regulations. While three-fourths of our trade was with Great Britain, only one-sixth of her trade was with us. That our supplies were more necessary to her than hers to us was a position which our self- love gave more credit to than facts would authorize. Well-informed men in other countries affirmed that Great Britain could obtain a supply of most of our productions as cheap and of as good quality elsewhere. On the other hand, where should the United States find a substitute for the vast supply of manufactures which it got from that country. No one would say that the United States could suddenly replace them by their own manufactures, or that this, if practicable, could be done without a violent distortion of the natural course of industry. The prosperity of the nation was not a plant to thrive in a hot bed. It was agreed on all hands that our great natural interests, our population, agriculture, manufactures, commerce, and navigation, were in a thriving and progressive state, and were advancing faster than was to have been expected, and as fast as could be reasonably desired. The additional duties were objectionable because the existing duties, averaging nearly twenty percent, were already, generally speaking, high enough for the state of mercantile capital and the safety of collection. To reciprocity, on the solid basis of treaties, there was no objection. But why should this young country throw down the gauntlet in favor of free trade against the world? There might be spirit in it, but there would certainly not be prudence.[185]

The position of agriculture and commerce was frankly stated during the debate. Hartley of Pennsylvania, who had made the first demand for a protective tariff in 1789, affirmed that while he had always been a friend to manufactures, and wished them every proper encouragement, he was sure they might go too fast. The manufacturers, he believed, were well satisfied with what had been done. On the other hand, the protecting duties had already en-hanced the price of labor very considerably, and this had extended to husbandry. If protective duties were increased the manufacturer would just add the difference to his price. Of course the farmers would have to bid higher for labor in order to prevent the coun-tryman or adventurer from going into a manufactory or workshop. The cultivation and improvement of the country were primary considerations, and no policy should be adopted which would disturb them.[186]

The most vigorous speech was made by Fisher Ames. In general he sustained Smith's (Hamilton's) position, and indi-rectly defended England's course. The good will and friendship of nations—"the jargon of romance"—he declared, were hollow foundations to build upon. Mutual interest was the solid rock of their connection with England. "If it is her interest to afford to our commerce more encouragement than France gives, if she does this when she is inveterate against us, as it is alleged, and when we are indulging an avowed hatred towards her, and partiality towards France, it shows that we have very solid ground to rely on." He hoped that they should never be so unwise as to put their good customers into a situation to be forced to make every exertion to do without them. If a trade was mutually beneficial, it was strange-ly absurd to consider the gains of others as our loss. "Trade flour-

185 Annals of 3rd Congress, 174-209.
186 H.R. Jan. 24, 1794.

ishes on our wharves," he declared, "although it droops in speeches. Manufactures have risen, under the shade of protecting duties, from almost nothing to such a state that we are even told it is safe to depend on the domestic supply, if the foreign should cease." "But the whole theory of balances of trade, of helping it by restraint, and protecting it by systems of prohibition and restriction against foreign nations, as well as the remedy for credit, are among the exploded dogmas which are equally refuted by the maxims of science and the authority of time." If he could have his way he would throw all the restrictive and prohibitory laws into the fire. But so many interests would be disturbed, and so many lost, by any violent change, that the idea of absolute freedom of commerce must be regarded as perfectly Utopian and wild.

The debate was adjourned until March, and by that time news had arrived of further British orders which swept the seas of all American commerce with the French West Indies.[187] An embargo was immediately laid; but Republicans were as loath as Federalists to follow this by adequate provisions for war, and Washington seized the opportunity to send a special mission to England. The result was the Jay treaty,[188] which though highly offensive to Jefferson and fiercely contested in the House, was satisfactory to commerce, and secured for ten years free course for development.

For the next decade there was little impulse toward protective tariffs. Manufactures indeed grew steadily, but without seriously lessening the dependence upon foreign manufacture. At the instance of the Treasury department the tariff was occasionally changed, and the rates slowly pushed upward: Hamilton found no occasion to remove the additional duties he had hoped would prove only temporary, and his successors did not even consider the question. But the pressure for government assistance was hardly felt at a time when commerce was growing at an unexampled rate and not only calling into its service every man who could be allured from agriculture and manufactures in America, but eagerly

---

187 H.R. Jan. 27, 1794; Annals of 3rd Congress, 328-349.
188 P.N. The Jay Treaty of 1794 "normalized" relations with Great Britain. It resolved territorial border issues, ended Royal Navy impressment of Americans, and opened up the West Indies to American trade. With some in the House and Senate supporting France, and others supporting Great Britain, it was a polarizing issue.

accepting English, French, and Spanish deserters, both ships and men. While Europe was distressed with wars, America, peculiarly and unexpectedly shielded by the Jay treaty, became the carriers for the direct and indirect trade between America and Europe, and even for the trade between one European country and another.[189]

In 1801 the Federalists, promoters of commerce and of close relations with England, gave way to the Republicans,[190] jealous of English influence and at best indifferent to commerce. Jefferson himself had in general a prejudice against commerce as entangling the United States with other nations, and as inconsistent with the Virginia ideal of republican and pastoral simplicity. He had begun by professing the vain wish of setting up a Chinese wall over against Europe, and his bitter experience in trying to protect commerce by destroying it, confirmed him in a hostility which he could not overcome. So much commerce as would carry off super-fluities, was his final as his first thought. He wanted the United States to become no mere city of London, he said, to carry on the business of half the world at the expense of eternal war with the other half. "Had we carried but our own produce, and brought back but our own wants, no nation would have troubled us."[191] However, on beginning his administration he recognized the absorption of the East in commercial pursuits as an inevitable part of human imperfection; and with his party in power and himself in the chief place, he felt no inconsistency in regarding commerce as very much less menacing to the Republic, and, indeed, in deference to the East, which he meant to purge of its old Federalism, as an industry to be cherished. "I am sensible," he replied to an address from the legislature of Rhode Island, "of the great interest which your State justly feels in the prosperity of commerce. It is of vital interest also to States more agricultural, whose produce, without commerce, could not be exchanged. As the handmaid of agriculture, therefore, commerce will be cherished by me both from

---

189 See 2 Henry Adams' History of the United States, 322-326.
190 P.N. While party politics was not formalized, Federalists were strong in New England, supported manufacture, trade, and Great Britain. The Democratic-Republicans, Jefferson's party, were more Southern, agricultural, and supported France.
191 See letter to Crawford, June 20, 1816; 7 Jefferson's Works, 6, 7.

principle and duty."[192]

All went well so long as only favorable winds were blowing. Jefferson dreamed the dream of republican simplicity, while his own initiative and the stress of events were drawing him nearer and nearer to the whirlpool of European complications. Until the First Consul unexpectedly put Louisiana into his hands he leaned toward England, protesting his friendship and even proposing an indissoluble British alliance.[193] Success in the Louisiana negotiation, and the prospect of Napoleon's assistance in obtaining the Floridas drew him to the side of France and into a cooler attitude toward England. He prepared to assert the full American rights against England, and when the English government courteously offered to renew the essential part of the expiring Jay treaty, Monroe, then minister to England, promptly declined, stating that the President wished to postpone the matter until he could include impressment and neutral rights in the treaty.[194] For a while Jefferson balanced himself unsteadily between the two European contestants, leading each to believe that the United States would take sides with that one in the struggle then going on. But both Napoleon and Canning soon understood that the last thing Jefferson meant to be forced into was war. He had started out with the idea that commerce was not worth a war,[195] but he had an even brighter illusion—the notion that the commerce of the United States was so necessary to Europe, and especially to England, that the mere threat to withdraw it would be sufficient to secure justice.[196] This persistent republican notion, clung to by Jefferson after everyone else had abandoned it, made the Republic contemptible abroad, completed the ruin of commerce at home, nearly severed the Union, and sent Jefferson into retirement with a stinging sense of defeat and public disapproval. Blow after blow fell heavily upon American commerce, orders in Council, Berlin and Milan decrees, even British ships blockading American harbors. Meantime, negotiations failing, goaded by taunts from Napoleon and insolence

---

192 May 26,1801; 4 Jefferson's Works, 398.
193 See 2 Henry Adams' History of the United States, 78.
194 2 Henry Adams' History of the United States, 421.
195 See 1 Henry Adams' History of the United States, 215.
196 See 1 Henry Adams' History of the United States, 214; and Jefferson's Works, *passim*.

from British ministers, Jefferson serenely prepared to take the last step to which his policy led—to lay an indefinite embargo and withdraw from all European intercourse until England and France were prepared to do him justice.

It is conceivable, as Jefferson always claimed, that had the embargo been persisted in it would have hastened, if had not brought about, commercial peace, though it could have gained the United States little respect among European nations. The success of the embargo, however, depended on the devotion of the people to the Jeffersonian policy; and unfortunately this policy bore most severely upon a section of the Union which had neither taste nor inclination for martyrdom. Old federalism stung to fury by the ruin of embargo, and new republicanism knowing little and caring less about Jeffersonian principles, united to pull down the embargo before England or France had relaxed in the slightest their obnoxious decrees. No further step could they take together, however, for the Federalists, hating Jefferson as the author of all their misfortunes, professed to believe that he was acting under direct orders from Bonaparte, and insisted that England was wholly in the right.

It is not necessary for our present purpose to trace the fate of commerce further. But one incidental effect of vast importance had already made itself manifest, The removal of the overshadowing importance of commerce, not less than the sudden monopoly of the home market noted as a powerful stimulus to manufactures, which now began to come forward, not so much for government encouragement as for protection against a return to the old state of things and consequent loss of their market. Toward this new phase of the situation the Republican leaders turned with constantly increasing interest and satisfaction. In his second inaugural address Jefferson, referring to a possible surplus revenue in the future, noted that the tariff was cheerfully paid by those who could afford to add foreign luxuries to domestic comforts, and raised the question whether, in time of peace, this revenue might not, by an amendment to the Constitution, be applied to rivers, canals, roads, arts, manufactures, education, and other great objects within each State.[197] In his annual message, December, 1806, he recommended

---

[197] 1 Statesman's Manual, 173, 174; Annals of 8th Congress, 2nd Session, 78; 8 Jefferson's Works, 41.

the continuation of the Mediterranean Fund,[198] remarking that the duties were laid chiefly on luxuries, and again broached the question as to what should be done when a surplus revenue began to accumulate. Shall it be abolished, he ventured to say, and thus give foreign manufactures that advantage over domestic, or since it is chiefly on luxuries, will not people rather have it expended on roads, education, and the like?[199] November, 1807, he noted with interest the establishment of the Merino breed of sheep in America, the beginnings of cotton manufacture, the general spirit of encouraging domestic manufactures, and the fact that Philadelphia was becoming more manufacturing than commercial.[200] In his last annual message he took a more positive stand, evidently foreseeing a new way out of commercial difficulties. "The situation into which we have thus been forced," referring to the European complications, "has impelled us to apply a portion of our industry and capital to internal manufactures and improvements. The extent of this conversion is daily increasing, and little doubt remains that the establishments formed and forming, will—under the auspices of cheaper materials and subsistence, the freedom of labor from taxation with us, and of protecting duties and prohibitions—become permanent."[201]

In retirement, Jefferson returned to his old notion of an equilibrium between agriculture, manufactures, and commerce, wanting of manufactures, he wrote Jay, simply enough to supply their own wants, of which the raw material was raised in the country.[202] To General Dearborn he wrote a year later regretting the repeal of the embargo, and affirming his belief that England could have been coerced to justice if the embargo had been honestly executed.

198 P.N. A separate Treasury fund used to pay for expenses from the Barbary War.
199 1 Statesman's Manual, 190, 191; 8 Jefferson's Works, 68. Since the rich alone used imported articles, the poor man, Jefferson reasoned, would have no taxes to pay. Then, "our revenues liberated by the discharge of the public debt, and its surplus applied to canals, roads, schools, etc., the farmer will see his government supported, his children educated, and the face of his country made a paradise by the contributions of the rich alone, without his being called to spent a cent on his earnings." (Jefferson to General Kosciusko, April 13, 1811; 5 Jefferson's Works, 586.)
200 Jefferson to Maury, Nov. 21, 1807; 5 Jefferson's Works, 214.
201 Nov. 8, 1808; 1 Statesman's Manual, 216; 8 Jefferson's Works, 109.
202 Jefferson to Governor Jay, April 7, 1809; 5 Jefferson's Works, 440.

But he found consolation in the thought that, after all, his essential policy would prevail through the new manufactures which England's policy was forcing into existence. "Radically hostile to our navigation and commerce, and fearing its rivalry," he wrote, referring to Great Britain, "she will completely crush it, and force us to resort to agriculture, not aware that we shall resort to manufactures also, and render her conquests over our navigation and commerce useless, at least, if not injurious to herself in the end, and perhaps salutary to us, as removing out of our way the chief causes and provocations to war."[203] Yet Jefferson in the retirement of Monticello got scarcely a glimpse of the 'manifest destiny' of manufactures, and presently, writing again to De Nemours, he reiterated his theory of the independence of commerce, agriculture, and manufactures, called attention to the fact that their new manufactures were mostly of the household kind, of which they should probably make enough for home use, and predicted that the attempt to make fine goods would prove abortive.[204]

Madison, in his first annual message, found consolation for the 'arbitrary and impolitic edicts of Europe' in the extension of useful manufactures, especially of household fabrics.[205] A year later he congratulated Congress on the 'highly interesting extension of useful manufactures,' declaring that in a national view the change was more than a recompense for the injustice which gave the impulse required for its accomplishment. How far it might be expedient to guard the infancy of this improvement in the distribution of labor, by regulations of the commercial tariff, he cautiously added, was a subject which could not fail to suggest itself to their patriotic reflections.[206] A year later he was more explicit, urging upon Congress the importance of a "just and sound policy of securing to our manufactures the success they have attained and are still attaining, in some degree, under the impulse of causes not permanent."[207] The robbery and theft of Bonaparte, and the effect of English monopoly, he wrote Jefferson, "are breaking the charm attached to what is called free trade, foolishly by some, wicked-

203 Jefferson to Gen. Dearborn, July 16, 1810; 5 Jefferson's Works, 529.
204 April 15, 1811; 5 Jefferson's Works, 583.
205 1 Statesman's Manual, 280 (Nov. 29, 1809).
206 Madison's Second Annual Message, Dec. 5, 1810; 1 Statesman's Manual, 283.
207 1 Statesman's Manual, 289.

ly by others."[208] Two years later when war had actually begun he declared that unrestricted intercourse with England, among other things, "would strangle in the cradle the manufactures which promise so vigorous a growth."[209]

Even Gallatin, who long afterward boasted of having been the first free trader in America,[210] fell easily into the current. As finance minister at a time when war was imminent he began to consider plans for such an emergency, and in his annual reports, beginning with 1807, laid down the general principles on which a war policy should be based.[211] Without reference to manufacturers, he turned to the tariff as the best means of raising revenue, and affirmed that a considerable increase of duties was perfectly feasible. In December, 1809, Seybert of Pennsylvania secured the reprinting of Hamilton's Report on Manufactures and the adoption of a resolution by the House of Representatives calling upon Gallatin for a similar statement regarding the present condition of manufactures. Gallatin replied, April 19,1810, with a detailed account of the existing manufactures, and an elaborate discussion of their prospects and needs which fell little behind Hamilton in the sweep of it's proposed measures. The debate which Gallatin's report precipitated did not find the House wholly unprepared. The subject had been coming to the front ever since the beginning of the commercial troubles, and a decidedly friendly attitude toward further legislation in the way of direct encouragement to manufactures had been reached.

"As the state of the country developed a more considerate feeling toward manufactures, petitions began to pour in upon Congress making firmer and more positive demands. Typical among these earlier memorials was that of the artisans and manufacturers of Philadelphia, communicated to the House December 9, 1803. On the whole, it was a rather frank confession of present weakness, with a vigorous assertion, along Hamiltonian lines, of the manufacturing resources and capabilities of the country. The fact that

---

208 May 25, 1810, 2 Madison's Works, 478.
209 Madison to the House of Representatives of South Carolina, July 8, 1812; 2 Madison's Works, 525.
210 See letter to J.R. Ingersoll, March 25, 1846; 2 Gallatin's Writings, 628.
211 See H.C. Adams' Public Debts, 112 et seq.

manufactures were already protected was scouted, as became so much the fashion later, and considering the small account which was then taken of a foreign market for American manufactures, a good deal was made of the prohibitions of European nations. "It is with deep concern," the memorial said, "that your memorialists have to represent that during the long period from the peace which terminated our Revolutionary war to the present time, they have seen the wealth of the nation sent to foreign countries to purchase a thousand articles which can be as well manufactured at home, and of which nature has abundantly supplied us with the raw materials." There were few articles of first necessity which could not be produced at home on equal terms if not prevented by certain reasons, which the memorial proceeded to give. *First*, foreign fashions stood in the way, especially with regard to clothing. It was impossible to keep pace with changes introduced by new patterns from foreign nations. *Second*, American markets were constantly over-stocked with foreign goods. The greater part of the manufactures of which iron, silk, wool, cotton, or flax, were the raw materials, ought to be established in the interior of the country, where provisions, house-rent, and fuel were cheap; but if the foreign manufacturer was permitted to keep merchants supplied with these goods on long credit, it would be impossible for citizens with small capital to persuade the storekeeper to purchase his goods for ready money. The *third* reason was the unjust competition with foreign manufacturers—unjust because the finished articles of our infant manufactures produced from raw materials found in the United States were generally either prohibited in foreign countries or more highly tariffed than similar goods coming into the United States. An infant manufacture must have some protection to enable it to contend with an old establishment; yet in the United States the reverse had taken place. *Fourth*, the expense necessarily attending the commencement of complicated manufactures. *Fifth*, injudicious duties on raw materials. "It is a position," the memorial went on confidently, "that will not be denied by the greatest enemies to domestic manufacturing, that as soon as any particular branch shall be established, foreign goods of the same kind ought to be prohibited or discouraged; and this is certainly the case with every manufactory of leather and fur; and yet your memorialists would be glad to know by what mode of reasoning it can be made to appear that the hatter and shoemaker, who have spent their youth in acquiring those arts, should every five or six years, be ruined by an excessive importation of foreign hats or shoes which may perhaps be the remaining estate of some European bankrupt?"

The memorial denied that the United States were too young to commence the manufacture of clothing, or that the development of the West would be retarded. As to the supposed vice of manufacturing towns, the facts of European manufactories denied it. The idea that if a manufacture did not take root of itself it was not fit for our climate or state of society, was true only of simple manufactures; where a combination of skill and capital was required it could only be secured by the fostering care of government. If there were not hands enough in America, it only proved the necessity of protective tariffs, which alone could give encouragement to men of genius to pursue complex and difficult manufactures.

Protection would benefit agriculture because the progress of agriculture was always in proportion to population, and agriculture alone would never concentrate population. Revenue likewise would be increased owing to the increase of population and increase of demand for luxuries; for nothing could be more appropriate than to tax foreign fashions and foreign luxuries.[212]

These various memorials and petitions received a favorable hearing from the committee on Commerce and Manufactures,[213] which reported January 25, 1804, expounding at some length the demands of the manufacturers of corks, coaches, harnesses, paper, gunpowder, hats, printing types, brushes, stoneware, hemp and sailduck, the calico printers and dyers, cordwainers, and shoemakers. Various specific measures were recommended tending to the release of raw materials from duty and to higher rates on certain competing articles.[214] Nothing came of this at the time, but the

---

212 Annals of 8th Congress, 2nd Session, (Appendix,) pp. 1467-1477.

213 Perhaps due to the Peace of Amiens, 1803, which threatened the supremacy of American shipping.

214 Annals of 8th Congress, 1st Session, 946-949. After referring to the "excellent and extensive" manufactures which the fostering part of the government had caused to "rise up and thrive in almost every part of the country," the Committee added: "And if we do not excel in the manufacture of the finer articles of cotton, silk, wool, and the metals, we may felicitate ourselves that, by reason of the ease

manufacturers lost no courage, and presently the fruits of non-intercourse and embargo dropped into their hands. Even the repeal of the salt tax was violently opposed by Quincy, nominally, at least, on the ground that the salt manufacturers of Barnstable and Cape Cod would be ruined.[215]

This upward movement toward manufacturing did not, of course, escape attention, and the very arguments used in support of protection were turned against it. Owing to the liberal price of wages, joined with the plenty and cheapness of land, it was declared to be impossible for manufactures to flourish in the United States in their present situation, although it was admitted that some of the Eastern and Middle States would eventually became manufacturing States, when peace returned in Europe and things name down to their natural standard.[216] In the debate on the non-importation act, Eppes of Virginia expressed the Southern sentiment that the total prohibition of British manufactures would be extremely injurious. It would put down at once the occupation and employment of the merchant of small capital, for commerce, particularly at the south, was carried on principally on credit furnished by Great Britain.[217] Macon of North Carolina reinforced Marsters' statement, and affirmed that Connecticut and Massachusetts had both tried the experiment of manufactures without success.[218] Bidwell of Massachusetts, quasi-republican leader, answered Quincy's argument for the repeal of the salt tax by saying that the interests of a few manufacturers ought not to be put in competition with the general interests of the country, and Holland

of gaining a subsistence and the high price of wages, our fellow citizens, born to happier destinies, are not doomed to the wretchedness of a strict discipline in such manufactories."

215 H. R. Jan. 12-13, 1807; Annals of 9th Congress, 2nd Session, pp. 290, 301. Jefferson recommended in his annual message, December, 1806, that the salt tax be abolished on the ground that "salt was a necessary of life." "Now I ask," said Quincy, in unanswerable protectionist logic, "which is the readiest means to 'the free use' of any article? To make it ourselves, or to be dependent for it on others? The strongest argument in the world, in favor of patronizing this manufacture, is the very one used by the President, in effect, for its destruction." 15., p. 302.

216 Marsters of New York in H. R. March 6, 1806; Annals of 9th Congress, 1st Session, p. 581.

217 H. R. March 10, 1806.

218 H.R. March, 10, 1806; Annals of 9th Congress, 1st Session, p. 692.

of North Carolina declared that if the salt manufacture was destroyed those only would be to blame who had been such forward speculators in the matter.[219]

But the tide was going the other way; and when Marsters indicted the administration by declaring that the embargo virtually inhibited all intercourse with foreign nations and that it would tear up by the roots and annihilate the commerce of the country, many silently acquiesced who totally dissented from his picture of resulting ruin and distress and wild state of nature to which the United States would return.[220] Bibb of Georgia, at this same session, introduced a resolution pledging the members of the House to appear at the next session clothed in the manufactures of their own country,[221] and though not taken seriously, it voiced a widely growing sentiment. "I rejoice," affirmed Giles, quasi-republican leader and afterwards a bitter opponent of the tariff, "to see our infant manufactures growing into importance, and that the most successful experiment has attended every attempt at improvement."[222]

To the manufactures which sprang up and flourished under the stimulus of embargo and non-intercourse, the lull in the storm accompanying the Erskine negotiations of 1809 was full of danger. In the joy which everywhere hailed the renewal of intercourse with Great Britain commerce hurried its ships and merchandise out of port without waiting for the day formally set by the President's proclamation; and in Congress all attempts to increase protective

---

219 H.R. Jan. 13, 1807; Annals of 9th Congress, 2nd Session, p. 307.

220 H.R. April 13, 1808; Annals of 10th Congress, 1st Session, p. 2169. Nelson of Maryland would never vote for the repeal or suspension of the non-importation law. He hoped to see the time when it should become a permanent regulation; he would not yield to any of the powers of Europe, and wished to be independent of them. There were many things now imported from Europe which could as well be made in this country (H.R. April 25, 1808.)

While Virginia was suffering most severely from the operations of the embargo, Giles declared that he was a farmer and that the embargo was a good thing for the farmer—it lessened his dependence on foreign nations.

221 H.R. April 25, 1808. Henry Clay offered a similar resolution in the Kentucky legislature this same year (1 Schurz's Clay, 51.)

222 Senate, Nov. 24, 1808; Annals of 10th Congress, 2nd Session, p. 102.

duties were defeated.[223] But manufacturers were not slow to move
along the strategic lines of their position. June 7, three days before
the Erskine arrangement was to go into effect, certain manufacturers of Kentucky set forth, in a petition to Congress, that they
had engaged in the manufacture of linen since the passage of the
embargo and non-importation acts, that they had put the greater part of their capital into machinery and buildings, and that,
while rejoicing in the returning sense of justice in Europe, which
afforded hope that the United States might escape the calamities
of war, they must be permitted to state that this cause of national
enjoyment would in all human probability, be greatly oppressive
to them. Their establishments had grown out of the difficulties
with foreign nations. The non-importation act, which was passed,
as they had always understood, as much to change the direction
of some of the national capital from commerce to manufacturing
pursuits as with the view to bring a great foreign power to a sense
of justice, by prohibiting the introduction of coarse linen and the
like into the United States, had given being to their manufactories. Such, however, was the superiority of European capital and
arts, such the cheapness of labor in Great Britain and Ireland,[224]
such the aid there given to manufactures by bounties from the
government, such the obstacles which an American manufacturer
had to combat and overcome, and such the lessons furnished by
experience, that the petitioners forbode the annihilation of their
respective establishments unless some aid was afforded them at
once by the interposition of Congress. Recalling the proceedings
of every Congress since the first, every act, every declaration had
shown it to be the wish of Congress to make the United States independent of the world as to articles of first necessity, as she was in
her political rights as a nation. For this purpose Congress had laid
duties upon all raw or manufactured articles to an extent sufficient
to prohibit their importation, whenever it was ascertained that the
country could produce a sufficiency for home consumption. Bounties even had been granted as in the case of fisheries, and Jeffer-

---

223 Henry Adams' History of the United States, 73, 81.

224 Perhaps the first instance of the manufacturers themselves avowed cheap
foreign labor as a reason for protection. It shows extreme confidence and some
miscalculation of the force of public opinion on their behalf, since for twenty years
yet the argument was to be effectively used on the other side.

son's Report of 1793 was cited in favor of this.

The present was the time to encourage manufactures effectually; If those which were already erected were suffered to go to waste, if those recently established died with the law which gave them being, an age would pass away before other citizens would embark in the same business. It was not an unimportant consideration that the encouragement of domestic manufactures would have a tendency to transplant the arts and capital of Europe to the United States; and returning to the particular argument, it was declared that Kentucky, rich in soil, but at a distance from the seas, was capable of producing hemp for the whole United States, and if sufficiently encouraged could induce farmers to cultivate it, so as to furnish a never-failing resource in peace or war. Kentucky, it was remarked, was subject to large drains annually for United States lands, owing to her proximity to Ohio and Indiana, and large sums were annually taken off for foreign productions; but protected as she was, by the Union, she was satisfied. Yet—and the anti-climax revealed the local bias which a fine argument had covered up—when fishermen East were not only encouraged by protective duties, but by bounties, when, comparatively speaking, no public moneys were expended in the State, Kentucky would be better pleased to be indemnified for these disadvantages by some encouragement of her industry.[225]

The repudiation of the Erskine arrangement by the English government and the consequent partial repairment of the Chinese wall of embargo, fortunately for the manufacturers, obviated the necessity of bringing their demands to an immediate trial before Congress. They did not, however, intend to lose any advantage already gained.[226] As has already been noted, Seybert of Pennsylvania secured the reprinting of Hamilton's Report on Manufactures, and a report covering similar ground from Gallatin. The chief sig-

225 Annals of 11th Congress, 1st and 2nd Sessions (Appendix), pp. 2170-2173.
226 At the opening of Congress in Dec. 1809, Sawyer of North Carolina introduced a resolution to create a separate Committee on Manufactures, alleging that one Committee could not properly attend to two such subjects as commerce and manufactures, and asserting that the subject of manufactures ought to engage the undivided energies of the best talents of the House. Only twenty-four members voted for the resolution, and the separate Committee was not created until 1820. (H. R. Dec. 4 and 12, 1809).

nificance of Gallatin's report lay in the great progress that he was able to show had been made within a few years. The total annual product of American manufactures had reached a hundred and twenty million, dollars, of which forty millions were credited to household manufactures, twenty millions to leather, twenty millions to wood, twelve to fifteen millions to iron, and ten millions each to hats and spirits. Nearly three times as many boots and shoes were exported as imported, ten times as many candles, and five times as much soap. From 1791 to 1808 the number of cotton mills in the country had increased from 1 to 15, working 8000 spindles. In the next two years the number of mills rose to 87, and by the beginning of 1811 Gallatin estimated that 80,000 spindles would be in operation. The increase in carding and spinning had been four-fold during the preceding two years. The principal obstacle to the extension of the manufacture was the want of wool, which was still deficient in quality and quantity; but these defects were daily and rapidly lessened by the introduction of merino and other superior breeds of sheep. Two-thirds of the clothing used in the United States outside of the cities was of household manufacture. Paper mills were in every part of the Union, and a great part of the consumption was of home manufacture.

The most prominent causes which impeded the introduction and retarded the progress of manufactures, Gallatin found to be the abundance of land compared with population, the high price of labor, and the want of sufficient capital. The superior attractions of agricultural pursuits, the great extension of American commerce during the late American wars, and the continuance of habits after the causes which produced them had ceased to exist, might also be enumerated. Several of these obstacles had, however, been removed or lessened. The cheapness of provisions had always to a certain extent counter-balanced the high price of manual labor; and this now, in many important branches, was nearly superseded by the introduction of machinery. A great American capital had been acquired during the last twenty years; and the injurious violations of neutral commerce, by forcing industry and capital into other channels, had broken inveterate habits and given a general impulse, to which must be ascribed the great increase of manufactures during the two last years. No cause, perhaps, had more promoted in every respect the general prosperity of the United States, than the absence of those systems of internal restrictions and monopoly which continued to disfigure the state of society in other countries. "It is believed that, even at this time, the only powerful obstacle against which American manufactures have to struggle, arises from the vastly superior capital of the first manufacturing nation of Europe, which enables her merchants to give very long credits, to sell on small profits, and to make occasional sacrifices."[227]

The information he had obtained, Gallatin explained, was not sufficient to warrant his submitting, in conformity to the request of the House, the plan best calculated to promote American manufactures. The most obvious means, he said, were bounties, increased duties on imports, and loans by government. Occasional premiums might be beneficial, but prohibitive duties were liable to the treble objection of destroying competition, taxing the consumer, and diverting capital and industry into channels generally less profitable to the nation than those which would naturally have been pursued by individual interest left to itself. A moderate Increase would be less dangerous, and if adopted, should be continued during a certain period; for the repeal of a duty once laid materially injured those who had relied on its permanency, as had been exemplified in the salt manufacture. Since, however, the comparative want of capital was the principal obstacle to the introduction and advancement of manufactures in America, it seemed that the most efficient and most obvious remedy would consist in supplying that capital. "The United States might create a circulating stock bearing a low rate of interest, and lend it at par to manufacturers, on principles somewhat similar to that formerly adopted by New York and Pennsylvania in their loan offices. It is believed that a plan might be devised by which five millions a year, but not to exceed twenty millions, might be thus lent, without any material

---

227 Cf. statement of Prof. R.E. Thompson in the Penn Monthly, Sept. 1874 (p. 653): "The day will come, if we have the wisdom to persist, when we will be as independent of tariffs to protect the great staples of manufacture, as the tides are of Parliamentary or Congressional legislation. ... But until the capital of our country has grown to such power and can afford to make such sacrifices as that of England, it will not be either wise or fair to expose it to the unfair competition, the wholesale underselling, which are among the best known weapons of industrial warfare practiced in modern Christendom."

risk of ultimate loss and without taxing or injuring any other part
of the community."

The debate far outran the report, as indeed it did not wait for
it. A bill was introduced advancing duties but the whole question became involved in the discussions over non-intercourse and
embargo, and, as far as protection was concerned, finally centered
in an amendment to Macon's Bill Number Two increasing duties
fifty percent. The advance line of argument for the manufacturers
was thrown out by Seybert, who brought a considerable battery of
flowery rhetoric to support his position. The tack taken was quite
the opposite of that followed by the Kentucky memorialists of the
previous year. Instead of finding in every act of Congress since the
first an evident attempt to encourage manufactures, he declared
that while Congress had lavished many millions annually upon a
rotten and inefficient naval establishment, while it had established
discriminating duties in favor of merchants, which amounted to
a bounty for their encouragement, and had incurred an enormous
annual expense to keep up its diplomatic intercourse with foreign
nations; while it was paying tribute to barbarians in support of
foreign commerce, and for this same commerce, was risking the
peace, honor, and independence of the nation, it had at the same
time, refused a justifiable aid to another class equally deserving its
notice and fostering care. He was no enemy to commerce, but he
regarded it as far less necessary to national independence than a
well-regulated manufacturing system. The United States should
manufacture to secure its independence, whereas abroad they
manufactured because they were dependents. At the present time,
the spirit and tendency of the nation was in favor of manufactures.
This might not always be the case. They ought to take advantage of
the present temper and disposition of the people and adopt such
branches as would promote the agriculture of the country. He did
not wish the government to create manufactories—only to protect
such as seemed requisite from the peculiarity of the times, and
such as were consistent with the nature of the climate, soil, habits,
and necessities of the people. They should not look to the supplying a foreign market for centuries to come. Still, if they could
count upon a constant and free commerce, and demand for their
agricultural productions in Europe, they might perhaps adopt less

zeal in the promotion of manufactures.

Done with theoretical concessions, Seybert was very positive as to the practical course to be taken. In the main he enforced Hamilton's general argument, with some modifications adapted to the turn of debate. Manufactures need not prejudice agriculture because almost everywhere in the United States there was a sufficient number of persons too young or too old for laborious employments who might without prejudice to agriculture or commerce, be well employed in manufactories.

Instead of regarding the high price of labor as an argument for protection, he declared that he should pay no attention to the clamor which had been raised. "Experience has taught me," he said, "that it is unfounded, and that very little difference exists here as to the price paid for labor, and that of the same kind in England. ... Intelligent workmen who have come from Great Britain assert that from four to six shillings sterling can be earned per day abroad, when for work done of the same kind they at most obtain one dollar in this country." Besides, those situations where living is cheap were always selected for manufactories. Wheat was fifty cents a bushel in Kentucky, as against two dollars in England, beef two dollars and a half per cwt. in Kentucky, and a shilling a pound in England. Indeed, the United States could manufacture so cheap as to warrant a profit on exportation to Europe, even should all the processes be effected by manual labor.

It might very well be asked if labor stood on such equality with the labor of Europe, and in all other respects Americans had such decided advantages, so that manufactures could even be exported to Europe at a profit, why protection was needed. Seybert forestalled such an objection by a statement still in vogue eighty years afterward: "Unless protected for a time, it is not to be supposed that our manufactures can compete with the enormous capital which foreigners can command, especially when connected with their skill and experience. Foreigners do all they can to destroy our infant establishments. They conspire and sell their articles for a loss for a time in our markets—when they have obtained their object by putting a stop to our efforts, they raise their prices and furnish us with articles of an inferior quality. They do not stop here, but resort to a system of deception, which could hardly be imagined. As soon as our establishments furnished our markets with a supply of excellent fabrics, the agents of foreign manufactures procured patterns of such as were most esteemed. These they with every possible haste dispatched to Europe, in order to have imitations as to appearance, but very inferior in quality—afterward sold as American fabrics at reduced prices."[228]

He regretted the difference of opinion between different sections of the Union. The South was opposed to additional duties because it considered their operation partial and oppressive. It did not possess the capital and requisite population to establish manufactures, and in this respect the Northern States had the advantage. Seybert held that the statement was not conclusive. Duties were laid in the North as well as in the South, and those who preferred foreign articles must in common pay duty upon them. But suppose the Northern manufacturer should sell to the South; in consequence of the increasing number of establishments the home articles would, in a short time, be as cheap, if not cheaper, than they could now be imported. The inconvenience to the planter would be temporary, while he would always, from the nature of things, possess the advantage of supplying the North with raw materials. We should not too closely view our immediate local interests when we were to legislate on great national questions. He favored the system because those who were most competent to judge declared that protection from the government was absolutely necessary in many instances. It was the mode which all foreign nations had adopted. He was perfectly willing that the protecting measures should continue only for a reasonable time, so that there might be some stability in the system to enable it to compete perfectly against foreigners. Our manufacturing establishments must be regarded as so many infants who needed a mother's care to bring them to maturity; then they would be the most certain guarantees of our liberty.[229]

---

228 The guileless Yankee is here made to appear in a very helpless condition. Cf. *infra*, p. 187, note where at least he assumes a more natural role.
229 H.R. April 18, 1810; Annals of 10th Congress, pp. 1891-1900.
The peroration gave a glowing picture of the natural resources of the country and its adaptability to a 'judicious manufacturing system,' closing with a reminder that he did not wish to convert the people into a nation of manufacturers; he merely

Lyon of Kentucky was even more pronounced as to the simplicity of tariff laws. He knew that whatever extra price was paid for manufactures would be a sacrifice for the nation's good. This sacrifice would be a mere trifle, of but short duration. The difficulties of competition with regard to many articles bad been already overcome, and the American manufacturer needed no extra duties to protect him. "When we have continued our duties long enough to enable our manufacturer to withstand the strong current against him, occasioned by the credit given by foreign capitalists, if the competition for sale among the American manufacturers does not bring the articles to a proper level with regard to price, we can lower or take off duties." The freight, insurance, and duty on raw materials, profits of exporter and importer of raw material, carriage of raw material to the place of manufacture, export duties, and the like, were all in the nature of a bounty to the American manufacturer, "which cannot fail after he is fairly set on his legs to be ample encouragement." Contrary to Seybert, he saw no reason why slaves could not manufacture, and declared that there was "nothing but pride, a perverse bias, prejudice, apathy, and indolence, to prevent the great good which the manufacturing system, on a moderate scale, would do in this nation, and more particularly the southern and western part of it."[230]

The counter argument was largely defensive, though not lacking in spirit. Key of Maryland declared that he was a friend to manufactures and would have them progress *pari passu* with agriculture and commerce; but he would never foster one in a hotbed at the expense of the other. The reason why they could send raw materials abroad to be manufactured was because they had land to cultivate, and agriculture was more congenial to the habits of the

asked for the introduction of a system that would confirm their independence, make them respected abroad, promote agriculture, bring the genius of the people into combination, reveal the immense resources of the country, and make every individual of the nation happy, respected, and independent.

230 H.R. April 18, 1810; Annals of 13th Congress, 1st and 2nd Sessions, pp. 1900-1902.

Richard M. Johnson of Kentucky supported the proposed regulations because they would lessen importation from Great Britain and France, beget habits of economy, and destroy those ancient ties of commerce which threatened to enslave them (H.R. April, 18, 1810; Annals of 11th Congress, 1st and 2nd Session, pp. 1909-1912). Cf. speech of Clay in Senate, April 6, (5 Clay's Works, 7).

American people than manufactures.[231]

If the purpose of the bill was revenue, rather than saddle his constituents with a tax to encourage manufactures, Macon of North Carolina would vote for a direct tax. "What does this system go to? To this: that you will go on by tax on tax until you manufacture within the limits of the United States everything that can there be raised for the purpose of manufacture. This may be a good thing to the part of the country which will be the manufacturing part. They may laugh and sing; but to the part that will never manufacture it will be death. The latter may wring their hands and cry, but in vain; for once but get the manufacturing mania fixed on the nation, and we shall be saddled with it as long as the nation exists."[232]

Admitting that manufactures were really necessary, the question, asserted Kennedy, also of North Carolina, was whether they should have them by taxing other classes of society, or on the other side of the Atlantic without taxation. He had always thought that regulations of a government which diverted labor from its usual and ordinary channel were an injury to individuals and a manifest loss to the nation; the people in all countries knew their own interest best, and when left unshackled by their government would pursue that kind of business which yielded them most clear profit. The United States were agricultural rather than manufacturing because of their extensive tracts of waste land. Less capital was required in agriculture and the profits were greater, even when manufactures had the advantage of transportation, freight, and from 15 percent to 20 percent duty—and this was owing altogether to the high price of labor in the United States. If this were not true, and the high price of labor presented no impediment to competition with European manufactures, then it followed of course that American manufactures needed no encouragement from the government.

He firmly believed, he said, that they would never be able to manufacture as cheaply as Europe until they were almost as thickly settled and consequently as nearly miserable as Europe was. Some thought the new policy would prevent us from getting into contact

---

231 H.R. April 18, 1810; Annals of 11th Congress, 1st and 2nd Sessions, p. 1905.
232 H.R. April 10, 1810; Annals of 11th Congress, 1st and 2nd Sessions, p. 1845.

with the belligerent powers of Europe; but he would ask what was
to be done with our surplus produce? Others thought we should
be enabled to supply ourselves with certain articles essential in
time of war; but why raise duties generally? "But, it is said, that
when, by encouragement, the manufactories get into operation,
they will be able to make out without this aid from the government, and that the duties may be taken off. Sir, I have no faith in
this doctrine. It may serve to amuse and deceive, but never will be
realized. Once raise the duties and common experience will teach
you that it is almost impossible to remove them"[233]

As to results, however, everything waited the uncertain issue of
foreign difficulties. Meanwhile the protectionist position was more
boldly and more tensely thrust forward as the struggle seemed
to turn upon the question whether commerce or manufactures
should be favored by the government. A petition from Lexington,
Kentucky, communicated to the Senate January 22, 1811, raised
the issue between commerce and manufactures and appealed for a
share of public encouragement. From the beginning, the petition
declared, Congress had shown a predilection for commerce, while
little had been done for the internal industry of the country. The
revenue system had indeed afforded some partial protection; but
the system appeared to have been calculated only for the purposes of revenue, and no act had been adopted with the view of
encouraging domestic manufactures. On the contrary, commerce
had met with its exclusive attention and support.[234] So far from
condemning the policy toward commerce the petitioners felt upon
such subjects as Americans should, and only complained because
the protection and encouragement of industry had not been made
universal and extended to every pursuit known to the country.

The unnatural extension of commerce brought about by the
<u>wars since the</u> French Revolution, could not be depended on, and

233 H.R. April 10, 1810; Annals of 11ᵗʰ Congress, 1ˢᵗ and 2ⁿᵈ Sessions, pp. 1847-
55. Cf. Remarks of Telfair of Georgia, H.R. April 3, 1816; *infra,* p. 175.
234 "To prove this, let us refer to the immense sums that have been expended in
the fortifications of the seaports; to the establishment of a navy; to the expenditures
occasioned by our intercourse with foreign nations; to the duties which have been
laid on foreign tonnage; to the bounties which protect the fisheries; to the credits
given to merchants at our custom-houses; and in fine, to the many sacrifices which
have been made to commerce." *Ib.*

steps should be taken to direct the capital to home industry and so provide a market when the foreign market was gone. No pursuit, agriculture excepted, was so productive as manufactures. The manufacturer worked up our raw material and consumed our provisions; what he earned was kept at home and almost immediately circulated again. The merchant was by no means so useful; part of his gains were sent abroad, and part paid to the foreigner.

Only Congress, it was urged, could effectually encourage manufactures. "The American manufacturer is at present poor; he has buildings to erect, workmen to teach, and powerful prejudices to overcome; his limited capital often makes it necessary for him to force markets, while his opponent can wait for or command one at pleasure. Indeed, it is to be feared that the foreigner will purposely seek opportunities to depress markets, in order to remove the American out of his way. Such have often been the effects of jealousy of trade." Imposts laid for the encouragement of manufactures were but taking from one pocket what was abundantly repaid to the other. Whatever gave life to the domestic industry of the country benefited every man in it. "When the domestic manufacturer shall have acquired experience, and his laborers are completely instructed in their business; and when by industry and success, he shall have acquired capital sufficient to enable him to extend his business, the natural effect will be to reduce his prices to a very moderate profit; and lower often than what the same article could be afforded for from abroad." Whether this protection should be afforded by bounties, or by prohibitive or protective duties, or in whole or in part by loans, as recommended by Gallatin, the petitioners did not presume to point out. But as capital, was much wanted they would suggest that a combination of these might be attended with salutary results.[235]

The question of increased duties was promptly brought forward on the assembling of Congress in November, 1811. But weightier measures had first to be attended to. The paralysis which the Jefferson policy of peace at any price had laid upon the country was at last overcome, and under the leadership of younger men the country regained its moral tone. War was finally declared. June 18,

235 Petition of Lewis Sanders and one hundred and twelve others, citizens of Lexington, Kentucky; Annals of 11th Congress, 3d Session (Appendix) pp. 1275-1281.

1812. This act had already been preceded by an embargo which showed war to be inevitable, and a bill to double duties had kept pace with other preparations. This last measure was put on its final passage, in the House June 22, in the Senate June 29, and received the President's signature July 1.

All other causes leading to the exaltation of the protective system were small compared to the extraordinary growth of manufactures during the war. Non-intercourse was practically complete, and under the stimulus of a ready home market and advanced prices, with the government itself a large purchaser, capital turned itself into manufacturing plants with astonishing rapidity. The papers teemed with notices of new manufactories.[236] Statistics are not available and estimates vary greatly, but the growth was unprecedented. In 1810, according to Niles, there was not a single cotton spindle in operation in Baltimore; three years later there were 9,000.[237] More than thirty charters were granted to manufacturing companies in 1813, in New York State alone, and as many more in Massachusetts the following year.[238] In 1815 there were a hundred and forty cotton manufactories in the vicinity of Providence, R.I., operating 130,000 spindles.[239] Wilmington, Del., had thirty cotton manufactories. Pittsburg, Steubenville, Cincinnati, Lexington, Ky., Rochester, and many other places either sprang into existence during this period or received an extraordinary impulse forward.[240] The number of cotton spindles in operation in the United States, which had increased from 3,000 in 1798 to only 20,000 in 1808, was now estimated at 500,000, employing $40,000,000 capital, 100,000 workmen, and paying $15,000,000 wages yearly.[241] The same estimate placed the capital employed in the woolen manufacture at $12,000,000, with 50,000 workmen, and an annual product

236 See 5 Niles, 380.
237 5 Niles, 207. A different version is given in 2 Bishop, 198, where it is said that there were 9000 spindles in operation in Baltimore in 1810.
238 2 Bishop, 198, 207.
239 Circular letter of the Cotton Manufacturers of Providence, dated Oct. 20, 1815; 9 Niles, 190. But see a lower estimate quoted in Taussig, p. 28.
240 See 6 Niles, 207-210; 8 Niles, 141, 233, 249, 452; 9 Niles, 35; also 2 Bishop.
241 Report of Committee on Commerce and Manufactures, Feb. 13, 1816; Annals of 14th Congress, 1st Session, pp. 960-967. But see a much lower estimate quoted in Taussig, p. 28; there is also a lower contemporary estimate of capital and workmen employed, in 8 Niles, 233.

of $19,000,000.[242] The total value of domestic manufactures, estimated in 1810 by Gallatin at $120,000,000, was placed by Tench Coxe, in 1813, at $200,000,000, and grew rapidly larger.[243]

Much of this enormous expansion was due to the advance in prices, which also accounts for a large part of the additional value of manufactured products. Thus wool rose in price from seventy-five cents to four dollars per pound, and cloth from eight to fourteen and even eighteen dollars per yard; Hyson tea advanced fifty percent, white Havana sugar half as much, while salt rose from fifty-five cents to three dollars per bushel. Wages in like manner increased from twenty to fifty percent.[244]

Prejudice against domestic fabrics seemed about to disappear. Governors in their annual messages began to notice these new manufacturing establishments and to speak of them in congratulatory terms.[245] The war itself took a decidedly industrial turn. In spite of the waste and expense, and almost unbroken disaster, prosperity was general and the land resounded with the hum of industry and improvement. Commerce alone was sullen and in ruins; but commerce by an opposition as unpatriotic as it was ill-timed was sealing its own fate. Almost unconsciously the idea grew that the struggle was, after all, not so much for "free trade and sailor's rights" as for industrial independence. New England protesting against the war was told that her people must be weaned from their commercial intercourse with England before they could possess any generous American feeling. Complaining of the exorbitant prices charged for domestic manufactures, they were reminded that if Massachusetts, under foreign influence, had not committed the gross political blunder of discountenancing manufactures thousands of her artisans and mechanics might have been retained and rendered unnecessary hundreds of the establishments then springing up as by magic in the Middle and Western States.[246] In the peace negotiations all those commercial and

242 See 2 Bishop, 214, 225.
243 See 2 Bishop, 191.
244 See 2 Bishop, 178, 179. Coton alone fell owing to the loss of the foreign market.
245 See Niles. The South, however, was silent.
246 Niles, 328; 5 *ib*. 3. "We must look not to the tape-sellers of our seaports, but to the independent farmers and manufacturers for republican virtue. It is they who

maritime rights for which embargo and war had been risked were silently abandoned; and when the British sloop Favorite sailed into New York Harbor late one Saturday night in April, 1815, bearing news of Jackson's victory at New Orleans and of the signing of the Treaty of Peace,[247] the bells which pealed out the twice glad tidings proclaimed, not indeed the triumph of " free trade and sailor's rights," but the supremacy of Nationalism and the dawn of a new industrial era.

---

feel they have a country." (9 Niles, 174).
247 See 6 Hildreth, 565.

CHAPTER IV

THE AMERICAN SYSTEM

The return of peace at the beginning of 1815 brought the manufacturers face to face with a serious danger. War had been their harvest time. Favored by double duties and abnormal conditions their industry had attained a marvelous though not always safe development. To many of these new enterprises, solely the result of unnatural stimulus, not yet deeply rooted or wisely administered, the renewal of old relations with Europe meant instant destruction. By limitation, the double duties were to expire one year after the conclusion of peace, and unless Congress intervened promptly and effectually their individual ruin was certain.

Apparently there was little to fear. Unable as they were to bear competition in the open market, the struggle for government intervention was no longer to be waged by a few weak industries. The manufacturing interest had become important and powerful, alive to its needs, and ready to take its part in legislation rather than to humbly petition an indifferent legislature. More than all else, the country had taken a new attitude toward manufactures. The only actively hostile section—New England—was thoroughly discredited by its disloyal attitude during the war. The indifference and hostility of the South was disarmed. Holding the scales more evenly than the impetuous manufacturing centers of the North, resisting what it deemed unnecessary demands, the South yet stood out generously in the enthusiasm of the new Nationalism, in the persons of Lowndes, Cheves, Calhoun, Crawford, and others, prepared to place upon a firm basis the manufactures which war had called into being. Wholly aside from the ordinary question of protection the argument for these was irresistible. They were the one material and tangible result of the war, and to suffer them to perish through British competition was to surrender all that had been gained. From suffering and mortification, as Dallas put it, had sprung the means of future safety and independence, in those manufactures which private citizens, under favorable auspices, had constituted the property of the nation.

This new manufacturing interest began early to fortify itself against the return of peace. As new industries sprang up, petitions were promptly laid before Congress praying for new duties, for the permanence of the war duties, and for certain prohibitions. When, after the war began, merchants asked for a remission of the bonds given on recent importations of British goods, they were sharply told that at a time when the people were fighting for commerce and free trade, no class of citizens could be licensed to carry on a trade with the enemy. The time had come for acting with energy. Non-importation, embargo, and non-intercourse had been too weak because the mercantile class were strong.[248]

An attempt was made in 1814 to secure a new tariff "conformably to the existing situation of the general and local interests of the United States," and the partial suspension of non-intercourse in the interest of revenue, as well as the repeal of the embargo, were resisted as hostile to the manufacturing interest.[249]

In laying before Congress the treaty of peace, February, 1815, Madison called attention to the 'unparalleled maturity' attained by manufactures, and 'anxiously recommended this source of national independence and wealth to the prompt and constant guardianship of Congress.'[250] This recommendation was repeated in his annual message in December of the same year, though in more guarded phrases. In adjusting the duties on imports to the object of revenue, the influence of the tariff on manufactures would, he said, necessarily present itself for consideration. However wise the theory which would leave to the sagacity and interest of individuals the application of their industry and resources, Madison went on in his own stereotyped phrases, there were in this, as in other cases, exceptions to the general rule. And further than these phrases he did not get.[251]

But it was not to Madison that Congress or the country looked for direction. The acquiescence of the President was enough. To

---

248 Speech of R.M. Johnson, H.R. Dec, 3, 1812; Annals of 12th Congress, 2nd Session, p. 224.
249 See Annals of Congress, 2nd Session, pp. 1062-1065, 1091; *ib.* 13th Congress, p. 1988 (H.R. April, 7, 1814).
250 1 Statesman's Manual, 326.
251 1 Statesman's Manual, 331.

Dallas, Secretary of the Treasury, the manufacturers had already turned. Six days after the treaty of peace was ratified, the House, February 23, 1815, called upon Dallas to report a general tariff bill at the next session of Congress. In making up his reply the Secretary was not left in doubt as to the fears and wishes of the manufacturers. Two days after the adoption of the resolution just referred to, Seybert presented a petition from Philadelphia which, while setting forth the joy and exultation with which the petitioners were filled, for the inestimable blessing of honorable peace, expressed also their anxiety and dread for the fate of the infant manufactures 'whose existence and prosperity were of vital import to the whole community.' Yet they looked forward with hope to the permanent establishment of such manufactures as should render the United States independent of foreign nations for the necessaries and comforts of life.[252] This petition was an earnest of many more and of addresses and newspaper appeals, setting forth with more or less definiteness the measures which it behooved Congress to adopt. A circular letter from the cotton manufacturers of Providence, R.I., dated October 20, 1815, declared that their mills had been erected at great expense, on account of the interruption of commerce and in reliance on the favorable disposition of the government toward domestic manufactures. Already the pressure had been so great as to force many to contract their business and some to suspend entirely. The present free and unrestricted admission of cotton fabrics of foreign production not only extinguished the hope of a reasonable profit in the future, but threatened the speedy destruction of the establishments already erected. It was suggested that the cheap cottons of India be prohibited and the duties on those of coarse texture from other parts of the world increased. As to the favorite maxim of some that commerce should be free and unrestricted, it might be a good general rule, but it was far safer to follow in the beaten track of successful experience. All manufacturing nations protected their citizens, and especially in England had this policy been crowned with unexampled success.[253]

In his annual report in December, 1815, Dallas had proposed the extension of the double duties until June 30, 1816, in order to

252 Annals of 13th Congress, vol. iii, p. 1195.
253 9 Niles, 190. For further tariff movements see Niles Register *passim*, 2 Bishop, and Appendices to Annals of 13th and 14th Congresses.

give time for the elaboration of a new tariff bill; and after some discussion Congress agreed to this plan. February 13 he transmitted his reply to the resolutions of the previous February, closing with a carefully prepared schedule of new tariff rates. This, after being worked over in the Ways and Means Committee, was embodied in a bill and introduced into the House March 12 by Lowndes of South Carolina. Debate began March 20 and continued until April 8, when the bill was finally passed by a vote of 88 to 54. April 20 it passed the Senate with some amendments, and April 27 received the approval of Madison.

In drawing up his tariff bill Dallas set before himself three objects: To secure the necessary revenue, to conciliate the interests of agriculture, manufactures, trade, and navigation, to render the collection of duties convenient, equal, and certain. The interests of agriculture, he said, stating the general problem, required a free and constant access to a market for its staples, and a ready supply on reasonable terms of the articles of use and consumption. But the national interest might require the establishment of a domestic in preference to a foreign market and the employment of domestic instead of foreign labor in furnishing the necessary supplies. There were few if any governments which did not regard the establishment of domestic manufactures as a chief object of public policy. Certainly the United States had always so regarded it, though it was emphatically during the period of the restrictive system and of war that the importance of domestic manufactures became conspicuous to the nation, and made a lasting impression upon the mind of every statesman and patriot. The weapons and munitions of war, the necessaries of clothing, and the comforts of living were at first but scantily provided. The American market seemed, for a while, to be converted into a scene of gambling and extortion. But out of these circumstances of suffering and mortification had sprung the means of future safety and independence. Whatever might be said in favor of the maxim that individuals should be left free to follow their own employment, it was sufficient to observe that American manufactures, particularly those introduced during the restrictive system and the war, owed their existence exclusively to the capital, skill, enterprise, and industry of private citizens. The demand, when cut off from foreign supplies, was a sufficient inducement for this investment of capital; but this inducement must fail when the day of competition returned. Upon that change in the condition of the country the preservation of the manufactures which private citizens, under favorable auspices had constituted the property of the nation, became a consideration of general policy, to be resolved by a recollection of past embarrassments, by the certainty of an increased difficulty of reinstating, upon any emergency, the manufactures allowed to perish and pass away, and by a just sense of the influence of domestic manufactures upon the wealth, power, and independence of the government.

There were three classes of manufactures to be considered. *First*, those firmly and permanently established and which wholly or almost wholly supplied the demand. Upon these duties might be freely imposed wholly or nearly to prohibition without endangering a scarcity in the supply, while the competition among the domestic manufactures would sufficiently protect the consumer from exorbitant prices. By imposing low duties, importation would be encouraged and revenue increased; but without adding to the comfort or deducting from the expense of the consumer, the consumption of the domestic manufacture would be diminished in an equal degree, and the manufacture itself perhaps entirely supplanted. *Second*, manufactures which recently or partially established did not at present supply the demand, but which with proper cultivation could be made to do so. These were a more embarrassing class, but Dallas thought it in the power of Congress, by a well-timed and well-directed patronage, to place them in a very short time upon the footing on which manufactures of the first class had been so happily placed. The sacrifice could not be either great or lasting. The agriculturist whose produce and whose flocks depended upon the fluctuations of a foreign market, would have no occasion eventually to regret the opportunity for a ready sale for his wool or his cotton in his own neighborhood, and it would soon be seen that the success of American manufactures, which tended to diminish the often excessive profit of imported articles, did not necessarily add to the price of articles in the hands of the consumer.[254] The amount of duties must be such as to allow the manufacturer to

254 There is here the common but gratuitous assumption of a perfect competition within, among American manufacturers, and a very imperfect competition without, among English manufacturers.

meet the importer in the American market upon equal terms. *Third*, manufactures so slightly cultivated as to leave the demand almost wholly dependent upon the foreign supply. The only question was to adjust the rates to the revenue required, except that raw materials coming under this classification should be free.[255]

The features of Dallas' proposed tariff were the enlarging of the *ad valorem* list from three groups at 124, 15, and 20 percent to eight groups at 7 4, 15, 20, 22, 28, 30, and 33J percent; the increase of specific duties by about 42 percent; and, most important of all, in the article of coarse cottons, the insertion of a minimum, by which, as far as the custom-house was concerned, no quality was to be regarded as costing less than 25 cents per square yard. Except in the case of coarse cottons the new rates on articles which it was desired to protect fell slightly below the double rates of the war.[256]

Three positions were brought out in debate—two extremes, seeking the formulation of economic reasons for and against the policy of protection, and a middle party, composed mainly of men indifferent to manufacturing as such, but accepting the establishment of manufactures as one of the chief results of the war. The conservation and—preservation of the manufactures already established became therefore a national duty, and it was to these men, high in the counsels of the Republican party, that the shaping of the new tariff was committed.

The two extremes, however, were far from taking the positions assumed later by extreme protectionism and extreme *laissez-faire*. Self-interest on the part of the manufacturers prompted a pretty comprehensive scheme of protective duties, but their outlook was after all very modest.[257]Household manufactures were still of great and increasing importance. The prejudice against manufacturing centers as derogatory to health, morals, and intelligence, was still

---

255 As to other means of protection recommended by Hamilton and Gallatin, Dallas dismissed the matter by the statement that "the policy of the government seems to have been to encourage by protective duties rather than by bounties and premiums"; and the question was never revived until the session of 1890.

256 For Dallas' Report, see Annals of 14th Congress, 1st Session, (Appendix) pp. 1674-1698.

257 The extent and meaning of the industrial revolution brought about by the great inventions was not perceived.

strong. Now and for many years it was common for even the most
enthusiastic friends of manufactures to disclaim any intention of
introducing a system of manufacturing. As Niles phrased it, they
wanted to accomplish the sublime independence of the new world
by relying chiefly on household manufactures.[258] Protectionists
indeed rejected the idea That factory life was detrimental to health
or morals, or that encouraging manufactures would depress any
other industry; but their strongest position was the insistence
upon making permanent what the nation had encouraged them to
undertake in time of war.

The opposite extreme did not base itself on any consistent
theory of *laissez-faire*. The policy of "let alone" was commended,
but it was rather as representatives of the hitherto powerful merchants and commercial classes that its champions protested against
the unjust discriminations of tariffs, expounded the evil effects of
manufacturing, and held up the delights of bucolic pursuits. There
was, finally, no party divisions, and the moderates and protectionists meeting on the common ground of making permanent the
results of the war, arranged what at the time was regarded as a
satisfactory solution of the problem.

The opposition to the tariff of 1816 found its extreme voicing,
so far as the imperfectly reported debates show, in Telfair of Georgia and John Randolph. Randolph, responsible to no one and in
his most querulous mood, talked for no purpose of influencing the
bill, yet with a keenness of perception that anticipated the con-

---

258 9 Niles, 2; see also 12 *ib.* 34, 268; Annals of 15th Congress, 1st Session, pp. 84-
89 (Speech of Sanford of New York, Senate, January 7, 1818.)
"Let no one imagine that a general system of manufactures is now proposed to be
introduced into the United States. We would be understood as limiting our view to
the manufactures already established; to save those which have not already fallen,
from the ruin which threatens them." (Memorandum of the Oneida Manufacturing Society, January 7, 1818; 13 Niles, 398-401). Clay's ideal of an American
home was the well regulated family of a farmer; where every member of the family
was clad with the produce of their own hands, and where the spinning wheel and
the loom were in motion by day-break; the opposite example, the house of a man
who manufactured nothing at home and whose family resorted to the store for
everything they consumed (5 Clay's Works, 226; speech on Protection in 1820).
This was Jefferson's idea of manufactures to the last (see 5 Jefferson's Works 583, *et
passim.*)

troversy of many years afterwards. Taking up a remark of Sheffey that the case of the manufacturers was not fairly before the House, he declared that it could never be fairly before the House; it must always come unfairly, "not as a spirit of health, but as a goblin damned." Protective duties amounted to nothing but a system of bounties to manufacturers in order to encourage them to do what, if it were advantageous to do at all, they would do, of course, for their own sakes; "a largess to men to exercise their own customary callings for their own emolument; and government devising plans and bestowing premiums out of the hard working cultivator of the soil to mold the productive labor of the country into a thousand fantastic shapes; barring up all the time for that perverted purpose, the great, deep, rich stream of our prosperous industry." "I will buy where I can get manufactures cheapest; I will not agree to lay a duty on the cultivators of the soil to encourage exotic manufactures; because, after all, we should only get worse things at a much higher price, and we, the cultivators of the country, would in the end pay for all. Sir, I am convinced that it would be impolitic as well as unjust to aggravate the burdens of the people for the purpose of favoring the manufacturers; for this government created and gave power to Congress to regulate commerce and equalize duties on the whole United States, and not to lay a duty but with a steady eye to revenue ... The manufacturer is the citizen of no place or any place. ... Even without your aid the agriculturist is no match for him. Alert, vigilant, enterprising, and active, the manufacturing interest are collected in masses, and ready to associate at a moment's warning for any purpose of general interest to their body. Do but ring the fire-bell and you can assemble all the manufacturing interest in fifteen minutes."[259] Later, in the debate on Lowndes' bill, he characterized the tariff as a scheme of public robbery,[260] and moved its postponement to the following December, in the belief, as he said, that the subject, originally not properly and maturely prepared by the Secretary, of the Treasury, had been precipitated through the House, and hinting at a mysterious connection between it and the bank bill.[261]

---

259 H.R. Jan. 16, 1816; Annals of 4th Congress, pp. 686-688 (debate on proposal to extend double duties to June 30).
260 H.R. April 4, 1816.
261 H.R. April 8, 1816.

Telfair declared that incidental protection was well enough, but in the present discussion the encouragement of manufactures was placed in the foreground and admitted to be the principal object for which so enormous a tax was to be laid upon the people. As to the claim that the action of the government had been in the nature of a pledge to the manufacturers, he called attention to the infinite order of pledges to which such a system would give rise. Other interests suffered by the war. The manufacturers exhibited no particular statements, but in general called for duties amounting almost to prohibition. Congress had not been advised of the expenses of establishing manufactories, of the price of labor, of the cost of raw material, of the profits now enjoyed, or necessary in order to outlive the storm. In a word, all articles foreign and domestic were to be made dear to the consumer merely that the manufacturer might have a profit upon his capital. Was the agriculture of the country, he asked, in a condition sufficiently thriving to make this sacrifice? After having advanced in prosperity and improvement far beyond the march of any other nation on the globe, in the same period of time, they were now called upon to reject the admonitions of experience, and adopt a part of the very policy which was congenial to the people of Europe because it denoted the absence of all ideas of self-government. They were about to abjure that principle which was peculiarly their own, and the offspring of freedom, of leaving industry free to its own pursuit and regulation. The extent of territory, exuberance of soil, genius of the people, principles of their political institutions, had decreed, as a law of nature, that for years to come the citizens of America should obtain their subsistence from agriculture and commerce. Their circumstances were totally different from the crowded countries of Europe. "Because monopolies have for ages become familiarized to them, are we to disregard the evidence in favor of an unshackled pursuit of our own interest, and in despite of the warning voice of these very nations, which attests the ruinous effects of such a policy upon every principle held sacred by the friends of freedom, are we to give aid to a favorite class of the community by a tax upon the rest?" Manufactures, like banks, had grown up while war gave a feverish heat to the political atmosphere. How would they control the mighty combination to which such a policy as had been advocated would give rise? Would they open the flood gates and let in the ocean of foreign goods threatening to overwhelm them? Certainly not; and yet this would be the only corrective left them.[262]

Much of this was too foreign to the general current of discussion to receive any consideration at the time. There was no very close examination of schedules, but various points were emphasized by Webster, then of New Hampshire, Ward of Massachusetts, and others—mostly in the way of a running fire upon what appeared most vulnerable in the argument of the majority. In the debate on the repeal of the embargo in 1814, Webster had declared himself a friend to manufactures, but as not in haste to plant Sheffields and Birminghams in America. He was not anxious, he had said, in grandiose phraseology, "to accelerate the approach of the period when the great mass of American labor shall not find its employment in the field; when the young men of the country shall be obliged to shut their eyes upon external nature, upon the heavens and the earth, and immerse themselves in close and unwholesome workshops; when they shall be obliged to shut their ears to the bleatings of their own flocks, upon their own hills, and to the voice of the lark that cheers them at the plow, that they may open them in dust, and smoke, and steam, to the perpetual whir of spools and spindles, and the grating of rasps and saws." It was the true policy of the government to suffer the different pursuits of society to take their own course, and not to give excessive bounties or encouragements to one over another.[263] In the present discussion, however, he confined himself closely to the details under consideration, seeking to modify and restrain the more pronounced features of the bill.

The manufacturer's position, carefully stated by Dallas, had been more vigorously urged in a special report from the Committee on Commerce and Manufactures, Newton of Virginia chairman, submitted the same day as Dallas' report. Emphasis was laid upon the foreigner's recognition of the importance of what was at stake, and the special and redoubled efforts he would make to crush American manufactures. Once struck down, the government might indeed relent, but could it raise the dead to life? Competition would make the price low, and the extension of manufactories

262 H.R. April 3, 1816.
263 H.R. April 6, 1814; Annals of 13th Congress, pp. 1971-1973.

in the United States would secure such competition.[264] Richard M. Johnson of Kentucky emphasized the statement that citizens had turned their capital into domestic manufactures not subject to the control of foreign nations, and hence there was a moral obligation upon the government to give reasonable protection to them. Upon this subject, he said, the mind must expand and act upon a policy enlarged and liberal.[265]

Ingham of Pennsylvania, afterward Jackson's first Secretary of the Treasury, declared that revenue was only an incidental consideration and ought not to have any influence in the decision upon the bill, which involved a great principle of national policy, and was not a mere contrivance to collect taxes from the people in the easiest way without their knowing it. As to the notion that protection ought to be confined to articles indispensable in time of war and of first necessity in time of peace (referring to Madison's annual message), it was a plausible theory, but not founded upon sound policy. In the first place, no two persons would agree as to the articles. Besides, the great object of the government ought to be to promote the prosperity and happiness of the people, because it surely promoted in some degree its own prosperity and durability. The doctrine about first necessity was fallacious. He advocated high duties because the more powerful the stimulus the sooner there would be a supply and a competition at home.

There were difficulties to be overcome, he urged, independent of mere cost. European fabrics of the same material had the advantage in appearance though not in durability, which gained them a preference, and prejudice against domestic fabrics pervaded the country. It was a fact that the paper used by the members of the House to enclose their newspapers in, had the water mark of the British crown upon it, though the paper was made in the District of Columbia. He thought it a bounden duty of Congress to protect the industry of the country from such discouragements. As to the demand for estimates and calculations to show the precise amount of duty that would enable the American manufacturer to come into the market upon equal terms with the importer, such demands were in their nature unreasonable and unfair, because it

264 H.R. Feb. 13, 1816; Annals of 14ᵗʰ Congress, pp. 960-967.
265 H.R. Feb. 2, 1816; Annals of 14ᵗʰ Congress, p. 802.

must be obvious that they could not be answered with any kind of certainty.[266]

The mercantilism of the argument was furnished mainly by Gold of New York, who, after dismissing Adam Smith with Madison's favorite formula, quoted liberally from Sir James Steuart[267] to the effect that a nation ought to restrain by a duty on importation that which might be produced at home, and to manufacture as much as possible of the raw material, that a new manufacture could not be established without such encouragement, and that if the balance of trade was against a nation, it was her interest to put a stop to it. He invoked Hamilton as "one of the brightest stars in our political hemisphere," and quoted Brougham and others to show the continued hostility of Great Britain to the manufactures of the United States. No friend of his country, he said, could look at the enormous importation of goods the past year without concern; a hundred and thirty million of imports from Great Britain and only twenty-one millions of exports to her! Instead of there being a concert among manufacturers to raise prices, competition and the spirit of underselling prevailed to such an extent that sales were often made without a profit. Finally, it was not a distinct class of manufacturers who had petitioned for relief, but almost all classes, and principally the farmers, had embarked in the manufacture of woolen and cotton. Let no one be alarmed that a general system of manufactures was about to be introduced; that this country was now to attempt the manufacture of the almost endless list of goods contained in the importer's invoice. The question was simply as to whether they would uphold the present manufactures of woolen and cotton against the inundation of foreign goods.[268]

Most noteworthy was the utterance of Calhoun as showing the broadly national ground on which these young Southerners based their support. In advocating the loan bill in 1814, Calhoun had taken the opportunity to call attention to the amazing growth of manufactures, which of itself, he said, would more than indemnify the country for its losses. He believed no country, however valuable

---

266 H.R. March 22, 1816; Annals of 14th Congress, pp. 1239-1247.
267 The last systematic expounder of mercantilism, whose treatise was published nine years before the *Wealth of Nations*.
268 H.R. April 3, 1816.

its staples, could acquire a state of great and permanent wealth without the aid of manufactures.[269] His advocacy of the tariff of 1816was not without certain reserves which showed that he partook of none of the enthusiasm for manufactures that pervaded the North. He based his argument upon the cautious foundation Madison had laid, and with a steady insistence that the navy, manufactures, and internal improvements were alike objects of national importance and must advance with equal step. Yet within these limits his support was not halting or restrained, but full of the generous fervor of youthful Southern blood fired with national patriotism, and as yet showing not the slightest taint of the leprosy of Nullification. "The question relating to manufactures," he said, "must not depend on the abstract principle that industry, left to pursue its own course, will find in its own interest all the encouragement that is necessary. I lay the claims of the manufacturers entirely out of view, but on general principles, without regard to their interest, a certain encouragement should be extended at least to our woolen and cotton manufactures."[270]

Later, in opposing Randolph's motion to strike out the minimum on cottons, Calhoun committed himself more unreservedly. The debate heretofore, be said, had been as to the degree of protection which ought to be afforded to the cotton and woolen manufactures, all professing to be friendly to those infant establishments and to be willing to extend to them adequate encouragement. But Randolph's motion was introduced on the ground that manufactures ought not to receive any encouragement whatever, thus leaving our cotton establishments exposed to the competition of the East Indies, which everyone acknowledged they could not successfully meet without the proposed minimum duty. He favored protection on the broad ground that it was connected with the security of the country. War interrupted commerce and agriculture, both depending on foreign markets. Without commerce, industry would have no stimulus; without manufactures, it would be

---

269 H.R. Feb 25, 1814; Annals of 13th Congress, p. 1694. In supporting the repeal of the embargo, however, Calhoun declared that the infant manufacturing institutions of the country would not be embarrassed, and that during a state of war too great a stimulus was naturally given to manufactures—a stimulus which they could not expect to be continued in a time of peace (H.R. April 7, 1814.)
270 H.R. Jan. 31, 1816; Annals of 4th Congress, p. 837.

without the means of production; and without agriculture neither of the others could subsist. When our manufactures were grown to a certain perfection, as they soon would be under the fostering care of the government, we would no longer experience these evils. The farmer would find a ready market for his surplus produce; and what was almost of equal consequence, a certain and cheap supply of all his wants. To give perfection to this state of things, it would be necessary to add as soon as possible a system of internal improvements, and at least such an extension of the navy as would prevent the cutting off of the coasting trade.

To the objection that the country was not prepared for manufactures, he could not yield for a moment; on the contrary, he firmly believed that the country was prepared even to maturity. A prosperous commerce had poured an immense amount of commercial capital into the country, which until lately had found occupation in commerce; but the state of the world which brought this about had passed away never to return. This capital would not be idle, it must find a new direction, and what channel could it take but that of manufactures? Besides, the greatest difficulty had already been surmounted. The restrictive measures of the war, though not intended for that purpose had, by the necessary operation of things, turned a large amount of capital to this new branch of industry. He had often heard it said, both in and out of Congress, that this effect alone would indemnify the country for all its losses.

What then was the necessity of protection? It was to put manufactures beyond the reach of contingency. Besides, capital was not yet, and could not for some time, be adjusted to the new state of thing. There was, in fact, from the operations of temporary causes, a great pressure on these establishments. They had extended so rapidly during the late war that many, he feared, were without the requisite capital or skill to meet the present crisis. Should the present owners be ruined, and workmen dispersed and turned to other pursuits, the country would sustain a great loss. He denied that manufacturing, with the aid of machinery, destroyed moral and physical powers. He could perceive no such tendency in manufacturing districts, but the exact contrary, as they furnished a new stimulus and means of subsistence to the laboring classes of the community. Another objection, and one better founded, was that capital employed in manufacturing produced a greater dependence on the part of the employed, than in commerce, navigation, or agriculture. This was Certainly an evil and to be regretted; but it was not a decisive objection to the system, especially when it had incidental political advantages which, in his opinion, more than counterbalanced it. It produced an interest strictly American, as much so as agriculture, and in this it had the decided advantage of commerce or navigation.

Finally, it was calculated to bind together more closely the widely separated Republic, greatly increasing mutual dependence and intercourse. He regarded the fact that it would make the parts adhere more closely, and that it would form a new and most powerful cement, as far outweighing any political objections that might be urged against the system. In his opinion the liberty and union of the country were inseparably united. He had critically examined into the causes that had destroyed the liberty of other States. There were none that applied to the United States or applied with a force to cause alarm. The basis of the Republic was too broad and its structure too strong to be shaken by them. But let it be deeply impressed on the heart of the House and country, that while they guarded against the old they exposed themselves to a new and terrible danger,—disunion. This single word comprehended almost the sum of their political dangers; and against it they ought to be perpetually guarded.[271]

Only a few articles occasioned any discussion, and these were items like sugar, cottons, and woolens, which had been reduced in the Ways and Means Committee from the rates proposed by Dallas. Dallas had fixed the duty on cottons at 33 1/3 percent, which was reduced to 30 percent in Lowndes' bill. Clay moved to restore the original rate, in order, he said, to see how far the House was willing to go in protecting domestic manufactures— there being no difference of opinion as to the propriety of the policy itself.[272] After some maneuvering, during which Lowndes firmly defended the amount of protection afforded by the bill, Clay's motion was rejected by a vote of 68 to 61. Later Webster proposed a sliding scale on cottons, the rate to be 30 percent for two years, then 25

271 H.R. April 4, 1816; Annals of 14th Congress, 1st Session, pp. 1329-1336.
272 H.R. March 21, 1816.

percent for two more, and then 20 percent. Clay moved to amend
by making the first period three years and the second one year. The
present, he said, was the time for encouragement, and his amendment would give an adequate protection at the time of the greatest
difficulty. Lowndes assented to the motion. He rejoiced to see the
strongest friends of the manufacturing interest the advocates of a
proposition which would, in prospect, produce a return to correct
principles. He was satisfied that 25 percent or even 20 percent was
a sufficient protection, but he would support the motion, persuaded that it would eventually produce the state of things he thought
most desirable. Root of New York thought this proposition was
worse than any other; the manufacturing establishments would
be sustained for two years and then left to their fate. Hulbert of
Massachusetts had consulted with the manufacturers and found
them satisfied with Clay's proposition. Webster was informed
that the manufacturers would be satisfied with 30 percent for one
year. He was not prepared to say that the government was bound
to adopt a permanent protection. From the course pursued by the
government for some years back the community had a right to
expect relief from the danger to which a sudden change of circumstances exposed manufactures. Yet the government had a right to
say whether that protection should be permanent or not, and to reduce protective duties if it thought proper. But he was opposed to
a changing and fluctuating policy, and the object of his motion was
to impose a duty so moderate as to insure its permanency and still
be an adequate one. Calhoun opposed Clay's amendment. He believed 20 percent was ample protection. Webster repeated that his
object was permanent protection. Twenty percent would exclude
India cottons forever. Manufacturing establishments could now
be erected at two-thirds the cost of those first erected. Clay said
the object of protection was to eventually get articles of necessity
made as cheap at home as abroad. In three years they could judge
of the ability of their establishments, and could then legislate with
the lights of experience. Ross of Pennsylvania thought 20 percent
enough. He did not believe in the rage for fostering manufactures
to the exclusion of every other pursuit. Manufacturing had a tendency to degrade and debase the human mind, and the only kind
of manufactures he wished to see flourish were those in families.
Clay's amendment was negatived, 61 to 47, and Webster's motion

agreed to by a large majority.[273]

Considerable friction was experienced in fixing the rate on sugar. Huger of South Carolina, seconded by Sheffey of Virginia, proposed to reduce the committee's rate of 4 cents on brown sugar to 2 1/2 cents. This was resisted by Robertson of Louisiana, Forsyth, Lowndes, and Calhoun. Forsyth demanded 5 cents, declaring that sugar would be extensively cultivated in Georgia if the government gave sufficient protection, and protesting with much warmth against the injustice of taxing the South to support the manufactures of the East, and yet denying the South any security in return. Gaston of North Carolina in opposing the duty entreated the House to consider those unfortunate states which were burdened, on the one hand, to encourage the manufactures of the East, and taxed, on the other, to protect the products of the South. The 4 cent rate was stricken out, 62 to 55, and on motion of Clay 3 1/2 cents substituted, 64 to 58.[274]

Dallas proposed 28 percent on woolens. The committee reduced this to 25 percent, and following the example set in the case of cottons, Lowndes moved that after two years the rate be fixed at 20 percent. He believed, he said, that the manufacture of woolens, and particularly of blankets, required a decided present encouragement; and after receiving that support his amendment would produce the reduction of duties to the correct standard. After some debate the first period was made three years, and Lowndes' amendment agreed to.[275]

The tariff of 1816 was a substantial victory for the manufacturers. Their interests were for the moment the concern of all, and the unanimity with which the measure was received indicated the general feeling that the problem had been settled for all time by the conservation and exaltation of manufacture. Possibly, under ordinary circumstances, this hope might have been fulfilled, though in any event the self-interest of manufacturers would have prompted

273 April 3, the rate on cottons was reduced to 25 percent for three years, dropping then to 20 percent. The war duty was 35 percent.
274 H.R. March 23, 1816. The rate was finally reduced to 2 cents, but raised by the Senate to 3 cents, the House concurring. The war duty was 5 cents.
275 The reduction never took place, the act of April 20, 1818, continuing the rate on both cottons and woolens at 25 percent.

them to a continual extension of the system. But what was necessary for the conservation of the manufactures raised up by the war was but vaguely realized, and in its working out the tariff of 1816 proved a bitter disappointment to the manufacturing interest. The causes, however, were widely varied, and the result could hardly have been foreseen by the most unequivocal protectionist.

A part of the failure was due to a miscalculation of the obstacles to be overcome. The abnormal conditions during the war had not been favorable to careful business methods. Such was the demand for home manufactures, and such the sudden expansion of prices, that as Dallas put it, the American market seemed for a while to be converted into a scene of gambling and extortion. Manufacturers were warned that these extraordinary profits could not last, that they must be careful and build their reputations on substantial goods.[276]

These warnings were unheeded. Manufactories went on increasing even beyond the home demand. Many were sanguine enough to believe that even without protection they were beyond the reach of competition. Cotton and woolen manufactures, it was boastingly said, would not be affected by the peace, and the United States could even undersell Great Britain.[277] In the nature of things neither this sanguine prospect, nor anything like it could be realized. Any considerable loss of market meant the immediate destruction, at least of those manufactories built up on insufficient capital and lacking trained workmen and supervision. Nothing short of absolute prohibition could have prevented at that time large importations of British goods. The long wars had pressed heavily upon the English manufacturer and the return of peace found enormous quantities of goods on his hands which must be sold at any price. Nor could advantage in price even have saved, temporarily, the home market. The old preference for foreign goods reasserted itself. American goods which in quantity and price compared favorably with imported goods seemed to have little chance in the open market. Even inferior English goods crowded out their American competitors.[278] American merchants were

276 See 6 Niles, 217. See also 34 Niles 337-339.
277 See 5 Niles, 368.
278 See 11 Niles, 386.

eager to import and American fashion to buy. Indeed, the first shiploads from England were to supply long outstanding orders.[279]

Yet it would be easy to exaggerate the distresses of the country. The years from 1816 to 1820 especially, were years of depression and hard times, but the steady growth of the country was hardly interrupted. In the main the tariff did not fail of its legitimate object. For the most part the new manufactures were conserved. True, many establishments went to the wall, but, owing perhaps to the expected operation of the tariff, the number of manufacturing plants rapidly increased. Home competition became sharp and disastrous to those unfavorably circumstanced. There was a considerable fall in prices due partly to over-competition and partly to the application of improved machinery, and so rapid was the progress of invention that establishments which could not afford a constant replacement of machinery were soon hopelessly distanced. Nor were manufactures alone affected. Two successive years of bad harvests in Europe kept agriculture prosperous, but in 1819 there was a corresponding fall in the price of agricultural products, and this following close upon a financial crisis, due largely to mismanagement of the United States Bank, made the stagnation complete.[280]

---

279 Cf. Speech of Ingram. Niles tells a story of how the Duponts, extensive cloth manufacturers of Brandywine, were unable during the war, to dispose of their superior cloths because of the prejudice against American cloths. They thereupon arranged with an English agent to sell for them as though their goods came from England. These were quickly sold and at large prices. Niles makes the story into an idyl by having the Duponts so patriotic and eager for an American reputation that they persisted in selling their best cloths under their proper name, though at a lower price (18 Niles, 401). Cf. also 14 Niles, 244, (supplement) 87; 16 *ib.* 106; 24 *ib.* 243; 36 *ib.* 283.

280 Some years afterwards Niles gave this recollection of the years succeeding 1815: Thousands of persons forsook their farms and workshops to become merchants. Whoever could raise a few hundred dollars in cash, hastened to expend it in the eastern cities, as well as to exhaust all the credit that he could obtain, in ill-advised purchases of foreign goods. These were hurried into the interior with as much promptitude as if every day's delay on the road was the loss of a little fortune—and so the cost of transportation was doubled, to be added to the originally imprudent expenditure. As the goods were bought on credit, they could be sold on credit—and who would wear an old coat when he might easily obtain a new one at "the store"—he could get credit and pay "when convenient." The hum of the spinning wheel was banished and the sound of the shuttle no longer disturbed *speculative* minds. There was plenty of everything because there was plenty of

The recovery, though necessarily slow, was seen to be certain. The United States Bank was righted, and under the presidency of Langdon Cheves of South Carolina started on a new career of usefulness. The tendency to hold the tariff accountable for all the ills of the country was resisted, especially by the non-manufacturers who had firmly sustained, though with some misgivings, the tariff of 1816. They pointed out the temporary nature of the causes of depression, the substantial resources and recuperative forces of the country, and the indications of reviving prosperity. In his last annual message; December; 1816, Madison noted that the depression in manufactures resulted from an excess of importation which could not last very long, and in 1819 he declared that the evil, though severe, must gradually cure itself, and that the root of it lay more particularly in the multitude and mismanagement of the banks.[281] The season of 1820 he noted as an abundantly fruitful one and predicted that even if the manufacturers failed entirely in their hopes from Congress, they would experience much encouragement from the cheapness of food, materials, and labor.[282] Monroe, whose opening message had been so friendly,[283] when times were worse, had no specific recommendations to make, and in 1821 was convinced that under the existing tariff the United States would

credit! The needless debts thus created amounted to millions!—but "pay day" came at last. The city merchants pressed the country dealers, an they pressed their customers—every one pulled and hauled. In this state of things it was found out that the whole difficulty was caused by the want of money! A "circulating medium" was required. Banks must be established, and there was nothing wanting for them but acts of incorporation and paper mills. The people called for banks and banks were made; they loaned money freely, and for a little season the oppressed, having by new credits paid off some of their old debts, rejoiced at the "relief" afford ... But this did not last long. The bills of the new-made banks would not "pass"—it was discovered that they were paper—mere paper ... Brokers and shavers jumped up like mushrooms, and they gave "relief," out of sheer kindness to suffering people. They began at 10 percent discount and ended at 95 percent!—shaving away the greater portion of the little means that were left for the honest payment of debts. Banks by this time had obtained judgments—sheriffs as busy as "Old Nick in a gale of wind,"—and a general sweep of ruin was threatened in several of the states. (23 Niles, 81, 82.)

281 Madison to Rush, May 10, 1819; 3 Madison's Works, 128-131. See also *ib*. 265, 266.

282 3 Madison's Works, 181, 195.

283 And whom Senator Morril calls by "precept and example, almost a fanatic as to the policy of encouraging American manufactures" (Senate, December 8, 1881.)

soon become a manufacturing country on a large scale. His tone, however, continued friendly, and in 1823 he felt the pressure of the manufacturing interest sufficiently to recommend "a review of the tariff for the purpose of affording such additional protection to those articles which we are prepared to manufacture, or which are more immediately connected with the defence and independence of the, country;"[284] but his Secretary of the Treasury, Crawford, discussed the tariff wholly with reference to revenue, and the influence of the administration was generally counted as indifferent, if not unfriendly to the interests of manufactures.[285] Governors in their messages, while complimenting manufactures, were often as non-committal;[286]and Judge Ross struck a popular chord when he declared to a Pennsylvania grand jury that the cure for hard times was not in a loan office, internal improvements, or the tariff, but in simple habits and the curtailing of the extravagance and foolish pride of sons and daughters.[287]

But the movement was the other way. More and more there was a growing impatience with the tariff of 1816, and a tendency to lay the bad times upon its shoulders, a tendency heightened by the success of coarse cottons, protected by the minimum rate, which eventually, owing to a fall in price due to the progress of inventions, etc., acted as a complete prohibition. At first, there was merely a note of alarm sounded at the continued depression of manufactures after the new tariff had gone into operation, with a blind groping about for reasons. In 1816 Governor John Cotton Smith of Connecticut declared that the advantages confidently expected from a restoration of peace had not been fully realized. Governor Galusha of Vermont referred to the depressed state of manufactures as of serious concern. Governor Dickerson of New Jersey was more explicit. The imprudence of merchants, he said, had plunged the country into new distress by a ruinous importation of European goods, greatly exceeding the means of payment.

---

284 1 Statesman's Manual 458.

285 See 20 Niles, 370-374; 21 *ib.* 325, 326; also speech of Clay, 1824: "The executive government, if any, affords us but a cold and equivocal support." (5 Clay's Works, 294.)

286 See 12 Niles, 268; 15 *ib.* (supplement) 45, 61.

287 18 Niles, 321; see also 11 *ib.* 129, where Niles comments on the alarming progress of luxury.

Many manufactures had received a protection, which, while not affording immediate relief, gave hope of final success; but this was not the case with all, notably bar iron, and many establishments were already involved in ruin. Governor and Vice-President-elect Tompkins of New York deplored the fact that establishments for domestic manufactures should have been suffered to be suspended or even to languish. The appeal to the general government had produced partial relief; but the utmost exertion of the state legislature was necessary to yield such further encouragement as would place the domestic manufacturers on an equal footing with the importers of foreign merchandise.[288]

Gradually the feeling became more intense. Lord Brougham was quoted as saying in Parliament that it was "well worth while to incur a loss upon the first exportation in order by the glut, to stifle in the cradle those rising manufactures in the United States which the war had forced into existence, contrary to the natural course of things"; and this bumptious saying was passed up and down as gauging the economic attitude of the English government and English capitalists toward America. While all the nations of Europe, it was bitterly said, were alive to their interest, and making the most powerful efforts to encourage their own manufactures and to create a home market among themselves, the United States were calmly looking on, talking about independence and quietly bending their necks to the yoke, being tributary to England and relieving her wants at the cost of their own distress.[289]

At the session of Congress, 1816-1817, more than forty memorials were received setting forth the distresses of manufacturers. A petition from merchants of New York City pointed out the sinking condition of the commercial interest and declared that nothing short of the protecting arm of the government could rescue it from ruin. And the same causes, they said, were fast precipitating their manufacturing brethren to the same abyss. They admitted that Congress 'had bestowed upon this subject a wise and liberal consideration, and had granted such encouragement as was by many then deemed sufficient'; but this had proved inadequate, and they suggested making permanent, the higher rates,

288 See 11 Niles, 132, 150, 174, 181.
289 11 Niles, 297 (editorial).

more stringent revenue laws, a duty of ten percent on all auction sales of foreign goods, and that the army and navy and all civil officers use American fabrics.[290] Simkins of South Carolina admitted that the tariff of 1816 meant well, but declared himself sick of the unnecessary foreign predilections and thought they should learn a lesson from England.[291] It was the true policy of every state, he said, to encourage and buy of its own citizens every essential article, as thereby it added to its riches by keeping its money at home. This was the true and unvarying policy of England, who well knew that capital laid out abroad for foreign productions which could be as well produced at home was forever lost, both principal and interest.[292] The memorial of the inhabitants of Oneida County, New York, adduced the testimony of Hamilton and Sir James Steuart that no new manufacture could be established in the present state of the world, without government aid. It also laid down as a principle of political economy that any nation which should open its ports to foreign importations, without a reciprocal privilege, would soon be ruined by the balance of trade.[293] The legislature of Pennsylvania was more explicit. It declared that there was no example in history of a manufacture being left to take care of itself, or of success unaided by government. The Committee did not believe, the report added sarcastically, that every maxim of national policy was reversed by crossing the Atlantic, and they could see no good reason why the United States should not follow in the path lighted by the experience of others.[294]

These were but beginnings. Under stress of misfortune language became bolder, the tariff of 1816 was proclaimed a failure, even intentionally so, and systematic efforts were put forward to obtain a tariff in accordance with what their interests demanded. December 31,1816, the American Society for the Encouragement of Domestic Manufactures issued an address to the people of the United States advocating the prompt establishment of societies for correspondence with itself and with each other, and urging

---

290 H.R. Feb. 4, 1817; Annals of 14th Congress, 2nd Session, pp. 848-851.
291 H.R. April, 14, 1818.
292 See also 20 Niles, 178. This was a favorite maxim of Niles.
293 Senate, Jan 7, 1818; Annals of 15th Congress, 1st Session, pp. 84-89. (13 Niles, 398-401.)
294 12 Niles, 39, 40.

Upon manufacturers, agriculturists, merchants, men of science, soldiers, and women everywhere, to unite in upbuilding American manufactures.[295] Niles noted, in 1817, the 'great and simultaneous exertions' then making to awaken public attention to the subject of home manufactures.[296] A Pittsburg committee on manufactures announced the utter failure of the new tariff, and disdaining what it called the 'subtleties of abstract speculatists,' declared it sufficient to refer to the practice of the most wealthy and powerful nations in the world as a test of the utility of protective tariffs.[297] A joint committee of the New York legislature complained that the cotton and woolen manufactories of the state were in a precarious condition, some prostrated and others tottering to the ground, and that the duty of 25 percent, even if sufficient, was not of long enough duration to produce confidence in men of capital.[298] Baltimore manufacturers affirmed that the object of the tariff had been entirely frustrated.[299] Iron manufacturers of Pennsylvania and New Jersey reported their interests as in a deplorable condition.[300] Three-fourths of the cotton and woolen factories of Oneida County, New York, were said to be closed permanently.[301] From forty to sixty thousand workmen were estimated as having been thrown out of employment, seven thousand in Philadelphia alone.[302] There was never such commercial embarrassment, Niles reported in 1821, and in 1822, when manufactures were depressed and commerce was reviving, it was asserted that the years, 1820, 1821, were years of convalescence, and that while the country was gradually recovering and felicitating itself on the favorable prospect of its affairs, this eulogized freedom of commerce had once more come into operation and dashed the cup from its lips, renewing the scenes of 1815-16.[303] If manufactures had been fostered and protected in 1816, it was said, we should have drawn from England

---

295 2 Bishop, 230.
296 12 Niles, 75.
297 12 Niles, 129-135.
298 12 Niles, 236.
299 13 Niles, 332.
300 14 Niles, 105.
301 13 Niles, 398-401.
302 2 Bishop, 250; 17 Niles 116-120.
303 20 Niles, 34; 23 *ib.* 42, 274.

tens of thousands of her best workingmen.[304] The policy hitherto pursued in the United States, which had exposed their manufactures, excluded from nearly all the markets of Europe, to an unavailing struggle with all the manufactures of that quarter, was the principal cause of the present calamitous state of affairs. This system was in direct hostility to that of every wise nation in Europe, and the tariff of 1816 had been fixed so low that it required but little sagacity to foresee the ruin of manufactures.[305] Finally, it was boldly asserted that the duties under the tariff of 1816 were laid for the sole purpose of raising a revenue.[306]

Such a current could end logically only in prohibition or prohibitive duties, and this point protectionist thought soon reached. Jefferson's predilection for a Chinese Wall is well known; and Richard M. Johnson had declared at the beginning of the war that it would be only a temporary evil to cut off intercourse with England forever.[307] It had not yet been the policy of the United States, Niles wrote in 1817, either to prohibit the import or export of anything as a permanent regulation, and so far perhaps, that policy had been a wise one. But circumstances altered cases, and they had the unanimous sanction of all the statesmen of Europe that a contrary course was best adapted to the situation of their

---

304 15 Niles, 420.

305 17 Niles, 87-92.

306 18 Niles, 170 (Editorial, May 6, 1820). Baldwin made the same statement in the House, April 21, and Dickerson in the Senate, May 4, 1820.

Later protectionists have been much puzzled as to how to characterize the tariff of 1816. Mallary of Vermont, chairman of the committee which prepared the tariff bill of 1828, declared (H.R. Jan. 31, 1823) that 'considering the circumstances of the times, the unsettled state of public and private concerns, the countless interests involved, a more prudent measure could not have been expected from human wisdom.' More recent protectionists have generally followed Henry C. Carey, who referred to 'British free trade as established in 1817, 1834, 1846, and 1857',—a characterization which would have been gratifying to Calhoun and the other Southern democrats, who were only too glad to have the tariff of 1816 regarded as a revenue tariff.

As seen through the medium of a presidential campaign this tariff assumes a very queer appearance: "In 1816 the Democratic party came to the front, and with its cranky ideas of economy, repealed the law of 1789 and 1812, very low duties being only allowed. Great distress followed everywhere" (Chas. E. Buell, in the New Haven *Palladium*—quoted in New York *Weekly Press*, Aug. 9, 1888).

307 H.R. Dec. 3, 1812.

several countries.[308] Rich of Vermont, in 1820, submitted to the House the 'propriety of prohibiting the importation of sundry commodities then allowed to the prejudice of a free and vigorous employment of the skill and capital of our citizens, and of fixing upon some future period beyond which the American manufacturer shall enjoy the benefit of the markets of his own country uninterrupted by foreign competitors who owe no allegiance to the country, and who will neither fight its battles nor contribute to the support of its institutions.'[309]

An examination was made of the English system of prohibitions and heavy tariffs, of Russian and German protection, and of Spanish and Portuguese free trade. The English tariff of 85 percent on cotton, 79 percent on earthenware, 142 1/2 percent on leather, and other high rates, were compared with the low rates in the United States, and it was declared that were England to abandon her system and adopt that of Adam Smith she could not fail in a few years to be reduced to the level of Spain and Portugal. "On a fair examination," wrote Matthew Carey, "we shall bestow the most unequalled plaudit on the English Parliament for the admirable and incomparable system it has devised. We may fairly assert without the least danger of contradiction, that there never existed a legislative body which bestowed more attention on the solid, substantial, and vital interests of its constituents, so far as respects industry in all its various forms." Great Britain, he said, although possessing machinery which increased her powers of manufacture at the rate of two hundred for one, did not rely on that for the protection of her domestic industry, but interposed the powerful shield of prohibition and enormous duties, to preserve them from danger; while the United States, which had at the close of the war, a great number of important and extensive manufacturing establishments, and invaluable machinery, erected and advantageously

---

308 12 Niles, 292.

309 19 Niles, 331. There were the usual 'resolutions' indicating a tense period, like that of the Lycurgam Society of Yale College pledging itself to wear only cloth of domestic manufacturers; of the ladies of Washington, Penn., to confine their apparel to articles manufactured in the United States; and the grim parody of the young men of Cross Creek (near Washington, Penn.), who resolved, in paying addresses to the young ladies, to give the most marked preference to those clothed in homespun (19 Niles, 43; 21 *ib*. 337; 22 *ib*, 195.)

employed during its continuance, and although blessed by a boun-
teous Heaven with a boundless capacity for such establishments,
had, for want of adequate protection, suffered a large portion of
them to go to decay, and their proprietors to be involved in ruin,
the helpless victims of a misplaced reliance on that protection.[310]

Russia, Mr. Carey affirmed, completely fulfilled the indispensable duty of fostering and protecting domestic industry, for she
prohibited, under penalty of confiscation, nearly all the articles
with which her own subjects could supply her. It was painful to
state that so far as respected this cardinal point, she was at least a
century in advance of the United States, and Americans must look
with envy at the paternal and fostering care bestowed by the Em-
peror of Russia upon industry. The contrast was immense, striking,
and decisive, and how the United States sank on the comparison!
It could never have entered into the mind of Hancock, Adams,
Franklin, Washington, or any of those illustrious men who in the
field or cabinet achieved the independence of their country, that
before the lapse of half a century, American citizens would be
forced to make invidious comparisons between their own situation
and that of the subjects of a despotic empire; and that the protection denied to their industry was liberally afforded to the subjects
of Russia. The American manufacturer, Mr. Carey went on, was
the victim of a policy long scouted out of all the wise nations of
Europe, and which only lingered in, and blighted and blasted the
happiness of Spain and Portugal.[311]

A system of prohibitive duties would of course antagonize the
revenue policy of the country, and as protectionism became more
and more convinced that its interests were sacrificed on the altar of
revenue, it came to denounce this element in tariff legislation and
to hold up excise and direct taxes as infinitely preferable.[312]

But prohibitive duties were too bald and too undisguised class
legislation to win any conservative support, and the recoil was so
severe that even protectionism hastened to disclaim any purpose
of interfering with revenue. The 'American system' built itself up

---

310 16 Niles, 169-172
311 16 Niles, 181-185.
312 See 20 Niles, 306, *et passim*.

around a logic that made no quarrel with Madison's "if," nor with the theory that protection was a temporary sustenance for infants but practically it widened more and more its range of industries, demanded higher and higher rates, and showed less and less disposition to consent to any lowering of protective duties. The grounds on which protection had hitherto rested were essentially different from the old mercantile foundation. Much of this reasoning was undoubtedly involved, but the arguments that were really powerful were those addressed to the need of independence, the implied pledge of government assistance, and the expediency of helping manufacturers, in time of special peril, to do what it would ultimately be their advantage to do independently of governmental interference. There was apparently no very clear idea that protection would sometime he withdrawn because the need of it was outgrown; for free competition, whose international regulating power was so vociferously denied, was implicitly relied on to produce all beneficial effects within the closed circle of the nation. When that time came it could scarcely matter whether the tariff were taken off or left on, and the question would take care of itself. It was promised, however, that in the end the consumer should not be harmed, for the invariable effect of protection was to make the price lower than it would otherwise have been. The various reasons urged as to why manufactures could not succeed in the existing condition of the country, were the very reasons, it was said, why they should be encouraged.[313]

All this did very well so long as protection was given as alms, or as food for infants. But when manufactures became extensive and under thorough organization, when they appealed for aid as the recognized promoters among all nations of independence, prosperity, and happiness, and when manufacturers in their own person confronted the representatives of other interests, the old basis would no longer do. The old arguments were not withdrawn, but they were supplemented by an exposition of political economy which squarely antagonized Adam Smith and planted itself firmly on the doctrines of the old mercantilism. Of this new protectionism Matthew Carey and Hezekiah Niles were the principal

---

313 With one notable exception; the validity of the argument that the high price of labor was an obstacle, was not admitted.

expounders, the one through pamphlets and books, the other in his newspaper essays; while in Congress Clay's eloquence played upon it, softening its asperities and baptizing it anew under the alluring title of "the American System." Early in 1819, through the Philadelphia society for the Promotion of American Industry, Matthew Carey began the issue of a series of pamphlets designed to overthrow the political economy of Adam Smith, and to establish the 'plain and clear' principles of the science as understood by all the wise nations of Europe, and as suited to the situation and circumstances of the United States. The preliminary task of Mr. Carey was "to establish the utter fallacy of two maxims, supported by the authority of the name of Adam Smith, but pregnant with certain ruin to any nation by which they may be carried into operation": First, 'that to give the monopoly of the home market to the produce of domestic industry was to direct private people in what manner they ought to employ their capitals, and must therefore in all cases be either a useless or a hurtful regulation'; and secondly, that a workman could easily transfer his industry from one 'branch of manufactures to some collateral branch, or to agriculture, and that 'the capital of the country remaining the same, the demand for labor will likewise be about the same though exerted in different places and occupations.'

Part of Mr. Carey's reasoning on these points was keen, and anticipated later criticism upon the defects of *laissez-faire*. He pointed out some of the difficulties in the transference of industry, which Adam Smith had imagined so easy, denied that there were any collateral manufactures, and that if there were, the workman would find them not merely full but with supernumaries in abundance, insisted that artisans were wholly unfit for agricultural labor, and if not, there would be no chance of market for their surplus, and finally, that in the reorganization of industries it was impossible for capital to remain the same—arguments, indeed, which if valid, for Mr. Carey's purpose would prove altogether too much.

Regarding Adam Smith, there was in his criticism a mixture of playful sarcasm and severity which showed that the lion felt sure of his prey. This Delphic Oracle of political economy, with his unsound reasoning and verbiage, he said, was like other visionaries and doubtless failed to see the hideous result to which his theories would lead. Adam Smith's statement, that the merchants of England, in pursuing the mercantile system, had not understood *how* foreign commerce enriched the country, he could not forbear to cover with the ridicule which in his opinion it justly deserved. A merchant's apprentice of six months could answer the question—by the simple process of selling more than was bought! The principle was well understood by the merchants of Tyre three thousand years before Adam Smith was born! Any plowman could understand it in fifteen minutes! Hamilton's Report on Manufactures he called "one of the most luminous and instructive public documents ever produced in this, or perhaps in any other country," and in respect to this point, "so essential to insure 'the *Wealth of Nations*,'" "light and darkness are not more opposite to each other than Adam Smith and Alexander Hamilton."

But Mr. Carey's main reliance was upon what he called history,—supplemented by a series of highly colored conjectures. Adam Smith's statement that "if a foreign country can supply us with a commodity cheaper than we ourselves can make it, better buy it of them with some part of the produce of our own industry, employed in a way. in which we have some advantage," he proposed to test by its effects. Look at the prosperity of England, he said, with more than a million people employed in the woolen and cotton manufactures and affording a market for a million agriculturists. From this cheering prospect turn the startled eye to the masses of misery which Dr. Smith's system would produce. Suppose France, where labor and expenses were much lower, had gone into the woolen manufacture and thus enabled herself to sell at half price, or even three-fourths or seven-eighths of the price in England. Suppose also that manufactured leather could be obtained from South America and iron from Russia, below the rates of England. Then apply Adam Smith's doctrine and open the ports freely. France and Flanders would supply the English with superior and cheaper woolens and linens, Sweden with iron and copper, Italy and China with silks, and so on. Who could contemplate the result without horror? What a wide-spread scene of ruin and desolation would take place; the wealth of the nation swept away to enrich probably hostile nations, the laboring and industrious classes at once bereft of employment, reduced to a degrading state of dependence and mendacity, and through misery and distress driven to prey upon each other, all for the grand purpose of procuring broadcloth and muslins a few shillings per yard, or piece, or pound cheaper!

Continuing his illustration, Mr. Carey supposed the United States, 'pursuing Adam Smith's sublime system—buying cheaper bargains of wheat or flour, from one nation, cotton from another,' etc., etc., 'while the country was rapidly impoverished, its industry paralyzed, laborers reduced to beggary, and farmers, planters, and manufacturers involved in one common mass of ruin!'

To this simple-minded and melodramatic exposition of political economy, were added a detailed examination of the protective system of Russia and of Frederick the Great, in comparison with that of Spain and Portugal, where the doctrines of Adam Smith were said to have had free course for centuries, and an answer to the various objections to a protective policy differing but slightly from the summary of Hamilton. The common notion that to secure a home market is merely to allow home manufacturers to prey upon and oppress their fellow citizens was sufficiently disproved by the fact that no country in the world carried prohibitions and protective duties farther than England, and yet she was able to undersell all the other nations of Christendom.

The maxim that trade will regulate itself ought to have been consigned to oblivion centuries ago, by the consideration that no trading or commercial nation had ever prospered without 'regulation of trade.' Number Six of these essays, which was addressed to the President and asked for an extra session of Congress, recited how agriculture was kept out of foreign markets, that the home market was deluged with foreign goods, while thousands of citizens were out of employment and manufacturing languishing or wholly abandoned, that the balance of trade was ruinously against the United States, real estate everywhere depreciated from 15 to 60 percent, and concluded with the warning that nations, like individuals, which buy more than they sell, must be reduced to bankruptcy. But this huge inverted pyramid was unconsciously given a severe push in the eleventh essay, where Mr. Carey declared that were he the agent for the promotion of English interests, and had supreme power over the tariff, he would have it so modified as to protect national industry; for even if carried to double or treble its present extent, there would be, as stated in the Oneida memorial, ample room for the importation of as much goods as the country could pay for.[314]

These essays in political economy were printed and reprinted, reproduced and reinforced in Niles' Register, in the publications of the great number of societies called into being by the action of the American Society for the Promotion of Industry, by larger gatherings of manufacturers, by petitions to Congress, and in the arena of congressional debate. Especially was Mr. Carey's statement regarding the high price of labor, that the industry where manual labor was most used had succeeded best, repeated in memorials and speeches almost in his identical words. It was admitted by every one, it was said, that coarse cottons had thoroughly succeeded. Why then should the duty on coarse cottons be 83 percent, while on linens, worsteds, stockings, silk, and iron, it was only 15 percent? Why leave glass at a rate of duty which did not equal the foreign bounty? Why make a nominal duty of 25 percent on cotton efficient for 83 percent, and leave a nominal duty on paper of 30 percent efficient for only 15 percent or 20 percent? In introducing the tariff bill of 1824, Tod, chairman of the Committee on Manufactures, declared that no new principle was proposed; nothing but to extend and equalize the system, giving a protection to manufactures equal to that accorded to agriculture. Although it was denied by the Pennsylvania Society that the prohibition of cottons and woolens had ever been intended, it was claimed that total prohibition would cause no monopoly, for any body in the country could engage in manufactures. The United States exchanged raw materials for finished manufactures— the labor of from two to thirty persons for that of one. The last five years of European peace had taken more from the resources of the people than was acquired in the twenty-two years of European war. Baltimore merchants and citizens, petitioning for cash duties, declared that foreign credit took the wealth out of the country, and that from the practice and habit of using foreign goods in such abun-

---

314 16 Niles, 134, 153, 169, 181, 197, 215, 219, 250, 263, 283, 299, 348, 373, 409.

dance an unwarrantable prejudice had been created in their favor, to the great moral injury of the American community, who were disposed to consider many of those articles, not only as matters of convenience and comfort, but also as the test of importance among their fellow citizens. They recommended cash duties also with a view to turn the balance of trade and thereby bring back a portion of the precious metals. 'Our extravagance in the importation and consumption of foreign luxuries must be checked,' was the solemn warning of Niles, 'or we are a ruined people.' 'Let the reformation go on,' he said in the hard times of 1819, with something of heresy toward Mr. Carey's economy and indulging a suspicion that, after all, nations do not lift themselves wholly by their bootstraps,—'let the reformation go on, that economy may be forced upon us, the "days of leather breeches" come into fashion, and a hardy, high-souled yeomanry take the place of petty shop-keepers, and retailers, and speculators, and manufacturers of paper money.' The defeat of the Tariff bill of 1820 had, after all, he thought, rendered a permanent benefit to the country. The extreme pecuniary pressure was rapidly curtailing the importation and consumption of foreign goods and bringing about, a home trade of incalculable advantage to the country, by rendering the importation of such goods less and less necessary; these habits once established from necessity would be continued from choice. On the other hand, he emphasized the folly of America's policy by declaring that if England permitted free importations the wheels of her government would be stopped in less than a twelve-month.[315]

These doctrines and appeals reached Congress in many forms and from all quarters. A convention of the "Friends of National Industry" at New York, with delegates from nine states, recounted to Congress the great natural advantages of the United States in soil, climate, industries, intelligent and enterprising population, contrasting these with the great embarrassment in all branches of

---

315 14 Niles, 243, 244.
"Free trade is a pretty thing to talk about, but it cannot exist. What if England were to agree to receive American bread-stuffs? The taxes on lands could not be paid, nor the poor rates, nor the bellies priests be filled with the product of the labor of others " (30 Niles, 36 [1826]). And again (1831): "all the mighty capital of England—all her skill, industry, and scientific power, could not maintain an open trade with France for two years" (40 Niles, 289).

industry,—real estate decreased one-half in value, farmers reduced to bankruptcy, a great portion of the mechanics and artisans
unemployed, and the country deeply indebted to foreign nations.
There was something unsound in their policy, the memorial said,
which required a radical remedy, and wisdom dictated to the United States to profit by the experience of other nations. Portugal had
exchanged her prohibitive tariff for a protective one of 23 percent,
and in three or four years her manufactories were destroyed, her
manufacturers ruined, her workmen idle and beggars, and her raw
materials sold at low rates to foreigners. For centuries Spain had
nourished the industry of other nations, while the mass of her own
subjects, unprotected in their industry, were in a state of abject
distress and misery. Russia and Austria, on the other hand, protected their industry and were prosperous, while England, which
protected with the most care, had amassed the most wealth. The
return of peace had been attended with ruinous consequences to
America. Their infant manufactures were blighted in the bud, and
the spirit of speculation spread abroad.[316] The specious idea of
Adam Smith of buying goods where they could be had the cheapest had been given a fair trial and its pernicious tendency clearly
demonstrated: the United States were buying cotton, wool, and
muslins in Hindoostan, and there was good reason to believe they
would soon have large importations of wheat from Odessa. The
memorials from Rhode Island, Pittsburg, Baltimore, and Oneida County, N. Y., were pronounced in a Pennsylvania memorial,
to be 'masterpieces of eloquence.'[317] The Pennsylvania Society
for the Encouragement of Manufactures, in a second memorial
to Congress, undertook to answer the "vainglorious and cavalier
statement" of the agricultural societies of Virginia, that agriculture
asked for no protection. They were astonished, the memorialists
said, at such "utter unacquaintance with the real state of the case."
The average of duties on such agricultural products as were usually
imported, had been from the commencement of the government,
they pointed out, far higher than those on manufactures. For
example, the duty on cheese in 1789 was 57 percent, on indigo 16

316 H.R. Dec. 20, 1819; Annals of 16th Congress, 1st Session (Appendix), pp.
2286-2293.
317 Senate, January 17, 1820; Annals of 16th Congress, 1st Session, (Appendix) pp.
2311-2323.

percent, on snuff 90 percent, on manufactured tobacco 100 percent, on coals 15 percent, on hemp and cotton 12 percent; while seven-eighths of all manufactures including cottons, woolens, and iron, were subject to only 5 percent. At present hemp was rated at 26 percent, cotton at 30 percent, cheese at 90 percent, spirits at 80 percent, snuff at 75 percent, tobacco at 100 percent, coal at 38 1/2 percent, sugar at 37 1/2 percent, potatoes at 15 percent—averaging 58 percent.[318]

March 22,1820, Baldwin of Pennsylvania, chairman of the newly created Committee on Manufactures, introduced a tariff bill embodying the general demand of the protected interests for the abolition of credits on duties, for a tax on auctions, and for increased duties. After a week's debate beginning April 21, the bill passed the House by a vote of 90 to 69; it was defeated in the Senate by one vote.

In opening the discussion Baldwin stated that the first intention of the Committee had been to report a bill relating only to manufactures. But in reply to a resolution of the House, the Secretary of the Treasury had reported that an increase of duty on woolens, cottons, and iron would impair the revenue, and tend to introduce smuggling. They had then called upon the Ways and Means Committee regarding plans for filling the Treasury, and received the reply that nothing would be adopted by that Committee except a recommendation for a loan of four million dollars. Baldwin did not approve of asking the Secretary of the Treasury to take part in this great national controversy, and thought it not right to call in the influence of that great department against a large portion of the nation, struggling against what they conceived to be the indifference of their own and the efforts of foreign governments. Therefore, called upon by petitions of thousands of individuals, the Committee had no alternative but to go to the extent of their jurisdiction and report a system, which, while it would not injure commerce, should aid revenue and save the manufactures of the country.

The general attempt was still to keep strictly within the bounds

---

318 Senate, April 15, 1820; Annals of 16th Congress, 1st Session, (Appendix) pp. 2411-2423.

of moderation, although the thrusts of the other side and the exhibition of *laissez-faire* economy pushed the protectionists farther out than they had ever gone before. Baldwin granted that if other nations would adopt the maxims of free trade the industry of the country would regulate itself; all that was asked was to meet regulation by regulation and thus make competition fair and equal. The tariff of 1816, he said, was a revenue bill, reported by the Ways and Means Committee more to aid the Treasury than to protect the industry of the country. A nation which relied for revenue solely on imposts must encourage the importation, and not the manufacture, of its articles of consumption. With decreased importations revenue must diminish, and this had been the reason all attempts to promote home manufactures had failed. This system must be changed; either perpetual loans must be made, or new sources of revenue opened by giving a new turn to the labor of the nation. The minimum on coarse cottons had excluded the coarser cottons of India; yet every one admitted that coarse domestic cottons were now made cheaper than they were ever imported. This was equally true of nails and of every other article of which the country commanded the consumption ; and domestic competition would have this effect on every article. He advocated an additional duty on cottons from beyond the Cape of Good Hope, because those countries consumed none of our raw materials, afforded no market for our produce, employed none of our labor, and exhausted the specie of the country.[319]

The ablest and keenest speech in support of the bill was made by McLane of Delaware, afterwards Secretary of the Treasury under Jackson, who continued the traditions of Madison, and pointed out some of the errors of *laissez-faire*. The object of the tariff, he maintained, was purely national, not sectional. *Laissez-faire* was a plausible theory founded upon a state of things which, in fact, had no existence. Labor and Capital would not of themselves become immediately or extensively employed in manufactures without the fostering aid of government, especially in seasons of great distress.

319 H.R. April 21, 1820; Annals of 16th Congress, 1st Session, pp. 1917-1936. Gross of New York was satisfied that manufactures would be established whether the bill was passed or not; but if the government did nothing years of suffering and embarrassment might pass away before the evil would be completely cured (H.R. April 24, 1820; Annals of 16th Congress, 1st Session, p. 1965.)

Manufacturers did not ask to sell at higher prices, but to sell at all. The profit of the manufacturer depended not less on the quantity sold than upon the price. Give the American his own market and he desired no increase of price.[320]

The comprehensive, and indeed, the eloquent presentation of the 'American System' was made by play. He too, professed himself a friend to free trade, but it must be the free trade of a perfect reciprocity. If the governing consideration were cheapness, if national independence were to weigh nothing, if honor nothing, why not subsidize foreign powers to defend us. As to revenue, could any one doubt the impolicy of government resting solely upon the precarious resource of a tariff. It was constantly fluctuating. It tempted by its enormous amount, at one time, into extravagant expenditure; then, by its sudden and unexpected depression, into the opposite extreme. It was a system under which there was a perpetual war between the interest of the government and the interest of the people. Large importations filled the coffers of the government, and emptied the pockets of the people; small importations implied prudence on the part of the people, and left the treasury open. On such a system the government would no be able much longer to exclusively to rely. By encouraging home industry a basis would be laid for internal taxation which, when it got strong, would be steady and uniform yielding alike in peace and in war. "We do not derive our ability from abroad to pay taxes. That depends upon our wealth and our industry; and it is the same, whatever may be the form of levying the public contributions." It had been Urged that to sustain manufacturers was to tax other interests of the state. But the business of manufacturing was open to all. If true that the price of the home fabric would be somewhat higher in the first instance than the rival foreign articles, that ought not to prevent a reasonable protection to the home fabric; prices would be ultimately brought down to a level with that of the foreign commodity.

Our foreign trade must be circumscribed by the altered state of the world. But it was not necessary or desirable to cut off all intercourse with foreign powers. Yet if we had adopted the policy of China, we should have no external wars. The late war would

320 H.R. April 28, 1820; Annals of 16th Congress, 1st Session, 2105 *et seq.*

not have existed if the counsels of the English manufacturers had been listened to by their government. The tendency of a reasonable encouragement would be favorable also to the preservation and strength of the confederacy. Now, the connection was merely political. There was scarcely any of that beneficial intercourse, the best basis of political connection, which consists of the exchange of the produce of our labor. There was too much stimulus on our maritime frontier, while in the interior was perfect paralysis. Encourage fabrication at home, and there would instantly arise animation and a healthful circulation throughout all parts of the Republic. He agreed with the other side that things would ultimately get right; but not until after a long period of disorder and distress, terminating in the impoverishment, and perhaps ruin, of the country.

As to the maxim of "let alone," it was everywhere proclaimed, but nowhere practiced. It was truth in the books of European political economists, but error in the practical code of every European state. It might work in Europe, but the policy of the American States was otherwise—everything was new and unfixed. The maxim would require perpetual peace, and to be universally respected. He would not give unreasonable encouragement by protective duties. Their growth ought to be gradual, but sure. He believed all the circumstances of the present period were highly favorable to their Success; but they were the youngest and weakest interest of the state.[321]

---

321 H. R. April 20, 1820; Annals of 16th Congress, 1st Session, pp. 2040-2049; also 5 Clay's Works, 219 *et seq.*

CHAPTER V

THE TARIFF AND NULLIFICATION

Both sides had strained a point over the tariff of 1816, but the South far more than the North. Had there been no South the commercial hostility of New England would not have been considered for a moment. The rates proposed by Dallas, or even higher ones, would have been accepted unquestioningly. Had there been no North there would have been no manufacturing establishments to conserve, and the tariff would have been placed on a strictly revenue basis. The South was traditionally jealous of manufactures, and opposed the tariff encouragement as partial and oppressive. The argument which had won success in 1789—the national argument—was still more powerful in 1816; and for the sake of national independence, to keep an implied pledge to capital, and to conserve the results of the war, the Southern leaders sank their local prejudices and generously, though with some misgivings, held together to give the manufacturers of the North such protection as was thought necessary to enable them to withstand the shock of competition from abroad.

The steady advance of the protected interests toward a systematic and permanent form of government encouragement, and the elaboration of an economic philosophy, founded in considerable part upon the old mercantile doctrines, was met by a no less rapid crystallization of thought in the opposite direction. The patriotic sentiment which had appealed so strongly in 1816 was ceasing to be felt. The North still addressed itself to the national argument, but no longer merely to secure the results of the war; the 'American system' proposed the creation of industries, and of all possible industries, in the country. We must naturalize the arts in our country, affirmed Clay, and by the only means which the wisdom of nations has yet discovered to be effectual. In 1816 the economic aspect of the tariff had been practically waived. It could be no longer so, for the stand of protection was arrogant and aggressive.

What the South hoped, rather than had reason to expect, namely, the gradual dropping off of the protective features of the tariff, had now no prospect of being realized. On the contrary, the demand for better protection was growing sharper and more uncompromising, and was backed by a compact, determined phalanx arguing from premises which the followers of Adam Smith everywhere regarded as exploded errors. The very home competition which the protectionists lauded, in true *laissez-faire* fashion, as the regulator of all internal derangements, was indeed doing its work only too well, and creating an appeal for further government assistance which could not be resisted.

At first there was merely a firm resistance to any attempt to advance the tariff of 1816. About the protective features of that measure, the South raised no question. The falsetto of protectionism, that manufactures had been betrayed in 1816 and the tariff of that year enacted solely in the interest of revenue, passed without challenge as the hysterics of demagogy. There was no disposition even, to escape responsibility for the protective features of that act, although this charge furnished an easy chance. Not yet had the South come to regard the tariff of 1816 merely as fulfilling the implied pledges of war by letting the manufacturers down gradually, and without shock, to the former condition of things. Calhoun and Crawford were in the cabinet, but they were suspected of no hostility to the abstract principle of protection, though the growing coolness of Monroe's administration in the cause of protection was indirectly connected with the Southern predominance in it.

As to the question of further protection, the South, and a large part of New England as well, was substantially unanimous. The government had already gone as far as sound policy would warrant or permit. The tariff of 1816 had been framed with a view not only to revenue, but to enable manufacturers to meet the importer in the home market, on terms of fair competition. Further than this Congress ought not to go. To commercial enterprise, to the keen sagacity of the business class of the community, sharpened by the sense of self-interest and enlightened by long experience, it should be left to explore the old, or seek new channels.[322] Opposition to the increase of duties on iron, in 1818, brought out more sharp-

322 Talbot of Kentucky, Senate, Jan 25. 1819.

ly the point of departure. The complaints, it was said, came from New York and Philadelphia where iron directly competed with undersold imported iron. There wood was scarce, labor high, and provisions higher. The works had grown up during the war and under the restrictive system; it was not to be expected that they could flourish at any other time.

The legislature had given no pledges, and was not bound to sacrifice the great interests of the country to prop such fungus establishments. Like other speculators they expected to profit by the necessities of their neighbors. If the present basis was not sufficient, let them go down; it was not the interest of the country to encourage the production of inferior iron. The works in the interior of the country asked no protection. Seven new states and two territories must get their iron from the North and interior, or from abroad. All had iron ore of the best quality and in the greatest abundance. Wood was inexhaustible, pit coal abundant, provisions cheaper than in any other part of the world, and the price of labor low. These people would soon supply themselves. The proposed duty on bar iron was taxing the raw material of our extensive domestic manufactories contrary to the explicit advice of Hamilton. But the wiseacres of the day, the new political economists of the North, had found out that Hamilton was wrong, and that the "*Wealth of Nations*" had been a curse to the country. The great agricultural interest must bend before these mercenary few—these fat capitalists. It had been said that the country could not prosper unless manufactures were encouraged. Had any country ever equalled the United States in the same time? When the population became dense, when emigration had ceased in a great degree, when the fine lands of the West and South were disposed of, then manufactures would raise their heads. It was not true policy or true economy to force this by bounties and protective duties.[323]

Holmes of Massachusetts brought out more pointedly the conventionalisms of *laissez-faire*. Nine-tenths of the evils upon mankind, he said, came from governing too much, "let alone" was the sound legitimate doctrine, every man understood his own interest and would pursue it. He admitted, however, as exceptions, the necessity of aiding young industries, of supporting those

323 Smith of South Carolina, H.R. April 14, 1818.

essential to national supply, and of using countervailing restrictions wherever there was a prospect of success. He recalled Clay's melancholy picture of the ruined cotton factories of New England, "with the glass broken out of the windows, the shutters hanging in ruinous disorder, without any appearance of activity, and enveloped in solitary gloom." He, too, he said, had passed by several dwelling-houses of very industrious farmers that never had any windows in them; and the reason was that the Boston and Pittsburg manufacturers had been so well protected that these farmers could not afford to purchase glass. The whole country was distressed, yet the facilities of manufacturers had never been greater. Clay had admitted that there was redundancy of capital in the United States, inactive and lifeless, and that the capitalists of Philadelphia had offered the government a loan of twenty millions at five percent. Yet it was said that manufacturers could not succeed for want of capital; and as though nothing had been done, they asked for a little relief! Was the last tariff nothing? Was the modification made two years before to the full satisfaction of the manufacturers, nothing? Pass the present bill, and in two years more this would be nothing. The manufacturers had caused the deficiency in the revenue, because the tariff had been regulated more with a view to the protection of manufactures than to the protection of Revenue. The deficiency would have to he made up by a direct tax on land, and he would never agree to tax the land to support manufactures. "Create a motive, force a necessity, and sailors, merchants, and farmers must become manufacturers or quit their country. Pass this bill and it is the winding sheet of the navy." For twenty years the manufacturing industry bad flourished and improved more than other branches, and was making progress sufficiently rapid. He hoped never to witness the period when manufactures should hold the pre-eminence.[324]

When the bill of 1820 reached the Senate, Otis declared himself prepared for a moderate measure, but Congress was not prepared on such short notice to decide upon the great controversy between the school of Adam Smith and the economists and encyclopedists of France. He wanted more time to ascertain in what degree the decline of manufactures had been accelerated by other

---

324 H.R. April 27, 1820.

causes. Should the bill be passed, no matter what its effect on the revenue, or its reception by the country, it could not be repealed without a breach of the public faith. It would be regarded as the foundation of a permanent structure, and as a pledge that the manufacturing interest should be supported whatever the sacrifice and expense.[325]

Silsbee of Massachusetts was also a friend to manufactures and disposed to afford every aid consistent with a due regard to the other great interests of the country. But in a time of general depression, he could not consent to build up any one interest upon the ruins of another. As to the alleged balance of trade against the United States, the custom-house returns were very imperfect. The East India trade was certainly profitable.[326] It was not a question, Lowndes declared, as to whether manufactures were useful; nobody denied that. Nor was it even a question whether it was the policy of the government to encourage them by duties upon foreign importations. The idea of raising the value of labor and capital employed in every pursuit was very patriotic, but impracticable. We could not create capital—could only produce a change in the distribution of labor among the different employments. The notion that a bounty could be given without at least a temporary sacrifice was utterly illusory. Admitting that it was the interest of the United States to manufacture articles, which it could procure cheaper abroad, it must be still more its interest to manufacture such as should prove themselves adapted to its circumstances by being able to bear foreign competition. The statesman could not raise the wages of the laborer, estimated in the produce of the earth, and by high duties must lower his wages, estimated in the manufactures which he must consume. Even if all nations admitted a free trade, the arguments, for restriction on the part of the United States would be just the same. Suppose England admitted American bread-stuffs when the price was low; would any friend of the bill avow that this policy, which would make the establishment of manufactures a matter of somewhat more difficulty, would incline him to dispense with protective duties? Whatever had been the encouragement which should be afforded to manufactures, it

---

325 Senate, May 4, 1820.
326 H.R. April 24, 1820.

had always hitherto been supposed that these were required to be greatest at their first establishment. Hamilton distinctly said that where any branch of industry continued long to require a bounty, it afforded proof that there were obstacles to its establishment which would make it unwise to persevere in it. Yet our system was not only to persevere but to increase.[327]

Tyler of Virginia declared that if any one believed this bill would secure the permanent interests of the manufacturers, that this was all that would be required from Congress, he was most grossly deceived. This was but the incipient measure of a system. No principle of political economy was more true than that capital would flow into those employments from which it could derive the greatest profits. Suffer things to take their own course and the time would come when manufactures would flourish without the factitious aid of government. Natural causes would produce this result. The duty on cotton and tobacco he characterized as pure deception.[328]

It was this supposed unerring instinct of capital, and the idea that protection was a tax on one industry for the benefit of another, that was more and more relied on. Active as the manufacturers were in sending petitions to Congress, the opponents of the tariff were hardly less so. From the commercial classes of Philadelphia, New York, Boston, and Maine, and from the agricultural societies of Virginia, a multitude of memorials reiterated to Congress these laws of political economy and the injustice of further raising the tariff. A memorial from Maine declared that the vital interests of the Union depended upon the commercial prosperity of the country, that the Federal government was ushered into existence with almost a single eye to it. Even the present rate of duties was embarrassing to commerce and injurious to revenue. There was a premature growth of manufactures during the war, and the government was compelled to protect them by the imposition of duties, well known at the time to be injurious to the revenue, and adding to the already appalling prospects of the merchant. The celebrated essay of Hamilton had been pressed into service. The protectionists had adopted his principles, but disregarded their ap-

327 H.R. April 28, 1820.
328 H.R. April 24, 1820.

plication. Duties were now nearly treble what they were when he wrote. Hamilton could never have imagined that the time would come when it would be deemed good policy to make the people pay from thirty to a hundred percent more for goods. Besides, duties were now fully adequate for the protection of manufactures, and steadiness in government regulations was highly essential. At present there was a perfect acquiescence in relation to what had already been done to favor manufactures.[329]

The merchants of Salem and vicinity professed themselves free to admit that the manufacturing interests of the country deserved the fostering care and patronage of the government, but the interests of commerce were not less vital, and it was never sound or safe policy to build up one at the expense of the other. No manufactures ought to be which could not grow up under ordinary duties. The attempt to increase duties was not only repugnant to those maxims of free trade which the United States had hitherto so forcibly and perseveringly contended for as the sure foundation of national prosperity, but they were pressed at a moment when the statesmen of the old world, in admiration of the success of the policy of the United States, were relaxing the vigor of their own system and yielding themselves to the rational doctrine, that national wealth is best promoted by a free interchange of commodities upon principles of perfect reciprocity. It was a strange anomaly in America to adopt a system which sound philosophy in Europe was exploding.[330]

An elaborate and inflated memorial from Philadelphia declared that it was impossible to compete with Sheffield, Birmingham, and Manchester, whose workmen were forced to labor from fourteen to seventeen hours, to live almost exclusively on a vegetable diet, in order to earn a miserable pittance of wages scarcely sufficient to keep body and soul together.[331] A memorial from

329 Memorial from Maine, Oct. 19, 1820; Annals of 16th Congress, 2nd Session (Appendix), pp. 1493-1498.
330 Memorial from merchants and inhabitants of Salem and vicinity towns, H.R. January 31, 1820; Annals of 16th Congress, 1st Session (Appendix), pp. 2335 *et seq.*
331 Memorials of merchants and others of Philadelphia, Senate, Nov. 27, 1820; Annals of 16th Congress, 2nd Session (Appendix), pp. 1498 *et seq.* This of course, was urged as an argument *against* protection, not in its favor, as would have been the case even a decade later.

Charleston, S. C., after declaring the maxim that labor and capital should be free to seek and find their own employment, too evident to permit of controversy, added that if bounties were to be given to fill Northern cities with manufactories to furnish articles with which they could well dispense—if this was necessary to independence, equally so would it be to cover the pine barrens of the South with hot houses to raise sugar, coffee, tea, pepper, and the like. The Southern states were not, and could not for a long series of years become a manufacturing nation, but must raise articles of first necessity. Therefore it was peculiarly their interest that interchange with the world should be free, and equally their interest that the articles they were compelled to consume should be procured on the most advantageous terms. The United States could only calculate to manufacture for the supply of its own wants, and this would not consume half the cotton crop. A duty of 30, 50, and 100 percent was called for on all foreign manufactures, a virtual admission that the productions of the foreign artisan could be sold in the American market at one-half or two-thirds of the home price. In conclusion, the Charleston citizens had no hostility to manufactures, but wished them to rise, flourish, and attain a vigorous and permanent maturity. But it was unwise to force them into premature being.[332]

Various agricultural societies of Virginia "invoked the protection of Congress against the wild speculations and ruinous schemes of an association denominating themselves friends of national industry."[333] The Roanoke Agricultural Societies quoted liberally from Adam Smith, and from the Edinburgh Review against the proposed tariff of 1820, contrasted the freedom and independence of agriculture with the hireling manufacturer, and declared that the identity of feeling and interest which was the cement of the Union, would be destroyed by a rigid system of prohibitive duties.[334] Fifteen agricultural societies of Virginia united

332 Remonstrance from citizens of Charleston, S. C., Senate, Dec. 8, 1820; Annals of 16th Congress, 2nd Session (Appendix), pp. 1505 *et seq.*

Senate, Dec. 22,1820; Annals of 16th Congress, 2nd Session (Appendix), pp. 1522-1524.

333 Petition of various Agricultural Societies of Virginia, Senate, Dec. 18, 1820; Annals of 16th Congress, 2nd Session (Appendix), pp. 1517-1522.

334 Senate, Dec. 22,1820; Annals of 16th Congress, 2nd Session (Appendix), pp.

in a remonstrance against the proposed tariff of 1820. Agriculture, they said, solicited not the fostering care and patronage of government to alleviate by bounties, monopolies, or protective duties, calamities inevitable in their nature. The tariff plus the freight already averaged 40 percent, and the necessaries of life were much cheaper than in Europe. The favorite argument that home manufactures were necessary to keep the great body of people firm in time of war was so offensive that indignation would not suffer them to pass it unnoticed.[335]

A remonstrance from Petersburg turned the historical tables by declaring that the advantages of a free trade were fully demonstrated in the commercial history of the nations of Europe, from the unexampled prosperity of the Hanse towns, under the influence of an unrestricted system of commerce, to the commercial ruin of Great Britain, under the most complete prohibitive system that had ever been devised. From Great Britain the remonstrants learned that a nation might become so deeply involved in the protective system as to be unable to extricate herself, though aware of the ruin to which it led. The tendency of protective duties, the remonstrance went on, was to ruin every one engaged in commerce direct or indirect, necessitating heavy internal taxes to make up the deficiency in revenue, and forcing our seamen to emigrate to commercial countries. As to the home market argufiers, they had not calculated how many manufacturers one agriculturist could feed, nor how immense an addition to the products of the soil and the number of its cultivators half a century of unrestricted agricultural enterprise would make. The evils of the prohibitive system were obvious, universal, and highly oppressive; its advantages limited to a few great capitalists. In conclusion, by adding to the average tariff of 25 percent, 15 percent for freight, 33 1/3 percent for taxes paid by the British artisan, and the increased value of money in the United States, the remonstrants were able to figure out a protection of over 100 percent.[336]

1522-1524.

335 H.R. Jan. 17, 1820; Annals of 16th Congress, 1st Session (Appendix), pp. 2323 *et seq.*

336 Senate, April 15, 1820; Annals of 16th Congress, 2nd Session (Appendix,) pp. 1490 *et seq.*

The report of the Committee on Agriculture, through Thomas Forest of Pennsylvania, to which had been referred the petitions and remonstrances of the Virginia Agricultural Societies, while dealing somewhat in *laissez-faire* abstractions, was yet an admirably tempered argument. The petitions were considered, the Committee said, from the point of view of the threatened interests of agriculture. The only way in which the government could render agriculture any service was to remove the restrictions which oppressed it. The question was not as to the desirability of manufactures, but as to the expediency and legality of the means of promoting them. It was not possible to buy of foreigners unless they bought of us in return. As long as capital continued to be employed in the foreign trade, it could only be because it was more profitably employed than it could be if withdrawn. If we could pay for what we bought, well and good; if we could pay only at a sacrifice, then we would cease to trade. The whole fallacy of the balance of trade proceeded from the fatal error in political economy that the commodity called money was regulated by different laws from all other commodities; or from the no less fatal error that a nation, in order to become rich, must sell more than it buys. Among sources of loss in the restrictive system was the constant tendency to diminish production, to drive commercial capital abroad and capital from one kind of manufactures to another, and population from one state to another. The restrictive system not only diminished the amount of national wealth, but must distribute it very unequally, which was by far the worst effect. England was prosperous not in consequence of this system, but in spite of it. The present low price of cotton goods was ascribed by the manufacturers to competition, by their opponents to the fall in price of raw material and of labor, the greater facility in production, and the general stagnation in trade. The fall had been general all over the world, and coarse cottons would be still lower if the duty were taken off.[337]

The demand for additional protection was in no way checked by the failure to pass the bill of 1820, though for a time the momentum was lost and all efforts were fruitless. Business slowly revived, interrupted indeed by occasional reverses, but the im-

---

337 H.R. Feb 2, 1821; Annals of 16th Congress, 2nd Session, pp. 1653-1681.

provement was so marked as to deprive the arguments of 1820 of much of their force. Niles noted especially, in 1822, the prosperity of Baltimore and Philadelphia. In spite of continued importations at Baltimore he rejoiced to see the market amply stocked with domestic goods and sales continually increasing. Great building activity was noticed in Philadelphia, and the city, Niles declared, owed much of her prosperity to the amount and success of her manufactures.[338] The growth of the cotton manufactures was especially rapid, and in 1823 a general revival of business set in.[339] Except the iron industry, 'which was still languishing and imperiously demanded the protection of the government,' domestic manufactures, Niles declared in 1822, were prosperous. The legislation of necessity and the balance of trade against us, he said, had given to several branches of business a large portion of that spirit which Mr. Baldwin's projected tariff was designed to afford. The woolen manufacturers were looking up, and great improvements were making in the quality of their cloth. Many farmers had more than a thousand head of sheep, some three to four thousand. The cultivation of flax was extending rapidly. American coarse cottons were better than the British, though extensively imitated and the flimsy English fabrics imposed on the ignorant.[340] The country in 1821 and 1822, he said, was in a state of convalescence. And such were her resources that no policy, however injudicious, could permanently depress her. Her native energies would enable her to rise with, or, as in the recent case, without the aid of government.[341] In his annual message, December 2, 1823, President Monroe recommended a revision of the tariff in the interest of further protection, but evidently without sharing Matthew Carey's envy of Russia. "If we compare the present condition of our Union with its actual state at the close of our Revolution," he wrote, "the history of the world furnishes no example of a progress in improvement, in all the important circumstances which constitute the happiness of a nation, which bears any resemblance to it."[342]

338 23 Niles, 1, 17. Cf. Statement by the Hon. W.D. Kelly, *Forum*, February, 1888.

339 2 Bishop, 268, 281; for further details see 2 Bishop, years 1821, 1822, 1823, see also 5 J.Q. Adams' memoirs, quoted in Taussig, p. 74 (note).

340 22 Niles, 225; see also 24 Niles, 243.

341 23 Niles, 42.

342 1 Statesmen's Manual 461. For adverse statements, see 23 Niles, 41, 97; 24 *ib.*,

In his annual report, December 21, 1821, Secretary Crawford advocated a general advance of duties in the interest of revenue, adding, however, that the increase on some articles might eventually cause a reduction of revenue, but only where similar articles were manufactured in the United States, in which event domestic manufactures would have been fostered and the general ability of the community to contribute to the public exigencies would have been proportionately increased? But Congress showed little disposition to act upon the Secretary's mild suggestion. The election of a new Speaker,[343] opposed to further protection, brought about a rearrangement of the Committee on Manufactures, and although Baldwin was still chairman, a majority of the Committee voted it inexpedient at that time to legislate on the subject of manufactures. Baldwin immediately introduced a resolution to add to all duties the amount of bounties granted in their own countries, increasing the rates on various articles, and instructing the Committee on Manufactures to prepare a bill accordingly. This failing, Rich of Vermont, relying on the saving clause in the Treasury report, introduced a similar resolution with regard to the Committee of Ways and Means.[344] March 12, the Committee reported a bill, but it was never taken up. Already intrigues regarding the next presidential election had begun and were engrossing the time and attention of Congressmen. Niles characterized this session as a "do nothing Congress," some members looking for an early adjournment to escape taking up certain important subjects, others because hopeless of accomplishing anything.[345]

The following year Crawford repeated his recommendations regarding the tariff, and January 9, 1823, Tod of Pennsylvania, the new chairman of the Committee on Manufactures, reported a measure somewhat milder than the bill of 1820. This too was smothered in Committee, because, as Niles insisted, so many members had embarked in president-making;[346] but it was confidently claimed that the next Congress, which under the new

161; Memorials to Congress; 5 Clay's Works, 256 *et seq.*, 440; and nearly all later protectionist literature.
343 P.P. Barbour of Virginia, Clay having retired to private life.
344 H.R. Jan. 7, 1822.
345 22 Niles, 20.
346 See 23 Niles, 146.

apportionment would contain a considerable accession of members from the agricultural and manufacturing states of the North and West, would surely come to the rescue of the manufacturers.[347]

The tariff measure of 1824, introduced by Tod from the Committee on Manufactures, January 9, was discussed on substantially the old grounds. The protectionists leaned more heavily on the doctrines of mercantilism, Clay especially holding up the example of England, declaring that "a people better fed, and clad, and housed, are not to be found under the sun than the British nation." The national argument, however, was continually emphasized, Tod declaring that no new principle was proposed—merely extending and equalizing a system, giving other departments of domestic industry, and other oppressed portions of the community, something of that protection which the laws had so liberally and wisely given to the cultivators of cotton, of sugar, and to all the interests of navigation. Clay, who made the principal argument for the bill, invested protection with the name "American System," and in general elaborated and amplified his argument of 1820. He referred to previous tariff legislation as a fatal policy, inevitably leading to impoverishment and ruin, dwelt upon the widespread distress of the country, denied that wages were in any considerable degree higher in the United States than in England, justified the English Corn Laws, quoted as in favor of the restrictive and prohibitive system, the Edwards, Henry the Eighth, Elisabeth, and the Colberts of Europe, and Franklin, Jefferson, Madison, and Hamilton, at home, and as a still higher authority that "master spirit of the age, Napoleon Bonaparte."

The opposing arguments showed how deeply the *laissez-faire* theory had impressed itself upon the South, though the specific points made by protectionists were answered in detail and generally in good temper. McDuffie of South Carolina took the ground that each item should stand on its own merits, and made his protest almost in the language of Tucker in 1789. Modify the measure as they might, he said, the South must sustain from its passage a vast and heavy pecuniary loss. But regarding the general interest of the Union, if it could be shown that the proposed duties were connected with the independence of the country, this consider-

347 23 Niles, 401.

ation Would always have great weight; and a system of protection to manufactures tending to these objects, although it might bear heavier on the South than on the North, would not be disapproved.[348] Garnett of Virginia declared, regarding the proposed duty of twenty-five cents per bushel on wheat, that this attempt to raise the price of wheat was one of the most remarkable examples of the progress of the American legislature in the science of political economy which had ever been exhibited.[349] He insisted that the bill was for the benefit of capitalists only, and if persisted in would drive the South to ruin or resistance. The policy of the general government from the commencement had been, as respected the South, one of unabating exaction. The South had as yet, he verily believed, derived no advantages whatever from the Constitution, and the consequence was a degree of distress altogether inconceivable.[350]

Webster, who bore the brunt of argument, sneered at Clay's "American System" as a purely foreign policy, denied that the country was not generally prosperous, enumerated many causes of the present evils, pronounced the balance of trade argument "jargon and nonsense," and the doctrine of prohibitions preposterous, reaffirmed the statement that the high price of labor hindered domestic manufactures, especially iron, and in general made a keen and exhaustive exposition of *laissez-faire*. He explained, however, that there were parts of the bill which he highly approved, others in which he should acquiesce, and that he should vote for increased duties on woolens because asked for by his constituents.[351]

As the protectionists gradually lost the sense of economic law, their opponents sank deeper and deeper into the bog of abstract *laissez-faire*. In general the lesson it taught the latter was that the amount of duty was always added to the price, at least of the foreign article, that protection meant merely the taxing of the many for the benefit of the few, and finally that the tariff was a partisan measure deadly hostile to the South.

This outburst of sectional jealousy coming up again and again

348 H.R., February 12, 1824.
349 H.R., February 27, 1824.
350 H.R., April 2, 1824; Annals of 18th Congress, 1st Session, p. 2098.
351 H.R., April 2, 1824; Annals of 18th Congress, 1st Session, pp. 2026-2068.

was the most significant and ominous feature of the debate. The struggle over the admission of Missouri[352] had roused an intense sectional feeling and slowly convinced the South that its peculiar institution was in danger from the manufacturing states of the North.[353] Madison was quick to see the close connection between the two, but not the danger. "The tariff," he wrote, "is another question not a little pregnant with animated discussion. But it divides the nation in so checkered a manner that its issue cannot be very serious, especially as it involves no great constitutional question."[354] To Jefferson, however, the Missouri struggle came like a firebell in the night sounding the knell of the Union and awakening him from his complacent dream of normal constitutional growth and of the infallibility of republican counsels.[355] Once more aroused to the importance of the constitutional doctrines he had so freely violated, he strove with what energy yet remained to stir up the old republican feeling. The administration of John Quincy Adams with its federal ideas regarding construction, and its bold attitude toward questions of the day, only deepened his terror until he died in profound gloom for the future of the Republic.[356]

In the debate on the tariff bill of 1820, Alexander of Virginia took occasion to warn those who thought by means of that or any other injustice to mount upon the backs of the Southern peo-

352 P.N. With Missouri, the issue of territories entering the Union as slave states and free states came to the fore and would dominate politics up to the civil war. Congress chose to postpone the issue repeatedly, by seeking to maintain balance between free states and slave states by admitting an equal number both. The 1820 Missouri Compromise grew out of this tension, which admitted Maine as a free state, and Missouri as a slave state, and demarcating the 36th parallel as a dividing line between future slave states and free states.

353 In the debate on the Missouri bill the growing sectionalism was often commented upon. See, for instances, H.R., January 26, February 17 and 19, 1820.

354 Madison to Rush, December 4, 1820; 3 Madison's Works, 195.

355 "I had for a long time ceased to read newspapers, or pay any attention to public affairs, confident they were in good hands, and content to be a passenger in our bark to the shore from which I am not distant. But this momentous question, like a firebell in the night, awakened and filled me with terror. I considered at once as the knell of the Union. ... A geographical line, coinciding with a marked principle, moral and political, once conceived and held up to the angry passions of men, will never be obliterated, and every new irritation will mark it deeper and deeper" (Jefferson to John Holmes, April 22, 1820; 7 Jefferson's Works, 169.)

356 See letter to Giles, December 26, 1825; 7 Jefferson's Works, 426.

ple, that they would find their seats neither pleasant nor entirely secure.[357]

But the Southern temper did not stop with the conviction that the interests of the South were being sacrificed. Nor was this to have been expected considering the broadest way in which Madison and Jefferson, in the Virginia and Kentucky Resolutions, had once sown the seed of the whirlwind. The constitutional question, timidly broached, and by a Massachusetts member, in 1820,[358] and as timidly enforced in the Salem and Maine Memorials, was taken up in earnest by societies and local leaders in the South, who, as yet far in advance of public sentiment, prepared the way for and hastened the approach of nullification. The Virginia Remonstrance of November 21, 1820, reasoned that to force a people to manufacture what they could purchase abroad at a lower price was equally repugnant to justice, to policy, and to the principles of the Constitution, and declared that the powers necessary to execute such measures were too despotic to have been delegated by the American people to their government. The Charleston Memorial of December 8, 1820, merely called attention to the fact that every system of restriction, of monopoly, of particular privilege, was hostile to the general spirit of the Constitution; while a committee of the South Carolina legislature, though denouncing the restrictive system in unmeasured terms, deprecated any factious resistance or mischievous assertion of state rights.[359]

After the enactment of the tariff of 1824 excitement gradually died out. The country continued generally prosperous and was rapidly growing. In the partisan exaggeration of Clay it was the beginning of the seven most prosperous years in the history of the United States up to 1832. Little was heard of the tariff, but

357 H.R. April 26, 1820.
358 See Clay's Speech, H.R. April 26, 1820; Annals of 16th Congress, 1st Session, p. 2049, also *ib.* p. 1998
359 10, Niles 346. This was quite the prevailing tone until after the passage of the tariff of 1824. Occasionally some one more irresponsible than the others ventured to announce, as did Smyth of Virginia, with all the éclat of a new discovery, that the Committee on Manufactures was an unconstitutional committee. Congress, he said, had nothing to do with manufactures, but to pass a law for giving up runaway apprentices; and nothing to do with agriculture, but to pass a law for giving up runaway slaves. (H.R. January 20, 1823.)

unfortunately the sectional and states rights feeling grew daily in intensity. The bitter feelings engendered by the presidential struggle of 1824-25 forbade all further idea of party harmony, and foretold the desperate opposition to the administration, though "pure as the angels." But it was Adams' frank and bold adoption of the federalistic principles of constitutional interpretation, long practiced indeed, and almost without compunction, by the Jeffersonian republicans, and his vigorous assertion of a national policy such as Calhoun had clung to in 1816, that crystallized Southern sentiment and veered it swiftly around to the point of the Virginia and Kentucky Resolutions. Once more John Randolph and other malcontents of Jeffersonian days found themselves in favor and installed as schoolmasters of a willing South.[360] Issue was joined upon the very first acts of the administration, the Jackson campaign was started almost immediately, and soon opposition presses and orators were ringing changes upon 'the alarming encroachments of the general government upon the rights of the states.'

The prominence of the tariff in this campaign of hysterics was almost accidental. The tariff bill of 1824, modified as it had been in Congress, was almost satisfactory as a revenue measure, and although the South freely denounced the tariff as unconstitutional along with other federalistic abominations, no special emphasis seemed likely to be laid upon it. But amid the general prosperity one emphatic plaint was heard. The arrangement of schedules with regard to wool and woolens had not proved satisfactory to the manufacturers. They pointed out that while the tariff of 1824 had increased the duty on wool 15 percent, it had added only 8 percent to that on woolens, and declared that a measure better calculated to ruin the manufacturers of woolens could not easily have been devised. More than a third of the wool manufactured in the United States was imported from Europe. Wool sold in Europe at 50 percent lower than in the United States. The low rate of wool and labor abroad and the inefficiency of the home tariff enabled foreigners to persevere in their system. Besides there was always a surplus of manufactures in a country like England, so it was profitable to the English at whatever price they sold it. The woolen manufacturers at Boston, September 14, 1826, pro-

---

360 See Henry Adam's John Randolph (American Statesmen Series).

posed to ask Congress for either an increase of duties on woolens
or a decrease on wool. But their memorial to Congress was more
wily, and expressing the hope that the supply of domestic wool
would soon be equal to the demand, declared that there was but
one resource left, a square yard duty and the establishment of a
minimum rate.[361] By their own confession the manufacturers had
expected too much from the tariff, and capital had been over-ven-
turesome, so that even domestic competition had unduly depressed
prices. To cap the climax, England practically removed her duty on
the raw material,—as the protectionists hotly maintained, for the
express purpose of breaking down the American manufacturer. At
any rate, while wool growers prospered and the number of sheep
rapidly increased, the manufacturers found themselves with nearly
half their machinery idle.

The appeal to Congress resulted in the introduction of a bill,
January 10, 1827, by Mallary of Vermont, chairman of the Committee on Manufactures, in conformity with the desires of the
manufacturers. The *ad valorem* rate on woolens was not touched,
but four minimums were established. All woolens whose actual
value at the place whence imported was 40 cents or less per square
yard were to be dutied at 40 cents; between 40 cents and $2.50,
at $2.50; between $2.50 and $4.00, at the latter figure. Raw wool
was to be advanced to 35 percent after June 1,1828, to 40 percent
one year later, and wool costing between 10 cents and 40 cents
per pound was to be dutied as costing 40 cents.[362] At first the bill
seemed likely to pass without decided opposition. The majority in
the House was eleven, but in the end, owing to political intrigues,
it was defeated in the Senate by the casting vote of Vice-President
Calhoun.[363]

So far the appeal had been on the old grounds and Solely
for the relief of the woolen manufacturers. The very next movement showed the juggler's art and disclosed the fact that the
tariff controversy had been swept into the whirlpool of partisan
politics, from which it could never be rescued. Concealed by the

---

361 See 31 Niles, 105; *ib.* 185; *ib.* 200. Another proposition was to introduce the
principles of the English Corn Laws (31 Niles, 217).
362 31 Niles, 319.
363 See 31 Niles, 393, 32 *ib.* 23; 34 *ib.* 187.

cloud which they presently raised, men like Van Buren managed to display a double front, combining Northern protectionists on non-partisan lines for one purpose, and Southern free traders and Jackson protectionists for another, but in all cases, with an eye single to political supremacy and the escape of unpleasant responsibilities. Simple minded protectionists like Niles were quite unable to comprehend the rapid evolutions which followed, and unconsciously played more or less into the hands of the intriguers.

The Harrisburg Convention which met in June, 1827, disclosed the silent opposition that had proved fatal to the woolens bill. The call for this convention, made by the Pennsylvania Society, was addressed to all manufacturers and farmers, and friends of both, and the woolens bill cautiously denounced because it had included only one class of manufacturers. This sentiment was voiced by the Pittsburg Convention to choose delegates to Harrisburg, which under the guidance of Baldwin, author of the tariff bill of 1820, and presently to be made a judge of the Supreme Court by Jackson, declared that every description of American manufactures wherever located, was an object of national concern, and earnestly recommended that the woolens bill be so amended as to include any other article which needed protection.[364]

The attempt to procure from the Harrisburg Convention a recommendation for a general advance in duties on protected articles was most puzzling to the uninitiated. The stories of distresses among manufacturers in general Niles pronounced to be pure British inventions designed to console British workmen for their own distresses, and he was not aware that any other than the manufacturers of wool desired the intervention of Congress.[365] The iron manufacturers, he declared afterwards, when he had become reconciled to the tariff of 1828, privately begged of the Harrisburg Convention to be let alone, as they were doing very well and feared the effects of further home competition.[366] While the bill of 1828 was under discussion Niles declared that it would not benefit

---

364 32 Niles, 294. See also 33 Niles, 391, 431; 34 *ib.* 290-294.
365 31 Niles, 55, 153.
366 38 Niles, 350-252. "But," added Niles, "they magnanimously consented, for general purposes, that an increased duty on hammered bar iron might be asked for."

either wool or woolens; that while it would do no harm to try an increase on iron, no increase was desired; that they ought to make hemp at home, but did not, and. an increased duty might destroy the manufacture of cotton bagging and interfere with cordage; that the proposed increase on molasses would destroy the market with the West Indies, while that on distilled spirits would simply increase the home brewing of French brandy and the like; and finally that the glass makers did not ask for further encouragement.[367]

A general bill was, however, drawn up by the Convention, and for the most part undoubtedly in perfect good faith. The bait was temptingly displayed, and protectionist logic could not detect the slightest flaw in such a scheme. Nor would its adoption *in toto* have been, probably, of very serious concern one way or the other to the manufacturers. But it formed a famous cover under which the intrigues of a particularly unsavory presidential campaign could be worked out. Van Buren appeared in the New York Convention for choosing delegates to Harrisburg, but presently retired from active sympathy in the movement with solemn warnings against mixing politics with the measure; while later he kept himself easy with the South by having instructions prepared in the New York legislature directing the senators from that state to vote for the bill of 1828. Simultaneously the Senate of New York lashed President Adams for his apathy in the cause of protection, though bis Secretary of the Treasury had cordially endorsed the Harrisburg bill and elaborately argued the cause of protection. Baldwin denounced the President because he had never recommended protection in his annual messages, and even Niles found himself scored as hostile to the American System.[368]

The Harrisburg bill, however, in recognizable shape was not destined to appear before Congress. A Pennsylvania-Southern combination in the interest of Jackson, and through Van Buren's influence, it was said, placed Andrew Stevenson of Virginia, an anti-tariff member, in the speaker's chair. He in turn, continued Mallary as chairman of the Committee on Manufactures, but with a hostile majority to preside over. The first indication was given

367 33 Niles, 431 *et seq.*
368 33 Niles, 351, 352; 34 *ib.* 75, 290-294. For Secretary Rush's Report, 1827, see 33 Niles, 247 *et seq.*

December 31, 1827, when the Committee, against the protest of the chairman, voted to send for persons and papers to examine into the condition of manufactures. This movement was considered hostile to the Harrisburg bill and was opposed by protectionists, who objected to delay and insisted that the facts were well known. But the resolution was sustained in the House, 102 to 88, by the same Pennsylvania-Southern combination. The protectionists were greatly startled. "It is manifest," Niles declared editorially, "that any proposed alteration in the tariff with a view to the protection of the agriculturists and manufacturers of our country, is to be defeated—without reference to the merits of the question at issue, and by the default of individuals hitherto counted upon as fast friends of the system. ... If they succeed, if the friends of domestic industry shall not rally themselves and speak in a voice that must be regarded,—our country will meet with a shock from which it will not easily recover itself. From fifty to sixty millions of dollars will be instantly sacrificed in the reduced value of lands and sheep and the manufactories of wool. Already the farmers stand with whetted knives to kill off these useful animals. ... The proprietors of woolen manufactories will be generally ruined."[369]

The next move on the part of the anti-tariff men was even bolder, though less fortunate in the end. A bill was prepared which, while modifying somewhat seriously the woolen schedule, admitted without discrimination items and rates obnoxious to all rational protectionists. The result was astounding. The bill as reported, Niles affirmed, could not pass, and if it did, it ought to be amended to read: "An act to prohibit the manufacture of certain woolen goods in the United States, and to prevent the increase of sheep, and for other purposes."[370] This was precisely what the enemies of the tariff wished to bring about, and with the aid of Pennsylvania they succeeded in retaining all the more objectionable features of the bill. The "tariff of abominations," as it was popularly called, they hoped to make so bad that enough tariff votes could be got to secure its final defeat. But here they were at fault. Pennsylvania was consistent to the last, and parted company with the South on the final vote; and although a number of tariff

---

369 33 Niles, 329.
370 33 Niles, 385.

men refused to accept it, the bill, abominations and all, passed and received the approval of President Adams.

The discussion brought out little that was new. The protection-ists had so much trouble with the Committee's bill, which proved, even after considerable amendment in the Senate, a very bitter draught, that they had little heart to expound the American Sys-tem. The British spectre appeared with the old doleful threaten-ings, though looking even worse from the point of view of the new tariff than from the old. Extra shiploads of goods would be sent to the United States, and the hammer of the auctioneer would hardly descend rapidly enough to force them upon the consumption of the country. The busy hum of industry would cease at the factories, and the beautiful villages which they had built up would be de-serted. The markets for the farmer must cease, and flocks of sheep no longer be preserved except for family purposes. It was fearful to calculate, Niles exclaimed, the depreciated value of property which would result.[371] The overwhelming error of the Committee, he said, was the protection of the raw material rather than the making of a market for it. He had no doubt that the effect would be to cut the throats of the sheep and delapidate the woolen factories.[372] On the other side, the formulation of the extreme *laissez-faire* argument was left principally to the Ways and Means Committee, which, through McDuffie, submitted an elaborate report against the proposed tariff.[373] In debate, however, ardent free traders like Cambreleng of New York City and the Southern leaders gave a firm though indecorous support to the abominations of the bill, derisively seconded by the leading *laissez-faire* newspaper, the New York *Evening Post*.

At the South indignation was intense, heightened perhaps be-cause there was no good answer to the taunt that the South itself was responsible for the worst provisions of the bill. Even before the Harrisburg Convention the extremists were discussing the question in no conciliatory mood. At an anti-tariff meeting in Co-lumbia, S. C., July 2,1827, President Thomas Cooper of the South Carolina College declared that the time had come to calculate the

---

371 34 Niles, 33.
372 34 Niles, 24, 33.
373 See 34 Niles, 81-95, 138.

value of the Union, and to inquire of what use to them was this most unequal alliance by which the South had always been the loser and the North always the gainer. "Is it worth our while," he asked, "to continue this union of States, where the North demand to be our masters, and we are required to be their tributaries?"[374] "It is the principle we object to; it is the right we deny; it is the usurpation we complain of," ran the South Carolina *Circular*. "If we do not at once seize upon the strong ground of principle, with a determination never to quit it, our cause is lost. ... Protection was never meant to become a permanent tax upon the consumer, but to give a start to a new undertaking for a few years; on the implied and understood provision that it would soon be capable of maintaining itself. ... Are our domestic manufactures to continue in perpetual infancy? ... We exist as a member of the Union merely as an object of taxation. ... Our national pact is broken."[375]

At a public dinner, McDuffie, in a speech wildly applauded, drew a gloomy picture of southern degradation. Taxed ten millions a year, her commerce destroyed, her staples depressed to nothing, her citizens in debt, and the general government regularly and progressively increasing these unbearable evils to enrich a set of mercenary, desperate politicians who regularly barter and sell the interest of the country at every presidential election. There was no hope of a change in the system. Two-thirds of Congress were actuated by selfish, ambitious, and avaricious motives, determined to pursue their reckless course in spite of all consequences and totally regardless of the ruin of that portion of the Union which produced more than two-thirds of the exports of the country. The South was tenfold more insulted, more injured, more disgraced and contemned, by the majority in Congress, than ever their forefathers had been by Great Britain. It would have been better for the South to have had no representatives in Washington the past winter. Their remaining there was only bearding and provoking the lion; for McDuffie was sure that if an angel from Heaven had come down upon earth, no truth, no argument even from his lips, would have prevailed with a set of men desperately bent on their own aggrandizement—upon the ruin of the South.[376] None but a

374 33 Niles, 32.
375 33 Niles, 59, 60.
376 34 Niles, 339. Later toast of McDuffie: "The Stamp Act of 1765, and the

coward, he said, could longer consent to bear such a state of things. The Southern states were bound to save themselves from utter ruin and disgraceful annihilation. But his recommendations only extended to laying a heavy state tax on Northern manufactures and on the livestock of Kentucky, and to citizens of South Carolina clothing themselves in homespun.

Southern excitement, however, did not stop with even such flatly inconsistent acts as these. The people of Colleton district, South Carolina, advised an attitude of open resistance to the tariff law, and called upon the governor to immediately convene the legislature.[377] No resort to violence was intended, it was explained, but the state should put forward a solemn declaration to the people of the United States plainly and unequivocally expressing their determination not to bear the impositions of the tariff, and should appoint an express deputation to appear before Congress, not to reason or to argue, but simply to *demand* a repeal of the tariff.[378] "When we do resist," declared the South Carolina *Mercury*, "let us resist as becomes men and freemen; not each one in his own way and without head or concert. Let the state legislature or a state convention, after the maturest deliberation, take measures, and in proper time, send on to the United States government its *ultimatum*. Should the general government refuse, let the governor by proclamation open the ports for the reception of vessels of all nations."[379] Congressman Hamilton declared that from 1816 the South had been drugged by the slow poison of the miserable empiricism of the prohibitive system, and there was no hope of returning justice, owing to the unrelenting avarice and selfishness of the manufacturing spirit.[380] But although they were without reme-

tariff of 1820—kindred acts of despotism; when our oppressors trace the parallel, let them remember that we are descendants of a noble ancestry, and profit by the admonitions of history." (35 Niles, 61-64.)

377 34 Niles, 288-290; see also *ib*. 300, remarks of the *Southron*.

378 34 Niles, 353.

379 34 Niles, 394.

380 "Do not lay the flattering unction to your souls," he said, "that we can find any refuge in the stern integrity and inflexible justice of that venerable patriot, on whom a grateful and indignant people are about to bestow the highest mark of their confidence. He cannot repeal a law. The government of the country is not in the executive, but in the despotic sectional majority of both houses. Your candidate for president will have scarcely taken the oath of office before that man who claims,

dy in the justice or mercy of their opponents, they had a remedy in themselves; upon the reserved rights of the States they might build as upon a rock which the tempest and billows might beat upon but could not shake. Their reliance was upon the Virginia and Kentucky Resolutions of '98. How should they interfere? Let Jefferson answer in the Kentucky Resolutions: 'The several States who formed the Constitution, being sovereign, independent, have the unquestionable right to judge its infractions; and a nullification by those sovereigns of all unauthorized acts done under color of that instrument, is the rightful remedy.' Regarding the various remedies that had been proposed, Hamilton considered State excises as worse than inefficient—a sort of domestic tariff against friends and enemies alike. Besides, such local excises would be decided against them by the Supreme Court, which would thus virtually pass on the sovereignty of the State, and he did not want South Carolina involved in a pitiful contest with the subordinate officers of the general government. He had still less faith in non-consumptive resolutions. They were so partial and inefficient that they would punish the non-consumers with grievous self-denial, and at best were but a sullen acquiescence in wrongs. The resolution to establish manufactures in South Carolina, he said, was quite as sensible and consoling a remedy as would have been the proposition during the Revolution to have resisted the tea tax by cultivating the plant in hot houses throughout the country. He came back, he said, to Jefferson's principle—nullification. But would not a dissolution of the Union inevitably follow? Not unless their opponents willed it so. One of three courses would be open to the national government after nullification was proclaimed. It could submit, leaving South Carolina alone, call a convention of the States, or apply direct coercion. The State paid too much tribute to admit of the first. The next resource ought to be the remedy. Three-fourths of the states must affirm the tariff before it could be constitutional. If this were done (as it would not be), it would be as competent for South Carolina to withdraw from the Union as to withhold its consent

with every just pretension that injustice and a malignant hostility to your interest can give him, the title of the champion of the 'American System,' will begin to push this question for the purple for himself, with renovated and uncompromising zeal; the party opposing him will not be outdone in this holy work, and the venerable patriot must remain in spite of his devoted patriotism and Roman honesty, a passive spectator."

in 1787. If force were used they had nothing to fear; other states would join them, though they did not need even that.[381]

But these overheated and contradictory propositions found little soil for immediate growth. There was no difference of opinion as to the malignant effect of the tariff on the South, and almost none as to its unconstitutionality. Southern leaders generally, however, were not yet ready to despair, nor had excitement and anger carried them beyond all bounds of reason. The Union sentiment was strong, and in the election of Jackson the South saw the prospect of relief. Ex-Governor Williams of South Carolina believed the tariff to be unwise, unjust, and unconstitutional, but resistance to legislation must end in disunion, and the legislature could not better the situation.[382] Governor Forsyth of Georgia had no faith in state tariffs to correct the evil. The law must perish where it was born, under the force of public opinion. The people should practice economy, substitute the manufactures of Europe for those of the North, encourage household manufactures, and the like.[383] Governor Murphy of Alabama was clear that the tariff checked their prosperity. He advocated manufactures, thought slave labor extremely well adapted to it, and maintaining the strictest principles of constitutional interpretation.[384]

381 35 Niles, 203-208.

382 35 Niles, 47-48.

383 35 Niles, 223.

384 Polk of Tennessee declared that Jackson "had planted himself upon the ramparts of the Constitution and had take the high responsibility upon himself to check the downward march," etc. P.P. Barbour of Virginia said that Jackson had done the state some service before; but in his opinion it was but dust in the balance compared with the good he had done now. Senator Hayne declared at Charleston, in a Fourth of July speech, that "General Jackson in putting his veto upon the Maysville road bill has opened the Southern states the first dawning of returning hope." The Georgia *Journal* declared that by this veto "the American System has received a blow which it is hoped will prostrate it forever." And Senator Blair of South Carolina wrote to his constituents three days after the veto: "Since writing my address our political prospects have, I think, become much better. Two days ago, we passed in our House a bill reducing the duty on salt, another reducing the duty on molasses. The Senate a few days ago laid on the table a bill authorizing a subscription of stock to the Lexington and Maysville road bill ... I should be better pleased with his message if it were a little 'tight-laced' as regards the powers of Congress to make roads, etc. But for political purposes, as regards the South, it is quite efficient. Thus I regard the system of internal improvements as completely

The majority of South Carolina's leaders, however, refused to be reassured by the message which gave so much hope to even her representatives in Congress. The Cheraw *Republican* declared that the reduction of duties on tea, coffee, salt, and molasses was intended as a propitiatory sacrifice to those states whose disaffection had increased, and was a plausible pretext for continuing the existing duties; while the Newburn (N. C.) *Sentinel* professed to regard the reduction as a specimen of Northern jugglery.[385] Niles explained the matter by saying that it was not a triumph for free trade, as the New York *Evening Post* put it, but an undoing of what the free trade folks had done in 1828. The increased duty on molasses, for instance, had been crammed into the bill against the consent of three-fourths of the avowed friends of the tariff, and retained by the almost unanimous vote of the South.[386]

Both sides were becoming aroused. Niles admitted the imminent danger, and was the more alarmed, as all his predictions regarding the tariff of 1828 had been unfulfilled. The respective forces were drawn up in line of battle, and considerable skirmishing was done in Congress. But the signal for action was given by Jackson's third annual message, December, 1831. He congratulated the country upon its great prosperity, and calling attention to the prospective extinction of the public debt, advocated a horizontal reduction of tariff rates. In three years the debt would be paid, leaving a surplus of more than eleven millions a year. The lull in the tariff controversy was over. The Southern opportunity had come, and the South sprang at once to the attack. Public meetings and dinners gave occasion for anti-tariff and nullification utterances, and resolutions and remonstrances began pouring in upon Congress. On the other hand, the near approach of a necessary reduction of duties aroused the manufacturers to the necessity of placing the protective system on grounds which could not be shaken by revenue considerations.

---

overthrown—and with that the prohibitive system must soon go down. South Carolina has ample cause for gratulation and rejoicing, and every reason to hope that by continuing to exercise a little forbearance all things will right come in a year or two." (38 Niles, 308-315; 319-321; 379.)

385 38 Niles, 340, 341.

386 38, Niles, 321, 322. According to the Charleston *Mercury* these reductions would benefit only the tariff states.

South Carolina was by no means unanimous in supporting the nullification doctrine, but on one point the State was thoroughly united. While the Union party deplored the angry political excitement and blamed the nullifiers for attempting to force their dangerous political measures upon the State, they were no less outspoken in regard to the tariff itself. The tariff of 1828, they agreed, was unequal and unjust in its operation and burdensome to the South, unwise and impolitic, and must be repealed.[387] And this position was substantially taken by Virginia, North Carolina, and Georgia, in Governors' messages, legislative resolutions, and public meetings. In South Carolina, in response to numerous petitions, Governor Hamilton appointed a day of fasting, humiliation, and prayer.[388]

This feeling of unbending hostility on the part of the Union men of the South was most ominous. "One of the most alarming features of the controversy," wrote Matthew Carey, "is the fact that a large portion of the most decided supporters of the Union and enemies of nullification, and its counterpart, a dissolution of the Union, with all its attendant horrors, are firm believers in the unconstitutionality of the protective system, and appear to require its total abolition."[389] Yet to the demands of the South there was no response. "Let Congress repeal the tariff—abandon the principles of protection, abolish internal improvements—enact none but *bona fide* revenue laws, and Southern excitement will instantly cease," was the language of the South. "What happened in the days of the Hartford Convention so immodest and outrageous!" was the Northern comment.[390] Nor were the tariff men less active than their enemies. Monster meetings were held at Boston, New York, Philadelphia, Albany, Pittsburg, Louisville, and elsewhere, to enforce in strongest terms the necessity of maintaining the American System intact. The tariff position was substantially defined at a tariff. convention held in New York, October, 1831, following closely a similar meeting of free traders at Philadelphia. In the Philadelphia convention nearly all the delegates were from the South; in the New York convention the South had scarcely a

387 41 Niles, 13.
388 41 Niles, 65.
389 41 Niles, 89.
390 See 41 Niles, 101.

representative.

The Philadelphia convention, first suggested by the New York *Evening Post*, presented two papers to the country—an address to the people of the United States, written by Jackson's ex-Attorney General, John M. Berrien of Georgia, and a memorial to Congress, the work of Albert Gallatin. The address declared that they came in faith that if their grievances were understood they would he remedied. The discontent with the tariff could not be overlooked. It was of long standing. A numerous and respectable portion of the United States did not merely condemn the system as unjust, they utterly denied its constitutionality. Then followed a long exposition of extreme *laissez-faire*, the demand for free trade being based on the "unquestionable right of every individual to apply his labor and capital in the mode which he may conceive best calculated to promote his own interest." The memorial of Gallatin, avoiding the constitutional question, was a far abler and more temperate defence of free trade.[391]

The New York address declared the American System to be national in its character. It was to rescue the labor of the American people from an inferiority, a subjection dishonorable, burdensome, and degrading, that protective laws were originally passed and still existed. To give up this power would be to give up the Constitution. The American System invited the application of American capital to stimulate American industry. It proposed a restriction, in the form of an impost duty, on certain products of foreign labor; but so far as related to American capital or American labor, it simply offered security and inducement to the one, and gave energy and vigor to the other. The fundamental principle of the opposite school was totally erroneous. It considered profits of capital as the only source of national wealth. It assumed that the wages of labor were barely sufficient to support the laborer, leaving him nothing for accumulation. Whether true or not in Europe it was totally

391 For the Address, see Niles, 41, 136, *et seq.* Gallatin's Memorial is printed in U.S. Documents, 22nd Congress, 1st session, Senate Documents, vol i., No. 55. Gallatin's motion to strike out the part relating to the constitutional question was rejected by a decided vote. Maine, Massachusetts, New York, New Jersey, and Pennsylvania, cast 35 votes against Gallatin's motion to 29 in its favor. Gallatin and twenty-six others voted against the final adoption of the address (41 Niles, 156, 157).

false in the United States. America had no class corresponding to the human machines of Europe. There was no question as to the advantages of free trade as a municipal principle. But as between foreign nations there was no free trade, never had been, and never could be. It would contravene the arrangements of Providence. Nations were adversary to each other. An unrestricted intercourse between two nations reduced the labor of one to the same scale of compensation as the other. In conclusion, after dwelling at length upon the beneficent operation of protection in the United States, it was affirmed that in reducing the revenue, the tariff should be taken off of articles not competing with American industries.[392] "Our other manufacturers," it was said, in the convention, "require a like protection. If refused they will be underworked by the half-starved miserable labor of foreign countries. We are not to place our population in comparison with the English and Asiatic laborer who works sixteen or eighteen hours a day. They cannot and will not be degraded to a level with such men."[393] A crisis had arrived; Southern agriculture and Northern navigation had united against the tariff. People were being tempted by the prospect of low prices, while in point of fact, the repeal of the tariff would result in the great and permanent enhancement of prices.[394]

Every one knew that a desperate struggle was coming. The protectionists still held an unquestioned majority in Congress, but as a reduction must be made somewhere, there could not help being a disposition on the part of conservative men to yield some-what to the undoubted deep feeling of the South. Compromise and conciliation were undoubtedly in the air. Even Niles began to talk of compromise as to the quantum of protection, though the system itself could not and would not be given up. For its aban-donment, he said, would produce general ruin among the Middle, Eastern, and Western States.[395]

But the firm and dictatorial tone of Mr. Clay reformed the wavering lines. Once more back in Congress and looked to as the leader against Jacksonism, he was in no compromising mood in

---

392 41, Niles, 204 *et seq.*

393 41 Niles, 181.

394 41 Niles, 186.

395 41 Niles, 61-66, 73-76, 105-110.

this flood tide of a current which was bearing him, as he believed, straight to the chair of Washington. His enemies were alert and vindictive, but he felt able to cope with them, and he soon subdued much of the conciliatory spirit which the desperate earnestness of the South had infused into the protectionist ranks. But he entirely underestimated the strength of the Southern feeling, and here, as pointed out by Adams, was his great error. The tariff must be reduced, and Adams inquired if in the gracious operation of remitting there would not be a mixture of harshness in extending the protective system, and a danger of increasing the discontents of the Southern States. Clay's reply was characteristic. The discontent, he said, was almost all, if not entirely, imaginary or fictitious, and in almost all the states had in great measure subsided.[396]

The tariff discussion began as soon as Congress met. If a reduction must be made the struggle could not be avoided. Clay, indeed, was inclined to oppose the further payment of the debt, but in this purely tactical move he was overruled by Adams, who felt that the country was against it. January 9, 1832, Clay introduced a resolution to the effect that duties upon imports, not coming into competition with articles produced in the United States, ought to be forthwith abolished, except upon wines and silks, and that these should be reduced. This resolution he supported in a two hours' speech, January 11, which Niles pronounced decisive as to the maintenance of the protective policy and that of internal improvements. February 2, 3, and 6, he followed this with an exhaustive exposition and defence of protection, in what is usually called his "great speech in defence of the American System." He claimed for the tariff: the people out of debt, land rising in value, ready though not extravagant market; innumerable flocks and herds browsing and gamboling on ten thousand hills and plains covered with rich and verdant grasses, cities expanded and whole villages springing up as it were by enchantment, exports and imports increased and increasing, the public debt of two wars nearly redeemed; and to crown all, the public treasury overflowing, embarrassing Congress, not to find subjects of taxation, but to select the objects which should be liberated from the impost.[397]

---

396 8 J.Q. Adam's Memoirs, 443.
397 41 Niles, 361; 42 Niles, 2-16; also 5 Clay's Works, 437-486.

January 19, the House called upon the Secretary of the Treasury for information regarding manufactures and for the plan of a tariff bill. Without waiting for this report, McDuffie, chairman of the Ways and Means Committee, introduced, February 8, a bill reducing generally and by degrees the protective duties to a level of 12 1/2 percent. April 27, McLane presented his report and tariff measure reducing the average rate of duty from 44 percent to 27 percent, repealing the tariff of 1828, reducing duty on wool to 5 percent and on woolens to 20 percent, abolishing the minimum system on woolens except as to the lowest qualities, and lowering "at one fell swoop," to quote Niles, the rates on a large number of articles.[398] McLane's idea was to harmonize opposing interests by preserving protection somewhat after the law of 1824, while conceding not a little to Southern feeling. But neither party was satisfied, and in this extremity conservatives of all classes turned to the Committee on Manufactures, of which Adams was chairman. Adams felt himself unable, or at least unwilling, to cope with the difficulty, and having been appointed a member of the select committee to investigate the United States Bank, had asked to be excused from further service on the Committee on Manufactures. This disposition was violently opposed. The Jackson members crowded around him in the House begging him to withdraw his request. Cambreleng declared that the harmony, if not the existence, of the confederation depended upon the arduous, prompt, and patriotic efforts of a few eminent men, of whom Adams was one. Bates of Maine declared that Adams was the only man in the Union capable of taking the high stand of umpire. Other members spoke quite as emphatically, and Southern papers began referring to him in cordial terms.[399]

Thus impelled Adams threw himself into the subject with great vigor, drew up an elaborate report, and on the 23d of May introduced a modification of the McLane bill, which, while not impairing its main features, was more acceptable to the manufacturing interest. The report was an able and unprejudiced attempt to bring together the opposing arguments and to get at their real

398 42 Niles, 182-184; 188-192.
399 See 42 Niles, 70, 87. On the other hand, the extreme protectionists feared that Adams was not fully enough committed to the American System and wished to take him at his word.

value. The protective system he planted on the broad ground of national defence and national welfare. He rejected the favorite protectionist doctrine that duties lowered prices, as opposed to common sense, declared that it had always been assumed, never proved, that duties were the *cause* of a fall in prices, and asserted that the same competition, and hence the same fall, would have taken place had the tariff of 1828 not been passed. On the other hand, he denied as positively the equally extravagant statement of the South that the producer of the exported article, instead of the consumer, paid the duty. The doctrine of an irreconcilable opposition of interest between North and South, he declared could not be true; it would make union impossible. Representing as they did the manufacturing interest of the country, the committee had anxiously desired to adapt their provisions, not only to the interests, but to the feelings of that portion of the country which had considered itself most aggrieved by the existing tariff; but at the same time, they had been equally anxious to make all concessions required without any essential sacrifice of the interest entrusted to them.[400]

The temperate and unpartisan nature of Adams' report doubtless did much to win acceptance of his bill.[401] South Carolina refused to accept it, and various tariff meetings denounced it because it sacrificed too much.[402] But in the midst of renewed excitement it finally passed, July 14, 1832, opposed by the great majority of Southern members and by a section of extreme protectionists.[403]

---

400 42 Niles, 244 *et seq*; 232 *et seq*.

401 J.S Barbour of Virginia declared that it seemed far more objectionable to Southern views than McLane's bill, but under all circumstances he thought it better to accept it than to hazard the acceptance of far greater evils (42 Niles, 247.)

402 A tariff meeting at Philadelphia, opposed to both the McLane bill and the Adam's bill, adopted the following resolution: "That the free American workman, who lives well, and commands all the comforts and many of the luxuries of life, cannot be expected to manufacture as cheaply as the ill-fed operative of Europe; that much as we deprecate any legislation that shall equalize the value of our free labor with that of foreign paupers, we deprecate sill more the *pauper morals* that must necessarily follow such a course, and we hold any man or party of men who seek to reduce our working classes to this state of poverty, dependence, and immorality, to be enemies of their welfare especially, and hostile to the prosperity of our common country." (42, Niles, 277.)

403 For vote in the House, see 42 Niles, 336.

The McDuffie bill had been regarded by South Carolina as a sort of ultimatum. Its rejection was clearly foreseen from the first, and the anger of the State rose hot against the gigantic oppression which they imagined the tariff to be. They had been, they affirmed, absolutely denied a hearing by the protectionists of the North, who had met them in a spirit that proposed, in the words of Clay, "to defy the South, the President, and the Devil."[404] Before the fate of the McDuffie bill was settled a great meeting of the Union and State Rights party at Charleston had agreed upon the calling of a Southern Convention, in case Congress should adjourn without a satisfactory adjustment of the tariff.[405] After the passage of the Adams' bill, meetings were held at which it was resolved to resist the law at every hazard. Immediately upon the passage of the measure, the senators and representatives from South Carolina drew up, in Washington, an address to the people of their state, in which, while no remedy violent or otherwise was suggested, it was declared that all hope of redress was irrecoverably gone, and that it only remained for the sovereign State of South Carolina to determine whether its rights and liberties should be maintained.[406]

Temperate discussion, however, was impossible. South Carolina in her resentment refused to listen to reason. Nullification and disunion were everywhere and openly preached. A Southern Convention, to which project Virginia, North Carolina, Georgia, and Alabama, had given favorable consideration, was altogether too slow and feeble a mode of expression, and South Carolina, without waiting for co-operation or approval, proclaimed, by the solemn declaration of a sovereign State, the nullity of the new tariff law.[407]

---

404 See Sumner's Jackson, 222.
405 42 Niles, 300.
406 See 42 Niles, 385,412.
407 Toasts drunk at Edisto, S.C.: 1. Andrew Jackson—his example when a boy has taught the youth of Carolina to despise his threats when a man. 2. Nullification is the rightful remedy—South Carolina will never submit to a Yankee tariff while there grows on her soil a palmetto tree. 3. Let us hesitate no longer—we ought, we must, and will resist the encroachments on our rights at any and every hazard. 4. Governor Hamilton—wherever there are on this day two or three gathered together in the name of nullification, would to God he could be in the midst of them. A seven striped flag was hoisted at Oglethorpe, Georgia,—in allusion to the seven Southern states. Among the toasts were the following: 1. Self-redress—let us have no more of the sickly cant about brotherly love and the sacredness of the Union;

But the precipitancy of South Carolina isolated her from all the rest of the Union. Attention was drawn from the enormities of the tariff to the enormity of the proposed remedy. Tennessee, Kentucky, Alabama, Virginia, North Carolina, Mississippi, and Louisiana, hastened to disavow all sympathy, and even Georgia drew back and returned to the proposal of a Southern Convention.[408]

When Congress met in December, the presidential election was over. Clay was defeated, and in his ruin seemed involved the ruin of the projects he had announced as at stake in the contest. Still there was hope that between the Northern democratic support of protection and the general horror of nullification, the tariff would come through unscathed.

Jackson met the crisis with a mixture of firmness and concession. A few days after his annual message, which barely alluded to the South Carolina troubles, he issued a proclamation denouncing nullification and warning the people of South Carolina that the laws would be enforced. South Carolina answered with spirit and defiance, while the North rang with applause for Jackson. The President had echoed the constitutional doctrines of Webster, and asked Congress to enforce them. Meanwhile his annual message had discussed the tariff problem at length, arguing that protection should be confined to articles of necessity in time of war. The Committee on Manufactures being unable to agree on a measure, Verplanck, from the Ways and Means Committee, brought forward a bill for generally reducing duties to the revenue standpoint, which was understood to have the approval of the President—a measure, Niles declared, marked by cold blooded insensibility or reckless cruelty, whose passage would seal the fate of the Union.[409]

The winter was one of feverish excitement. Webster cordially supported the Force bill, but resolutely resisted any changes in the tariff; and this was the general protectionist attitude. The South Carolina Convention solemnly denounced the President's proclamation, but postponed, in view of the tariff discussion, the execution of the ordinance of nullification. Protectionists stood

they who shook off the tyrannical oppression of their mother country will not hesitate to resist that of their sister States. See 43, Niles, 77 *et seq.*
408 See 43 Niles, 209, 219, 220.
409 43 Niles, 313.

firm, believing that the Verplanck tariff would be the death blow to the American System,[410] and looking to Jackson to make good his proclamation. On the other side, South Carolina was sullen and determined, and without a reduction of the tariff could count on the active sympathy of Virginia, North Carolina, Georgia, and Alabama.

While affairs were in this unsettled state, Clay appeared, three weeks before the end of the session, with his compromise tariff. It hardly differed from the Verplanck bill except in postponing the evil day and gradually letting all protected articles down to a general level of 20 percent. Viewed purely from its economic side the measure was sound enough and could have no serious results. But it came too late and too much as a forced measure to have its full and healthful effect. It was introduced without the approval or even knowledge of his party, and came to most of its members like thunder out of a clear sky. Webster denounced it to the last, and when it finally passed it was mainly by Southern votes and against the almost solid front of Clay's own party. Clay was naturally a partisan and fond of political strife; but in moments of real or supposed national peril his mind took the easy but not always clear course of compromise. In this case he declared that the measure was necessary to save any part of the American System. But Webster's logic was unanswerable: "The honorable member from Kentucky says the tariff is in imminent danger; that if not destroyed this session it cannot survive the next. This may be so, sir. This may be so. But if it be so, it is because the American people will not sanction the tariff; and if they will not, why then, sir, it cannot be sustained at all."[411] But all he could do was to insist that the Compromise bill should not pass until after the Force bill, and that Calhoun, bitter as it was to him, should first vote for the Force bill.

As to who really won was long a matter of dispute. The flame

---

410 43, Niles, 297.

411 43, Niles, 417. The compromise tariff provided that one-tenth of the excess of all duties above 20 percent should be struck off Sept. 30, 1835, and so on each alternate year until 1841; then one-half of the remaining excess; and in 1842 the remainder, leaving a horizontal rate of 20 percent. The bill was very loosely worded, and much difficulty was experienced in administering it.

of nullification blazed out fiercely at dinners and Fourth of July celebrations, but it had no present meaning. South Carolina exultantly claimed the victory, while the North applauded to the echo Jackson's bold vindication of the Constitution. Clay and Calhoun long after wrangled over the matter in the Senate. Calhoun declared that Clay, flat on his back, had perceived in the Compromise the only chance of saving his political future, and but for Calhoun, would have sunk to rise no more. Clay retorted that it was he who had kept the rope from Calhoun's neck, which Jackson had ready for him. The truth is that both sides wavered when the crisis came, and to the majority in Congress, Clay's Compromise seemed a happy issue out of all their afflictions. The tariff question was made quiescent and postponed to a more convenient season, when, at least, it might be dissociated from the irrelevant and dangerous question of constitutional interpretation.

LIST OF AUTHORITIES CITED.

Adams, Henry. History of the United States, 1801-1817. 9 vols. New York, 1890-91.—Life of John Randolph. (American Statesmen Series.) Boston, 1882.

Adams, Henry Carter. Public Debts. New York, 1887.

Adams, John. Works, edited by C. F. Adams. 10 vols. Boston, 185H6.

Adams, John Quincy. Memoirs, etc., edited by C. F. Adams. 12 vols. Philadelphia, 1874-77.

Ames, Fisher. Life, edited by 8. Ames. 2 vols. Boston, 1854.

Annals of Congress, 1789-1824. 42 vols. Washington, 1834-56.

Bancroft, George. History of the United States. 6 vols. New York, 1888.

Bishop, J. Leander. History of American Manufactures, 1608-1860. 3 vols. Philadelphia, 1861-1868.

Chalmers, George. Political Annals. Book L London, 1770.

Clay, Henry. Works, edited by C. Colton. 6 vols. New York, 1857.

Cunningham, J. (?). Essay on Trade and Commerce. London, 1770.

Cunningham, W. Politics and Economics. London, 1885.

Dickinson, John. Political Writings. 2 vols. Wilmington, 1801.

Documents Relating to the Colonial History of New York. 10 vols. Albany, 1856-58.

Elliot, Jonathan. Debates on the Adoption of the Federal Constitution. 5 vols. Philadelphia, 1861.

Fisher, Willard Clark. American Trade Regulations before 1789.

Printed in vol. iii of Publications of the American Historical Association. New York, 1889.

Fiske, John. The Critical Period of American History. Boston, 1888.

Franklin, Benjamin. Works, edited by John Bigelow. 10 vols. New York, 1887-89.

Gallatin, Albert. Writings, edited by Henry Adams. 3 vols. Philadelphia, 1879.

Hamilton, Alexander. Works, edited by H. C. Lodge. 9 vols. New York, 1885-86.

Hildreth, Richard. History of the United States. 6 vols. New York, 1851-56.

Jefferson, Thomas. Works. 9 vols. Washington, 1853.

Lecky, W. E. H. History of England in the Eighteenth Century, vols. i-ix. New York, 1888-90.

Maclay, William. Sketches of Debate in the First Senate of the United States, edited by G. W. Harris. New York, 1882.

McMaster, John Bach. History of the People of the United States, vols. i-iii. New York, 1883-91.

Macpherson, David. Annals of Commerce. 4 vols. London, 1805.

Madison, James. Letters and other writings. 4 vols. Philadelphia, 1865.

Niles' Weekly Register. 50 vols. Baltimore, 1811-1836.

Pownall, Thomas. The Administration of the Colonies. London, 1764.

—Considerations on Taxing the Colonies. London, 1766.

Schouler, James. History of the United States, vols. i-iv. Washington, 1887. [vol. v. and new edition, New York, 1890-91.]

Schurz, Carl. Life of Henry Clay. (American Statesmen Series.) 2 vols. Boston, 1890.

Smith, Adam. Inquiry into the Nature and Causes of the Wealth of Nations, edited by J. E. T. Rogers. 2 vols. Oxford, 1880.

Statesman's Manual. 2 vols. New York, 1846.

Statutes at Large of Great Britain. 46 vols. Cambridge, 1762-1807.

Sumner, William Graham. Life of Andrew Jackson. (American Statesmen Series.) Boston, 1882.—Life of Alexander Hamilton. (Makers of America Series.) New York, 1890.

Taussig, F. W. Tariff History of the United States. New York, 1888.

Washington, George. Works, edited by Jared Sparks. 12 vols. Boston, 1834-38.

Winsor, Justin. Narrative and Critical History of America. 8 vols. Boston, 1886-89.

Young, Edward. Customs-Tariff Legislation of the United States. Washington, 1872.

Explicit iste liber, scriptor sit crimine liber, Christus scriptorem custodiat ac det honorem

Ὥσπερ ξένοι χαίρουσιν ἰδεῖν πατρίδα, οὕτως καὶ οἱ γράφοντες ἰδεῖν βιβλίου τέλος

श्रीकृष्णार्पणमस्तु

書成矣，感盡天地

סלוע ארוב לאל חבש סלשנו סת

"of making many books there is no end; and much study is a wareiness of the flesh"
- Ecclesiastes 12:12

BULKINGTON BOOKS